D1591169

DE VALERA, FIANNA FAIL AND THE *IRISH PRESS*

De Valera, Fianna Fáil and the *Irish Press*

Mark O'Brien

National University of Ireland, Maynooth

IRISH ACADEMIC PRESS
DUBLIN • PORTLAND, OR

First published in 2001 by
IRISH ACADEMIC PRESS
44 Northumberland Road, Dublin 4, Ireland

and in the United States of America by
IRISH ACADEMIC PRESS
c/o ISBS, 5824 N.E. Hassalo Street, Portland
Oregon 97213–3644

Website: www.iap.ie

British Library Cataloguing in Publication Data
A catalogue record of this book is available from the British Library.
ISBN 0–7165–2733–2

Library of Congress Cataloging-in-Publication Data
A catalogue record of this book is available from the Library of Congress.

Typeset by Carrigboy Typesetting Services, County Cork
Printed by ColourBooks, Dublin

This book is dedicated to my father, Dominick,
and to the memory of my mother, Mary

Freedom of the press is only guaranteed to those who own one.

A.J. Liebling

Contents

List of Illustrations

Foreword

Mark O'Brien's story of the birth, life and death of the *Irish Press* is not merely, in my opinion, the tale of how a great newspaper group fell before the forces of those two mules spawned by The Four Horses of the Apocalypse, Ego and Incompetence. It is also part of the warp and woof of twentieth-century Irish history. I believe he has told the story well and commend his book to anyone interested in that history.

The *Irish Press* was forged in the white heat of the struggle for Irish independence, when Eamon de Valera was touring America in 1919 and 1920, collecting money so that Ireland might be free. Inspired by this vision of a century fought for Holy Grail, tens of thousands of Irish and Irish-Americans contributed from their slender resources to a bond drive. Some of these people, like the lady who scrubbed the floors in a Boston University did so at great cost to themselves – the Jesuits fired her for subscribing to such a radical cause. Sadly, as the record shows, after Ireland achieved the amount of independence possible at the time, and de Valera had come to power, the scrubbing lady subsequently had great difficulty in retrieving her money, which she had intended as a loan.

Her story is a paradigm of how the *Irish Press*, its readers and staff were treated.

Founded in a flush of revolutionary enthusiasm, most *Irish Press* readers and staff saw the paper as part of 'The Cause'. Where the readers were concerned, a visitor to Ireland wishing to know the political allegiances of any Irish county, town or village, had only to enter the local newsagents and see who bought the *Irish Press* and who the *Irish Independent*. Immediately, one could tell whether this family or that had supported de Valera or Cumman na nGael during the Irish Civil War.

To the people who worked for the paper, figures like its first editor, Frank Gallagher, who seems to have discovered the art of the twenty-five hour day, service to the *Irish Press* was a continuation of the Civil War effort. Just as Gallagher's diaries record him getting up on his bicycle in sleet filled January to cycle home to Sutton, along the spray filled Clontarf seafront at three o'clock in the morning, so too did the average reporter, compositor or circulation clerk give his or her all for the paper.

Standards of excellence were set in journalism and in the distribution arm of the paper that have not yet been exceeded, although of course, methodologies have changed.

In remote, Republican Kerry, late into the thirties, my father, who had asked for an *Irish Independent*, was replied to wonderingly by the shop-owner: 'You mean there's *another* paper in Dublin?' The *Irish Press* may have landed at his shop courtesy of the local postman, bus-driver or Fianna Fáil activist. In one extreme case, Padraig O'Criogáin, who in my years, was the legendary and well-loved circulation manager, used to recall how after train, bus and bicycle had done their work, the final lap of the journey to a remote mountainous Kerry village was completed by ass and cart. Yet however it was done, the paper always landed at its destination at the appointed hour of the morning.

This circulation expertise was so well recognised that I once got a call from an executive in Guinness' Brewery, who explained that the company was overhauling its transport arrangements and wondered if it could send observers down to the *Irish Press* to see how 'the best distribution network in the country worked'.

The nature of what was happening may be summarised by an incident that befell me in Eyre Square, Galway, a few years before the *Press* finally died. A passing taxi driver who recognised me from television pulled up and enquired 'Jaysus, Tim Pat, what's going on up there? The other papers landed here as usual at 6 o'clock this morning, but your's didn't arrive until after 9. I'm just after coming back from Ballyvaughan'. Then he took out his notebook showing all the little villages at which he had dropped off papers along the Galway–Clare coast, added up the total cost and asked me: Jaysus, Tim Pat, how can you'se stick it?'

The answer is of course we could not. It was then after 1 p.m. and most of the papers the taxi man had dropped off were lying unread, their prospective readers having gone home paperless from school or creamery runs. As this was happening of course, the impact of competition from the other Dublin papers, television, the growth of the transistor radio, and the English papers, were also being felt.

The reply of the management to these forces was to produce not alone the Galway situation, but similar happenings all around the country. By that day (in the early 1980s) the battle for city circulation had also been lost. The management–labour relationship continued to deteriorate to such an extent that one was never quite sure whether or not a labour stoppage, or go-slow, in either the caseroom or on the printing floor would result in the taxi drivers' being deprived of their revenues, because an entire edition might be cancelled at short notice.

The death of the *Irish Press* occurred, like bankruptcy, in two ways, gradually and suddenly. A mortal blow was struck some years before the paper died, when, on the eve of a general election in 1973, the *Irish Times* pulled out of a 'one out, all out' cartel operated by the Dublin Newspapers Management Committee. Up to this, a combination of 'The Cause' mentality and the fact that all the newspapers concerned brought pressure to bear on the unions, largely the print unions, to settle disputes. The economic importance of some of the Press Group's publications helped also.

The great printers' strike of 1965 was settled when prominent Dublin traders came to see Jack Dempsey, the Press Group general manager, and negotiated a settlement whereby they agreed to take sufficient extra advertising to compensate for meeting the printers' demands. The dominance of the *Evening Press* at the time was such that Clery's, amongst other centre city stores, was recording a thirty per cent drop in trading volumes. Bereft of the famous full page ads interspersed with tiny pen and ink drawings of suits, dresses and coats, to be perused leisurely over long evenings, the country was no longer coming to the landmark Dublin store to purchase communion outfits, wedding dresses, and clerical outfits.

However, the means by which the paper was brought to birth contained within it the seeds of its death also. Eamon de Valera persuaded the people who had subscribed to Irish independence bonds to deed these over to him so that when they were redeemed he could use them as collateral to found the paper. Subsequently, he also used his dominant political position to force through the Dáil a provision that not only repaid monies owning on these bonds, but a twenty-five per cent premium, ostensibly because of the delay in payment. This gave him, as the dominant *Irish Press* shareholder, much-needed funds to save the paper from financial ruin.

The vast majority of the public, however, certainly the Fianna Fáil public, acquiesced in this manoeuvre which in our day would assuredly have brought about the attention of a Tribunal. They saw de Valera's actions in terms of 'The Cause', an integral part of the fight for the Republic and of the changes that de Valera intended to make in Irish society.

The paper, however, was not merely operated for the benefit of 'The Cause'. Had anyone troubled to consult the small print of its Articles of Association, they would have discovered that, as befitted a pious Catholic, Eamon de Valera had manipulated matters, so that the *Irish Press* was modelled on the doctrine of the Holy Trinity – with de Valera as Father, Son and Holy Ghost. He was the controlling director who could also be the managing director and editor-in-chief. There was the fiction of a board of directors, but in fact, when the crunch came, only one vote counted – de Valera's.

Other votes counted also. There was an Irish Press Corporation in America that took full advantage of the notoriously lax company laws of Delaware. The Corporation allegedly looked after the voting rights of the original Irish-American shareholders. But in fact, the Delaware shares that carried vital voting rights were actually controlled by – Eamon de Valera.

However, in those pre-television days of limited secondary education and white hat Civil War passions, the faithful Fianna Fáilers did little to question de Valera's demonstration of how efficiently Christ and Caesar could function hand in glove. The protestations of his political foes could be shrugged off in de Valera's own words, uttered during a bitter Dáil debate on his appropriation of tax-payers' money for *Irish Press* purposes as 'gall and wormwood' at the fact that he was now running the country.

De Valera's 'stroke', while it benefited his position, did nothing for that of the shareholders. Incredibly, in light of today's commercial attitudes, apart from a brief period in the 1970s, the Press Group, which in its day became a very valuable company, never paid a dividend. To the even more faithful staff, the atrocious wages and conditions were in general offered up on the alter of 'The Cause'. The work of the early *Irish Press* journalists is a story of unsung heroes. I had the privilege of knowing some of these survivors of the early days, and their stories of the foundation of the paper and many subsequent years were truly Homeric. Labour relations were always gladiatorial. Sean MacBride for example, left the sub-editor's desk for the law and politics after refusing to pass a picket.

But the talents of the staff and the hours worked were little short of marvellous. The *Irish Press* made the difference in the election campaign that first brought de Valera to power. It largely made the Gaelic Athletic Association what it is today through reporting GAA games that at the time were downplayed by the other two papers in Dublin, the *Irish Times* and the *Irish Independent*. Its first edition was deliberately timed to coincide with the 1931 All-Ireland hurling final. Unfortunately, the legendary Joe Sherwood, Yorkshire man and sports editor, slightly spoilt the effect by furnishing a puff for page one that informed readers that: 'the kick off will take place at 3.15 p.m. . . . '. Many phones rang over that one. But for sheer hard news reporting, it had no equal. Its literary pages, where standards were set by M.J. MacManus, yielded a rich crop of writers and anecdotes. A favourite of mine was that concerning Patrick Kavanagh, who after an article of his was rejected (thereby depriving him of desperately needed drinking money) stood at the head of the stairs, outside what later became my office, tearing up the pages intoning the mantra: 'Shite, pure shite'.

Another true story involved Maurice Liston, a legendary shorthand note taker and stalwart of the early National Union of Journalists, for whom it was commonplace to work a fourteen-hour day and then get on a bus to Waterford or some such to found a branch of the NUJ. Maurice, who always wore a long IRA-type trench coat, possibly a throwback to the days when a Fianna Fáil Cumann by day was an IRA flying column by night, was on 'night town' duty one evening after a long tiring day in the courts, when word came through that a dreadful fire had occurred in a girls' boarding school in Co. Cavan.

Arthur Hunter, the acting editor on the night, persuaded the exhausted Maurice to forgo his nightcap and go into one of the airless, claustrophobic telephone booths to perform the delicate task of ringing the convent to find out the awful details. Meanwhile, the country edition was delayed, and delayed, and delayed while Arthur despairingly walked up and down outside the booth vainly gesticulating to Maurice through the glass doors to get a move on.

Finally, the doors swung open, and a perspiring Liston emerged fumbling in his trench coat pocket for his glasses case. Inserting his glasses carefully into the case, he returned them to his pocket, quelling the frantic Hunter's gyrations in his broad west-Limerick accent with the immortal words: 'The Reverend Mother says the fire's not worth a fuck.' Liston, like many another member of the staff, Brian O'Neill for example, of the Republican Congress Movement, or Paddy Clare, the normal 'night town' reporter, was a convinced Republican in the Wolfe Tone / Rousseau mould.

As a young journalist coming from a Free State family, I was fascinated by the stories, and more importantly the perspectives, that these men gave me into the Republican motivation. They and figures like Angus O'Dálaigh, the librarian and brother of the President, Cearbhall O'Dálaigh, a former Irish editor of the *Irish Press*, were of invaluable assistance to me when I came to write my book on the IRA.

Unfortunately, their assistance to the *Irish Press* was not appreciated by its management. Until I managed to get the salaries brought into line, the pay of the Irish editor was something like half that of the English language literary editor. And Paddy Clare, for example, was even more shabbily treated.

Clare, who had a fund of War of Independence and Civil War stories, used to say of himself: 'Ah sure, I remember Arthur Griffith and the lot of them coming to our house. But when the Civil War came, sure where was Paddy – out on the barricades!' When the *Irish Press* came, Paddy, one of the most resourceful and professional reporters I ever met, joined the paper and incredibly served on the 'night town' or graveyard shift from 10 p.m. to 6 a.m. for approximately thirty years – 'on a docket'. In other words, he was never staffed, and was retained on a week-to-week basis. Eventually, with the aid of NUJ house agreements, it became possible to manoeuvre Paddy to a position where he received £1,500 a year, ex gratia pension.

However, he developed emphysema and came to see me one day to enquire if I could get his pension increased by £5 a week so that he could go to Spain for the winter. 'The oul winters here is killing me' he said. But kill him, it did. Vivion de Valera refused to concede the necessary £5 because it might do the unthinkable: 'Set a Precedent'. By then, the mid-1970s, the effects of the changes in the outside world were beginning to be noted, though not acted upon in the Press Group boardroom.

Broadly speaking, Vivion de Valera had taken over from his father in the 'Three Divine Persons in One' role. To his Caliph, a great newspaper man, Jack Dempsey, played the role of the Grand Vizier. When Dempsey retired, and at a rather chilly and inadequate ceremony in the Royal Dublin Hotel, was presented with a not overly large piece of silver, Vivion remarked truly:

> 'This is the House that Jack built'.

In terms of management style, what he meant was that he put the frighteners into Jack, as his father had done with *Irish Press* executives before him and Jack put the frighteners into everyone else. In face of the eroding spirit of 'The Cause', and the changes in Irish society and technology, this was no way to run a railroad. However, Vivion chose to replicate this formula, appointing Colm Traynor, a son of the respected Civil War veteran and Fianna Fáil cabinet minister, to replace Dempsey. Traynor was, and is, a man of classical 'Cause', loyalty, integrity, shrewdness and ability.

He carried on as best he could. But the task of transforming the Press Group called for a whole new approach in installing computerised typesetting, in broadening the base of the company to include diverse activities in the communication world, such as publishing, broadcasting, disseminating news and financial information, for business and other purposes.

The *Irish Press* still had the journalistic talent. It was particularly well placed to branch into publishing, for example. Its 'New Irish Writing' page literally printed early work from every Irish writer of consequence from 1968 onwards. Its sports and political coverage was still unrivalled. Some of us had won national reputations as broadcasters. The litany of *Irish Press* journalists who came and went – because they were not paid properly – onto stardom in the newsrooms, television and radio stations of the world, shines by its own light.

But the management structures were archaic. Marketing was a thing unknown. Compared to the other papers, the publicity and promotion efforts would have been a joke had they not been so tragically inefficient. Internally, labour problems multiplied, and externally, a new 'free education' generation was successfully wooed by the *Irish Times* or the English tabloids. It is a sobering thought that over six out of ten newspapers now bought in Ireland are English owned. And then there's Sky TV . . .

Vivion de Valera, in some ways, was a much-underestimated man. Possessing wit, intelligence and energy, he nevertheless suffered from what he once described to me as 'the same disease that affects Liam Cosgrave – 'Growing up in the Shade'. He was the Hamlet of the Irish newspaper industry. He knew what had to be done, but he hesitated. Worse, as editor-in-chief of a major communications empire, with a great past, a rocky present and a highly uncertain future, he continued under another hat as a Fianna Fáil backbencher.

This had an inevitably inhibiting influence on political comment. Working under him as an editor was an unending waste of emotional scar tissue that would have been far better employed working for oneself. Even what would appear to be self-evidently necessary decisions outraged him if he felt in some way that he did not have a proper controlling input into them. For example, when Northern Ireland finally exploded in August 1968, Sean Ward, later editor of the *Evening Press* but then a group news editor, had a brief chat with me and within minutes had deployed staff northwards. This inaugurated a period wherein it can be argued that the *Irish Press* coverage of the conflict became the best in the country. Vivion de Valera took a different view. For months, Sean and I had to listen to recriminations about the cost involved.

Vivion was at heart a conservative of deepest dye, in the Irish sense. That is, he was editorially adverse to contraception but practised it in real life. Needless to say, divorce, abortion, or making alterations to Daddy's Constitution to accommodate Northern Unionists were anathema to him. In many respects, the Press Group and a younger generation were travelling in opposite directions.

Worse was to befall. The unfortunate man, who had a brief glimpse of happiness after a long period of widowerhood, though marrying his lifelong friend, Vera Rock, but only after his father and mother were safely dead (second marriages were not favoured in that household) contracted cancer. What the papers needed was a strong board and a first-class chief executive.

What it got, as the storm of the Hunger Strikes broke in the North, was his son Eamon, who now became the 'Three Divine Persons in One'. In all honesty, the only one of the Three whose role he fitted, was that of the Ghost. He had virtually no background in journalism, and came to the Press from a rather obscure position working for Tom Roche, the then Roadstone magnate, who was a neighbour and friend of his father's. Eamon's fate was to become the Irish version of Warwick Fairfax, who inherited the Australian Fairfax newspaper empire, and in a short space of time let it slip through his fingers. As I remember remarking during a rather sad conversation with Warwick's mother, Lady Mary Fairfax, in Sydney: 'newspapers are like any other form of property, they don't care who inherits them'.

But the staff, and the board, of the Press Group did care. The circulation figures and revenue from all three newspapers were clearly going south. Finally, after a period of dissension within the boardroom, Coopers and Lybrand were appointed as consultants to draw up a report on the Group to make recommendations for the future.

I remember well a conversation I had with the executive responsible, who said: 'I've done a zillion of these reports, but I never found myself in the situation where in effect I was recommending to the man whose name goes on the cheque that he place himself out of a job.' However, that was in effect what the report proposed. On a day in May 1985, it was brought up for decision by the board.

D.P. Flinn, a rather domineering personality, whom Vincent Jennings, the editor of the *Sunday Press*, dubbed 'the suit' because of his sartorial elegance, with another board member whom he had been responsible for bringing in, Sean McHale, argued strongly for the adoption of the report, which the banks were also more than eager to see implemented.

However, Eamon, with a rare flash of his illustrious ancestors' Machiavellian brilliance, had another item on the agenda – the election of a new director, Elio Malocco. He (Eamon) had bought half of his uncle Terry's shares in the Delaware Corporation, and now had an impregnable holding. A future development was that on becoming a director, Malocco, a solicitor, was given the firm's legal business, which was transferred from the hands of Tommy O'Connor, who had been the firm's devoted legal adviser for decades.

Initially, Eamon's stroke-pulling meant that the now outvoted Flinn and McHale resigned and Eamon became chairman. Another consequence would see Malocco being sent to jail, for misappropriation of the monies that the appointment as company solicitor placed at his disposal. But the most damaging consequence of that May afternoon would be the demise of the Irish Press Group.

Eamon made a number of cataclysmic decisions. One involved the purchase of a give-away newspaper, *Southside*. The actual circulation of this publication, as opposed to whatever he was told or believed, may be gauged from the fact that one day I discovered a vast pile of the paper dumped right across the road from my home, over an old railway bridge. The sort of diversification that the Group required this wasn't.

By 1986, a number of pressures had built up. One was the state of the *Sunday Press* sales in particular. When Vincent Jennings became editor of the paper, its circulation figure stood at 408,000 per issue. This had fallen to 256,792 by 1986. While Jack Dempsey ran things, the paper, which was his baby in particular, had prospered. He had gone with Vivion to argue with Eamon de Valera I that a firm was like a tree or a family. Either it grew or it died. The old man saw the logic of this and sanctioned the flotation of the new paper in 1949. In furtherance of this policy, in 1954 the highly successful *Evening Press* followed.

However, with Dempsey's departure from the scene, the *Sunday Press* increasingly became a formulaic publication, dependent on book serialisation and old-fashioned approaches. For a short period, a gifted layout journalist, Andrew Berkley, revolutionised its appearance, but he was soon poached by the *Irish Times*. Unlike the *Irish Press*, relatively generous finances were available to the *Sunday Press*. I remember when the paper found itself unable to run a series of Nixon memoirs, these were given to the *Irish Press* and it turned out that they had cost £4,000 to purchase. In my twenty years as editor, no series or set of series came within an ass' roar of that sum. But the better financing did nothing to halt the circulation slide.

A second pressure was for the implementation of the Coopers and Lybrand report. De Valera decided to combine an attempt to do something to stop the rot on the *Sunday Press* front by appointing a new CEO. This appointment had become particularly necessary because even the faithful Colm Traynor had had enough, and was getting out. Eamon de Valera chose Vincent Jennings for the role. Thus a journalist who had presided over the loss of the best part of forty per cent of his newspaper's circulation was now going to turn around the fortunes of not alone his own paper, but those of the Group's two other publications. The fairly predictable chickens soon came home to roost.

Labour relations were worsening all the time. Alone of all the major Irish newspaper groups, the Press papers managed to create a strike over the introduction of computerised typesetting. To the people who had to operate the visual display units as opposed to the old hot metal typesetting, the new technology was the equivalent of going from driving Volkswagen cars to flying Concorde. Yet a derisory couple of weeks was all that was allowed for training.

If Eamon de Valera had deliberately set out to wreck the company, he could not have done better. After the print unions withdrew their co-operation from the hopelessly inadequate effort to introduce the new technology, without either strikes or loss of circulation through missed deadlines, it was only a question of when, not if, the Group collapsed.

When the new technology strike ended, de Valera decided to keep the *Irish Press* off the streets while the other two publications were re-introduced. I only found out about this decision when by accident I blundered into a meeting at which he was informing my colleagues of the return of the *Evening Press* and the *Sunday Press*. Both the staff and the reading public drew the obvious conclusions from the lack of respect accorded to what was perceived as the company's flagship publication.

This contempt for a significant Irish institution was heightened by the manner in which the various deals were concluded with the unions involved. Personnel were allowed to go with no regard either for their level of skill or the lack of it on the part of those who were retained.

Sometimes this lack occurred through no fault of their own. For example, in 1985 I was assigned the task of re-designing the *Irish Press* in the interregnum between the technology strike and the return of the paper to the streets. As the printer assigned to me worked to cut up a bromide, the scalpel he was using fell from his grasp and luckily struck my watch strap. It could just as easily have hit a vein. The unfortunate man's reaction was: 'Don't be too hard on me, Tim Pat, I'm only waiting for the call to go into hospital to have both eyes operated on for cataracts . . . '.

Not surprisingly, the delayed return of the *Irish Press* was a disaster. The ill-trained printers, some of them men in their fifties and early sixties who must have suffered from the 'techo-fear' that any of us who turn to computers in middle age must necessarily suffer from, just didn't have the experience to produce the paper from the numbers allocated. By the time output improved, the Galway taxi driver anecdote was being replicated all over the country and the paper was littered with misprints.

A final nail was driven into the coffin of the fortunes of the Group by the appalling decision to turn the *Irish Press* into a tabloid. I took my copper handshake and left in 1987. Behind me, nature took its course. There occurred a haemorrhage of journalistic talent from Burgh Quay that no newspaper group could hope to survive. Like men poking their fingers in the holes in the dyke to keep out the tide, Jennings and de Valera transferred people from the Group's other publications to fill the void in the *Irish Press*, often as a consequence making some decisions that, to say the least of it, were questionable. The end came in 1995, amidst recrimination and a poisonous industrial relations climate.

At the time of writing, Jennings and de Valera enjoy, if that is the correct term, a strange sort of afterlife, sitting amidst a plethora of companies that have grown out of the original *Irish Press*, in pleasant offices, drawing as far as one can see from such accounts as are published, large salaries, and claiming to be intent on finding some purchasers who will return the Press publications to the streets.

Whether this ambition is ever likely to be achieved lies totally in the realm of speculation. As far back as 27 August 1995, Vincent Browne, writing in the *Sunday Tribune*, had this to say:

> Eamon de Valera faces formidable obstacles to any attempt by him to revive any of the Irish Press newspapers. Richard Bruton, the minister, made it clear on Friday evening that he would prohibit any involvement by Independent Newspapers in the relaunch of any of the titles. It is unlikely that any other investor would join with de Valera and his associate, Vincent Jennings, in a revival of the newspapers – given their track record. And the journalists have said that they would not work for newspapers involving de Valera and Jennings.

Six years further on, any prospect of the papers' return seems even more 'unlikely'. A company is like a tree or a family . . . But in its day, the *Irish Press* was a good paper, produced by good men and good women. So good in fact, that certainly, while it was still alive, I, as a journalist, would have been tempted to eye up the competition, and echoing Patrick Sarsfield's words, say, 'change kings and we'll fight you again'. However, though it may be too late to re-run the fight, Mark O'Brien has done well to recall for us the story of the *Irish Press*' many battles and how the war was finally lost.

TIM PAT COOGAN
Dublin, October 2001

Acknowledgements

This book would not have been written without the support, generosity and hospitality of a number of individuals and institutions that helped me over the last few years. I am grateful to the National University of Ireland for its award of a grant towards the publication of this book. I would like to thank the directors of Irish Academic Press and managing editor Linda Longmore for their faith in the project. I owe an immense debt of gratitude to Dr Mary Corcoran, Sociology Department, NUI Maynooth, under whose supervision the Ph.D. thesis on which this book is based was completed. Thanks also to Professor Liam Ryan, Dr Peter Murray, Professor John Horgan and Senator Maurice Manning for their insightful comments on early versions of the text.

For granting me interviews and sharing with me their experiences of working for the Irish Press Group, I would like to thank David Andrews, John Brophy, Tim Pat Coogan, Douglas Gageby, Michael Keane, John Kelly, Hugh Lambert, Michael Mills, Emily O'Reilly, Michael O'Toole and Jim Walsh. Thanks also to Conor Brady, Vincent Doyle and Mary O'Rourke, all of whom were generous with their time. In particular, I am indebted to John Kelly whose keen memory was unfailing on several occasions. John was among the first to encourage me to commit the story of the Irish Press Group to paper and his introductions to many former Press Group personnel were much appreciated. In turn, their warm encouragement was a constant source of motivation.

I am deeply indebted to the late Michael O'Toole whose generosity in granting me access to his considerable collection of Press Group documents added immeasurable weight to the research. His untimely death in April 1999 deprived his family and Irish journalism of a warm and generous personality. Similarly, John Brophy, Pat Cashman, Maureen Browne-O'Toole, Dr Martin Mansergh and Colm Rapple were generous in allowing me to consult and quote from various documents. I am grateful to Ann Gallagher for permission to quote from her father's papers held in the National Library and her kindness in providing photographic material.

The research was greatly enhanced by access to the records of the Irish Press Chapel of the National Union of Journalists. My thanks to Seamus Dooley, Eoin Ronayne and the staff of the NUJ. The Archive Department of University College Dublin has become a researcher's utopia due to its immense manuscript collection. The collection now contains the archives of Cumann na nGaedheal, Fine Gael and Fianna Fáil as well as the papers of Frank Aiken, Eamon de Valera and Sean MacEntee. My thanks to Seamus Helferty for his help and to Fianna Fáil and Fine Gael for granting access to the material. Grateful thanks also to the Franciscan trustees of the Eamon de Valera Papers, for their permission to quote from the collection.

For granting me permission to quote from various sources, I extend my thanks to the Council of Trustees of the National Library of Ireland. I would also like to thank the managements and staffs of the National Archives and the Companies Registration Office. Dublin Corporation's Gilbert Newspaper Library is an invaluable resource to any researcher and its news clippings collection was one of the highlights of the research. Thanks also to the ever helpful staff of the John Paul II Library NUI Maynooth, particularly Patrica Harkin, Emma Boyce and Nicole Murphy. Illustrations and photographs were kindly supplied by Cyril Byrne, Pat Cashman, Ann Gallagher, Thomas Mulvihill, the Irish Times Photo-Library and the National Union of Journalists. Computer facilities were kindly supplied by Dominick O'Brien. For proof-reading various versions of the text I extend my thanks to Jarlath Burke, Tadhg Healy, Cornelius Marshall, Helen McDermott, Shane Morris and Robert Ross. The final thanks must go to my family and friends who put up with me talking about the *Irish Press* for what must have seemed like an eternity.

MARK O'BRIEN
Maynooth, June 2001

CHAPTER ONE

The Origins of the Irish Press

For de Valera the launching of the *Irish Press* was the fulfilment of a long cherished hope. Like all his associates and colleagues, both before and after 1916, he fully appreciated the importance of a newspaper in the fostering and developing of the Irish mind. He had lived through the sterilising period of the Irish Parliamentary Party and had seen the effects of the *Freeman's Journal* in bolstering up that party's control of the country. He, more than most, had suffered from misrepresentation and misinterpretation and what was of greater importance to him, he had realised the power of the press to mould and guide the people for good or ill. That early morning of the 5 September 1931, when the first copies of the *Irish Press* began to come off the machines, was a memorable one for de Valera, probably the most notable date in his diary next to Easter Monday 1916.[1]

Senator Joseph Connolly on de Valera and the Irish Press

If any man felt the need to establish a newspaper to counter the bad publicity and blame that political opponents were levelling at his feet in the aftermath of the bitter Irish civil war, Eamon de Valera was foremost in feeling that need. With his political career in pieces and his former allies now major political opponents, de Valera needed a medium through which he could respond to the accusations that the civil war was his fault. Sinn Féin's continued abstention from Dáil Éireann only increased de Valera's alienation from mainstream politics, and although breaking away from that party eased the problem of parliamentary abstentionism, the foundation of his own political entity, what Sean Lemass called the 'slightly constitutional' Fianna Fáil presented its own problems.[2] The new party badly needed publicity if it were to establish a foothold in the newly formed political landscape. Immediately after its foundation, de Valera and other leading members of Fianna Fáil decided to publish a national daily newspaper that would reflect their views and generate popular support for the party and the Ireland they envisaged. After its inaugural meeting in Dublin's La Scala Theatre in May 1926, the first party headquarters was opened in a building opposite Dublin's GPO, and it was from here that the rise of both Fianna Fáil and the *Irish Press* were planned. Working alongside de Valera at this office were Sean T. O'Kelly, Sean MacEntee, Frank Aiken, James Ryan, Sean Lemass, Gerry Boland, Tommy Mullins and Frank Gallagher – all of whom played central roles in the birth of both Fianna Fáil and the *Irish Press*. In particular, Sean Lemass realised the support a partisan newspaper could command. According to Lemass, Fianna Fáil was 'only beating the air without a press' behind it. The *Irish Independent* had 'become more definitely hostile than ever' and its 'power to do harm' was being 'repeatedly demonstrated'.[3] The expressed role of the new paper was to help establish Fianna Fáil as a legitimate political force and win support for it among the electorate.

The fortunes of the *Irish Press* were irrevocably intertwined with the fortunes of Fianna Fáil. In the early years, de Valera mobilised the party's grass root support to promote the idea of the newspaper around the country and in later years the paper paid back this debt by consistently promoting de Valera, the Fianna Fáil party and its objectives. To this end, the *Irish Press* played a crucial role in the development of the party by providing a forum for the dissemination of ideology to the masses while conversely giving supporters something practical to affiliate to. Since de Valera was the founder of both party and paper, he ultimately controlled both. During his terms as Taoiseach, the support of the *Irish Press* was unwavering as successive de Valera governments pursued policies of social conservatism, protectionism, self-sufficiency and neutrality. Since these were the doctrines of Fianna Fáil, so too were they the doctrines of the *Irish Press*. As the first edition of the paper stated, it would support Fianna Fáil, 'but only because the philosophy and aspirations' of the party were 'identical with its own philosophy and aspirations'.[4] The idea for founding a national newspaper to promote his ideologies had always been on de Valera's mind since the end of the civil war. As far back as 1922 de Valera had told a colleague that 'the propaganda against' him was 'overwhelming' simply because the anti-Treaty faction did not have 'a single daily newspaper' on its side.[5] Indeed, de Valera had learned at first hand the power of the media during the Treaty debates when he was condemned for not accepting the Anglo-Irish Treaty by the *Irish Independent*, the *Irish Times* and the *Freeman's Journal*. So severe was the media hostility to de Valera that anti-Treaty supporters burst into the latter paper's premises and smashed its printing presses in April 1922. When the paper ceased publishing in 1924, the only other indigenous national daily titles were the *Irish Times* which 'still thought and spoke in terms of Unionism', and the *Irish Independent* which 'was a strong supporter of the Commonwealth connection'. Both were 'violently anti-de Valera'.[6] Therefore de Valera's founding of the *Irish Press* 'could be justified solely in terms of the hostility of the newspaper establishment'.[7]

Indeed, the *Irish Independent*'s origins lay within the tradition of the Irish Parliamentary Party. Originally titled the *Irish Daily Independent*, it had been launched in 1891 as the organ of the party faction that had continued to support Charles Stuart Parnell after his position as leader was compromised by the Kitty O'Shea divorce revelations. By 1900 the paper was bankrupt and when the *Freeman's Journal* made a bid for the paper, John Redmond, the chairman of the Irish Parliamentary Party, asked William Martin Murphy, a wealthy Dublin businessman and relative of party stalwart Tim Healy, to buy the title. Murphy did so and revamped it along commercial lines, imitating the style of contemporary British mass circulation daily newspapers. Retitled as the *Irish Independent*, Murphy relaunched it in January 1905 as Ireland's first half-penny newspaper. He later acquired an evening title, the *Evening Herald* that dated from 1891 and added a Sunday title, the *Sunday Independent*, in 1906, thereby firmly establishing the Independent Newspaper legacy. While the *Irish Independent* 'could be and was at times severely critical of many aspects of the Cosgrave administration' it was also 'consistently hostile to any of the movements favouring republicanism'.[8] Conversely, most republicans harboured a severe loathing for the *Irish Independent*. Its 'past record was remembered' and very few republicans forgot 'the attitude of the paper in 1916' or its 'infamous leading article which preceded the executions of Sean MacDermott and James Connolly'.[9] Although Cumann na nGaedheal claimed its descent from Sinn Féin, the Independent company viewed the party as less antagonistic than Fianna Fáil and so lent it the support of its titles. Just as the Press titles became associated with and supported Fianna Fáil, so too did the Independent titles become associated with and supported Cumann na nGaedheal and its successor Fine Gael. But despite its obvious strong aversion to de Valera and Fianna Fáil and its support for Cumann na nGaedheal, the Independent company continuously boasted of its papers 'not being tied to any political party'.[10] Although commercialism rather than politics was always more important to the company, ideologically the papers were highly sympathetic to Cumann na nGaedheal. The several generations of the Murphy family who inherited the papers were equally supportive of Cumann na nGaedheal and Fine Gael and just as anti-Fianna Fáil. While William Lombard Murphy outbid de Valera in the purchase of the *Freeman's Journal* to prevent it falling into the hands of republicans, his successor T. V. Murphy was an active chairman, often walking around the premises 'at two in the morning to let the staff see who was in control . . . he also admitted that he blue-pencilled copy, particularly at election time'.[11]

The *Irish Times* was equally anti-de Valera. Since the paper's foundation in 1859, it had been a pro-union and conservative paper, with one owner, Sir John Arnott, describing himself as a 'staunch supporter of law and order and imperial government in Ireland'.[12] After independence, the paper immediately took to supporting Cumann na nGaedheal, which it viewed as more moderate, less nationalist and less hostile towards Britain than de Valera's Fianna Fáil. According to one reviewer, the popular perception of the *Irish Times* at that time was of 'a dyed-in-the-wool, dry-as-dust, dead-in-the-last-ditch ascendancy organ, the sworn enemy of the Irish people'.[13] Despite this, the reviewer acknowledged that the paper's political stance and readership profile were often misrepresented. While its politics were that of home rule rather than unionism, its readership consisted not of unionist minded individuals, but of home rule protagonists. A somewhat similar description of the *Irish Times* was also given by the paper's first Catholic editor, Conor Brady; 'at its inception it was a home-rule newspaper rather than a unionist one. Its unionism became a feature of the early years of this century and peaked around the 1920s'.[14] Indeed, it was during the 1930s that the paper finally ditched its hard-line unionist posturing. After having being appointed editor in 1934, it was Robert Smyllie who 'instinctively saw that the old style unionism was finished, that to pursue it would bring down the paper'.[15] Almost immediately, the space devoted to 'news of the doings of the titled people' was cut back to 'make space for real news'.[16] Despite this however, the paper still remained essentially hostile to de Valera and Fianna Fáil, being especially critical of de Valera's dismantling of the Treaty from 1932 onwards.

As a result of such media hostility, de Valera attempted to raise enough money to buy the titles of the *Freeman's Journal* in 1926. His plan came to nothing, however, when despite representations on his behalf from Sean T. O'Kelly, de Valera failed to secure the financial backing of the Irish-American republican movement, Clan na nGael, which was of the 'opinion that if the *Freeman's Journal* was not a paying proposition, the burden for republicans would be too much and eat up their resources'. Instead, the Clan suggested that de Valera 'try and interest Hearst in projecting a paper in Ireland'. Media magnate William Hearst owned several anti-British newspapers in America and, according to the Clan, it was 'worth feeling him out on the matter'.[17] De Valera, knowing that he could never fully control a newspaper that involved Hearst, declined the advice and in the end was outbid by Lombard Murphy, who integrated the title into the *Irish Independent*. It was this failure that resulted in the strategic planning by de Valera and his followers to launch their own newspaper. The funding of the new paper and its unique financial structure would always be a source of controversy and much of its origins lay in de Valera's 1919 visit to America on behalf of Dáil Éireann to raise funds and recruit support for the creation of an Irish republic. It was during this period that he collected the money that was later used to part-finance the founding of the *Irish Press*. At the start of the 1919 visit, de Valera was well received by the influential leaders of the main Irish-American organisation, Clan na nGael. This organisation had established several newspapers to promote its viewpoint and no doubt de Valera was impressed by the effectiveness of partisan newspapers and the influence that they could command in a community. Prominent Clan na nGael leaders and newspapers included John Devoy, editor of the primary Irish-American newspaper *The Gaelic American*, Judge Daniel Cohalan of the New York Supreme Court, and Joseph McGarrity who had founded another Irish-American newspaper in Philadelphia called the *Irish Press*.

Although de Valera toured America as a guest of this organisation, as far as fund raising ventures were concerned disagreements soon evolved. By February 1919, Clan na nGael had raised a quarter of a million dollars for the Irish Republic. While Devoy and Cohalan saw the amount as sufficient, both McGarrity and de Valera thought it too little. Thus when de Valera proposed his idea for a loan based on a bond issue for several million dollars in the name of the Irish Republic, some animosity arose. Both Devoy and Cohalan objected to the idea, claiming that the proposal would violate American anti-fraud laws that prohibited the sale of bonds on behalf of countries not officially recognised by Congress. Not to be outdone, however, de Valera found a loophole in the law. By issuing bond certificates that could be exchanged for real bonds when the Irish Republic was recognised by America, de Valera managed to sidestep the law and begin the sale of bonds, the proceeds of which, ten years later, would to be used to part-finance the foundation of the *Irish Press*. While Devoy and Cohalan still objected, McGarrity enthusiastically supported de Valera's unique method of fund raising. He found a bank to handle the money, rented premises from which to run the bond drive and brought on board Martin Conbey, a New York based attorney, to iron out any legal difficulties. Conbey suggested that an independent, American legal opinion be obtained. Accordingly, de Valera approached another rising politician, a partner in the New York law firm Emmet, Marvin and Martin, named Franklin Delano Roosevelt. After examining the issues involved, Roosevelt, who would lead America during the Second World War, pronounced favourably on the scheme.[18] The position of national director for the bond drive went to another New York attorney and high profile Irish-American, Frank Walsh. In later years, as chairman of the American branch of the Irish Press Ltd, Walsh would play a central role in fund raising for the *Irish Press*.

De Valera then began a high profile cross-country tour of America organised by James O'Mara, a Kilkenny TD renowned for his business sense and organisational ability. At de Valera's request, O'Mara set to work co-ordinating welcoming committees across the various states. Beginning with a huge outdoor meeting in New York, de Valera was awarded the freedom of the city by its mayor, John Hylan. In return de Valera presented him with a bond certificate. The first bond certificate was sold to the Carmelite School in New York. De Valera's tour also included speeches to Irish-American communities in Boston, Chicago, San Francisco and Philadelphia, and earned him much front-page coverage from newspapers such as the *Boston Globe* and the *San Francisco Leader*.[19] Indeed the American press 'faithfully reported all functions at which money was collected for the cause and prodded emigrants and natives alike to help Ireland's fight for freedom'.[20] The bond certificates were sold on a scale that rose in cost from ten dollars to ten thousand dollars. Those who subscribed to the fund were described in the *Wall Street Journal* as 'Irish domestic servants, and others of the like or lower standards of intelligence'.[21] Indeed, de Valera very much exploited the sentimentality of the Irish-American population. It was, he said in a press release, 'a sentimental appeal and not an appeal to investors'.[22] In later years, he would replace sentimentality with business sense by requesting bondholders to invest the money in the *Irish Press* rather than cash the bonds in. Although de Valera had originally been sent to America to raise one million dollars, his high profile tour enabled him to raise just over five million dollars. Eventually the row over the bonds issue polarised de Valera and the leaders of the Irish-American community so much that in 1920, de Valera with the help of O'Mara,

McGarrity, Conbey, Walsh and Harry Boland set up his own Irish-American organisation, the American Association for the Recognition of the Irish Republic (AARIR). Its chairman was John Hearn, a staunch de Valera supporter. Membership of the organisation grew steadily to several hundred thousand Irish-Americans who, in later years, would subscribe funds to the *Irish Press*. A committee to represent those who had contributed to the Dáil loan was also set up by de Valera. Called the 'American Bondholders Committee', again de Valera made his presence felt by appointing John Hearn as treasurer. When de Valera returned to Ireland in December 1920, he left approximately three million dollars of the Dáil Loan on deposit in several New York banks. James O'Mara stayed behind and attempted to develop the AARIR into an Irish-American lobby group to campaign for the recognition of the Irish republic by the American government. De Valera, however, viewed the organisation solely as a fund raising one and resisted O'Mara's plans. He later precipitated O'Mara's resignation by demanding an auditor's report into the finances of the organisation. The final straw came at the AARIR convention in Chicago in April 1921, during which a cable from de Valera to Joseph McGarrity suggesting that a levy be put on membership of the organisation was read out. This immediately provoked O'Mara's resignation. He had not been consulted and pointed out that de Valera had left almost three million dollars of the original bond drive in American banks when he returned to Ireland. This money was still on deposit, therefore a new levy was not necessary. Losing faith, O'Mara also resigned his Dáil seat and returned to his business interests. His brother Stephen, another businessman (who would later become an *Irish Press* director), was then dispatched from Ireland by de Valera to take over the AARIR.[23]

A year later, in August 1922, the Free State government led by William Cosgrave successfully applied to the New York High Court for an injunction to prevent the New York banks from handing over any of the money to de Valera or anyone acting for him. Concurrently, in Ireland the Cosgrave administration applied to the Irish High Court for a declaration that it, as the legitimate government of the Free State, was entitled to the £81,000 that was on deposit in Irish banks. De Valera, in his capacity as trustee, objected and argued that the money had been subscribed for the purposes of a republican government only. He was supported in his objection by one of the other trustees, Stephen O'Mara, and opposed by the third, Bishop Michael Fogarty of Killaloe, who along with most of the Irish banks supported the government. In July 1924, the High Court ruled in the government's favour. Although de Valera appealed to the Supreme Court, his appeal was rejected in

December 1925 and the Irish banks subsequently handed the money over to the Free State government. Following this success, the government applied on the same grounds to the New York Supreme Court for a declaration that it was entitled to the money on deposit in the New York banks. De Valera again contested the action and galvanised better support this time round. While the Bondholders Committee supported de Valera's assertion that the money was for the exclusive use of a republican government, the New York banks remained neutral and maintained that the money should be returned to the original subscribers. However, the case was not to be heard until March 1927.

Back home in Ireland, the political battle for the hearts and minds of the Irish people continued. In post-independence Ireland with the 'heady days of revolution over', the work of reconstruction and nation building had begun and a population educated for generations in a nationalist faith had come to expect 'that a golden age would follow the ending of British rule'.[24] While in the past all political, economic and cultural grievances had been laid at the door of the alien ruler, it now fell on the shoulders of Cumann na nGaedheal to provide this golden age. Forging a distinct Irish identity proved beyond the capabilities of the party, however. In formulating its vision of Irishness, Cumann na nGaedheal severely under-emphasised the cultural identity of the Irish people and it was this omission that later allowed Fianna Fáil via the *Irish Press* to exploit the hunger for cultural cohesiveness in the new nation state. During the civil war, Cumann na nGaedheal had found a strong and influential ally in the Catholic Church. It had strongly castigated de Valera and the anti-Treaty faction for causing the civil war and had overtly supported the pro-Treaty faction. When the Free State was established, Cumann na nGaedheal increasingly turned to the Church for political support. After many years of war, partition and the bitter divisions of the civil war, the new government could not easily appeal to the cohesiveness that nationalism provided. Instead, the government turned to religion to provide that inclusive feeling of nationhood. Indeed, as successor to the Irish Parliamentary Party, Cumann na nGaedheal inherited the latter's inability to play cultural politics. Its relatively narrow support base, chiefly the urban middle class, big farmers, shopkeepers and former unionists, accentuated its problems of legitimation and political appeal.

The party thus lacked cultural authority and after seventy-seven civil war executions it could hardly claim to have charismatic authority. Therefore the new government could only rely on legal authority; authority that was sanctioned by the former coloniser and so it increasingly turned to the Church to provide it with legitimation. Indeed, before independence the Church already had a significant input into areas such as health, education, art and welfare but this input was later magnified by Cumann na nGaedheal's dependence on it for legitimacy. In the absence of a social programme of its own, the party adopted that of the Church and 'transferred the church's social authoritarianism into the state's basic attitude'.[25] Largely neglecting to develop and highlight crucial nation building characteristics and distinct cultural attributes such as language, political economy, race or political ideology, the party adopted and propagated the cultural interpretative models of the Catholic Church as its own. As regards the economy, both the government and the Church were non-interventionist. The government did not believe that it had a duty to find work for the unemployed, while the Church believed it had the sole right to control social services. The end result was a strong partnership of social and cultural conservatism and agreed authoritarianism. This prevailing conservatism resulted in a litany of conservative public watchdogs being established and a glut of conservative legislation being passed by the government. These included a law censoring films in 1923, the forcing of a debate on matrimonial law in 1925 that eventually led to the prohibition of divorce, the establishment of a Committee on Evil Literature in 1926, and the Censorship of Publications Act of 1929.

Alongside its failure to develop a distinct Irish nationality, the Cumann na nGaedheal government also failed to radically alter Ireland's political or economic relationship with the former coloniser. Negating the old Sinn Féin ideal of self-sufficiency, the government left intact the policy of free trade that it had inherited from the British. Indeed, in its economic policy, the government 'gave no indication that it wished to alter the traditional role of Ireland as the agricultural complement to industrial England'.[26] Despite its success in securing equality for dominions within their relationship with Britain and appointing ambassadors abroad, the government's policy was one of conservatism and not the radical nationalism that had defined the old Sinn Féin. Stressing the benefits of membership of the Commonwealth, the party's attitude 'differed little from that of the British Conservative party between 1895–1905; a well governed Ireland would receive positive economic benefits from its association with Britain and quickly forget old passions and hatreds'.[27] Even among its staunchest adherents 'Cumann na nGaedheal was not seen as a party 'serving the nationalist aspirations of the Irish people'.[28]

Thus the Free State government's attempt to formulate a distinct Irish national identity came to little or nothing. Lacking any creative vision, the party merely made Irish nationality a reflection of the Catholic ethos of the time. It failed to foster a distinct Irish identity due to its inability to highlight and develop distinct cultural attributes such as language, political economy or political ideology. With the arrival of Fianna Fáil, Cumann na nGaedheal faced an ever increasing battle to maintain its credibility with the electorate. From 1926 onwards, Fianna Fáil began a game of cultural nationalist politics that Cumann na nGaedheal found it could not compete in.

For its part, Fianna Fáil drew its inspiration for a distinct Irish identity from the cultural nationalist revival that had begun in the 1880s. This revival had as its aim an 'Irish Ireland', to eliminate all that was English in Irish life and to make Irish people aware of their own cultural heritage and identity. The cultural stagnation prevalent at the time was perhaps best summed up by Archbishop Croke who declared in 1884 that the Irish were 'daily importing from England, not only her manufactured goods, but together with her fashions, her accents, her vicious literature, her music, her dances, and her manifold mannerisms, her games also and her pastimes, to the utter discredit of our own grand national sports as though we were ashamed of them'.[29] The revival resulted in the foundation of several cultural nationalist institutions. These included the Gaelic Athletic Association which had as its main aim 'the organisation of Irish sport by Irishmen, not Englishmen',[30] the Gaelic League which promoted the revival of the Irish Language, and the Irish Literary Theatre which nurtured a national literary revival. Emphasising its commitment to a simple, frugal and virtuous rural Gaelic civilisation, the revival mobilised the masses to engage in nationalist politics. Economically, the revival argued against the over-concentration of industry and stressed that protectionism would allow Irish industries to flourish when freed from the debilitating competition of British imports. Later, neutrality through the guise of conscription became an issue. After 1914, support for the Irish Parliamentary Party declined rapidly, caused mainly by John Redmond's recruitment of Irishmen to fight in the British army during the First World War. Since one of the main principle beliefs of the cultural nationalist revival was that the British connection was the source of all Ireland's political, economic and cultural ills, Fianna Fáil based its vision of Ireland and Irishness on that very same manifesto. The identity project that de Valera consolidated was a mixture of despair directed at the existing order as maintained by

Cumann na nGaedheal and of the political action that would take place under a Fianna Fáil government. Acknowledging the power that mass media could contribute to such a project, the party established the *Irish Press* to codify its identity project for mass consumption. When setting out its aims and objectives, Fianna Fáil sought to regenerate the national consciousness that Cumann na nGaedheal had failed to revive. Such a national consciousness was defined in terms of highlighting commonalities such as language, religion, culture and shared history. It was also defined in terms of differentiation from another nation or a perceived internal enemy. Fianna Fáil's objectives were a combination of both. Its aims were:

1) To secure the unity and independence of Ireland as a Republic.
2) To restore the Irish language as the spoken language of the people and to develop a distinctive national life in accordance with Irish traditions and ideals.
3) To make the resources and wealth of Ireland subservient to the needs and welfare of all the people of Ireland.
4) To make Ireland, as far as possible, economically self-contained and self-sufficing.
5) To establish as many families as practicable on the land.
6) By suitable distribution of power, to promote the ruralisation of essential industries as opposed to their concentration in cities.[31]

Such objectives heralded a return to the objectives of the cultural nationalists of the 1880s. All the crucial cultural characteristics were there: restoring the language, self-sufficiency, ruralism and familism. Indeed, by the mid-1940s, Irish society would be 'reconstructed according to the model of a Catholic and radical nationalist imaginary, an imaginary that had been decisively forged before independence'.[32] According to Fianna Fáil, its manifesto was the cure for the ills of the Free State and would give Ireland a distinct and independent national identity based on Irish nationalism and culture. The objective of the party was, as such, to differentiate Ireland from England as much as possible. The notion of a united, independent republic represented an undoing of partition and the creation of a sovereign thirty-two county republic – as opposed to the British monarchy. The prominence given to restoring the Irish language and developing a distinctive national life in accordance with Irish cultural traditions again highlighted the linguistic and cultural differences between the two states.

A different and distinct economic policy was also propagated. The policy of protectionism was at complete variance with the British policy of free trade. Not only was the policy perceived as patriotic, but by eliminating foreign competition, the hope was to build up an indigenous industrial base. This in turn would lead to an expansion of the economy, increased employment and increased spending that would ultimately benefit agriculture. The policy offered something to everyone, from native industrialists and farmers to the unemployed. Likewise, the 1927 addition of a pledge to withhold payment of the land annuities was portrayed as a matter of national pride. While Cumann na nGaedheal had meekly handed over the money amid the depression of the 1920s, Fianna Fáil gained the upper hand by arguing that the money should be invested in Irish industry and agriculture. The final objectives of ruralism and familism were also differentiations from the urbanised and highly industrialised England. The party's programme of ruralism and the diffusion of property ownership was portrayed as the creation of a nation of small property owners, with each family having its own stake in the nation. The party also made a pitch for the support of the Catholic Church by calling for prayers to be said in the Dáil and for it not to sit on Church holidays. It also criticised the Cumann na nGaedheal government for its failure to consult the hierarchy over its attempts to have a papal nunciature established in Dublin. Fianna Fáil's vision celebrated and propagated that 'uniquely puritanical variant of Irish Catholicism' by emphasising that Ireland could not live beyond its means. The aim instead was to develop 'a self-sufficient Ireland neither dependent on any other nation nor expectant of a rich, luxurious life. The vision was of the rural, frugal, family-orientated Catholic society, cognisant of its limits and not envious of the wealth or economic security of other modern nations'.[33]

The appeal of the Fianna Fáil programme lay in its ability to evoke powerful nationalist sentiments while simultaneously responding to specific political, economic and cultural problems. While the party's vision resonated with the sentiments of the cultural nationalists of the 1880s, it also offered a practical political programme that would deliver that vision. The connection made between the cultural vision and political policy was to prove a potent force over the succeeding decades. While Fianna Fáil became 'the party of the people and the nation, in contrast Cumann na nGaedheal was seen as the party of particular and privileged interests'.[34] Such a theme would resonate through general elections for decades after. The party system, like the newspaper media of the time, did not divide right from left but 'divided from each other over issues of national and cultural identity, over relationships with the ex-imperial power and over what might be best described as different strategies towards national development'.[35] Fianna Fáil represented more than a political alternative; it was simultaneously a cultural alternative. Indeed, Cumann na nGaedheal's inability to promote Irish identity resulted in a marked increase in the circulation of British newspapers in Ireland – a fact that several prominent academics feared would dilute or even destroy what was left of the Irish language and Irish way of life. De Valera's announcement at the second Fianna Fáil ard fheis in 1927, that the party intended to launch a new national newspaper, was well timed. It was in that year that the Report of the Evil Literature Committee was completed. After its release, several academic and religious personnel spoke out against the prominence of English publications in Ireland and their fear of the 'dominating influence of an alien press'.[36] Among those who spoke out were professors Eoin MacNeill and Thomas O'Rahilly, Fr Richard Devane and Reverend Michael MacInerny. Their objections to the English publications were based on four grounds; those of economics, religion, culture and nationality. Firstly, the Irish newspaper and printing trades were threatened by the unfair competition posed by the English publications, whose printing costs amounted to virtually nothing when their print costs were absorbed into the overall production costs. The publications were then dumped on the Irish market where the continuous advertising of English goods and services also posed a threat to indigenous industry. The publications were also of the wrong religion, as most espoused Protestant or secular morals that did nothing to enhance the Catholic way of life. Finally, despite political independence, the continued presence of English publications in large numbers ensured that Irish nationality was formed under the influence of the English ideological dominance that the publications represented. Although the Irish were 'spending a great amount of money in trying to revive the Irish language and Irish culture', if Irish children had 'only English magazines for the development and entertainment of their young minds' the effort seemed 'doomed to failure'. According to the academics, 'against such propaganda of the English language and English ideas' any attempt at a national revival resembled an 'effort to beat back an avalanche with a sweeping brush'.[37]

The sheer volume of English publications sold in Ireland at the time gave some validity to their concerns, as 'a glance at the counter of any newsagent's shop' would convince even the most sceptical that the Irish were 'in a condition of mental bondage' through purchasing 'from our former masters practically all the food consumed by our minds'.[38] During the 1920s, there were eighteen English dailies with a combined circulation of between 135,000–165,000, twelve English Sunday titles with a circulation of 429,411 and fifty-three weekly and twenty-four fortnightly or monthly English publications available in Ireland.[39] As a result of this intense competition, the number of Irish daily newspapers had fallen from seven to three and the remaining native newspapers had begun to imitate the worst aspects of the imported newspapers by incorporating sensationalist crime reporting and political and society gossip into their publications. According to the academics, while the main function of newspapers was the dissemination of ideas and the promotion and fostering of a national identity, the English publications had no understanding of the problems faced by the Irish state or its people and instead concentrated on the institutions and policies of the English state, with no regard for Irish readers. While the Irish people were 'engaged in an heroic effort to revive our national language, national customs, national values and national culture', these objectives could not 'be achieved without a cheap, healthy and independent native press'. In the face of English competition, such a press was 'an impossibility'.[40] Thus the academics called for a tariff to be imposed on all imported publications to 'protect the products of Irish hands and workers and the products of Irish brains and writers' and to 'break the stranglehold the English press' had on Ireland.[41] The call fell on the deaf ears of Cumann na nGaedheal. Within a few years, however, de Valera would have addressed all their concerns through the establishment of the *Irish Press*.

Indeed, that same year, 1927, saw the Fianna Fáil ard fheis pass a resolution pledging 'its ardent and practical support to the projected new daily paper' and a worldwide campaign to raise the necessary capital began immediately.[42] In Ireland a nationwide subscription campaign began, while in Australia a friend of de Valera's, Archbishop Daniel Mannix of Melbourne, a former President of Maynooth College, sold bonds and urged support for the new nationalist venture. De Valera, accompanied by Frank Gallagher, spent the spring and summer of 1927 touring America, seeking financial backing for his new enterprise. According to de Valera, he went to America to 'organise the support of our people for complete independence . . . One of the means by which the movement for Irish independence could best be organised and supported in my opinion was through an Irish newspaper, a newspaper that would really represent the Irish people and I went to America to get subscriptions for the capital of that newspaper.'[43] However, de Valera sold the idea of a newspaper very differently in America and Ireland. In America, 'he sold the idea as a national Irish newspaper, but at home in Ireland, he wore a different hat, selling the idea to party supporters as "our paper" with people like Gerry Boland knocking on doors collecting subscriptions. The company was public but was not quoted and many subscribers believed it was a cause rather than a business operation, but that did not give de Valera the right to grab control.'[44] Indeed, it was during this American trip that the issue of who was entitled to ownership of the Dáil bonds was resolved. De Valera began his tour by giving evidence as three legal teams, representing the Bondholders Committee, the Free State and de Valera, fought for control of the fund. The case proved a complex one for the presiding judge who had to listen to arguments about the differences between the First and Second Dáil, and whether Cosgrave's government was republican or not. In the end, Judge Curtis Peters ruled that neither party was entitled to the money and ordered that receivers be appointed to ensure that subscribers got back whatever money was still in the accounts less any expenses. In effect, each subscriber was to receive fifty-eight per cent of what they had originally subscribed. The Irish government then opened an office in New York for the purpose of repaying the bondholders. Commenting on the decision, de Valera stated that he was not 'dissatisfied' with the decision as 'the Free State's claim to this money was audacious merely and untenable in the explicit representations made to the subscribers when the money was being subscribed'. His actions had been merely 'confined to resisting that claim'.[45]

In the wake of the judgement, however, there began a concerted effort by de Valera and the Bondholders Committee to persuade bondholders to sign over their bonds to de Valera rather than cash them in. Unknown to Martin Conbey (de Valera's American lawyer), Frank Walsh, lawyer to the Bondholders Committee and chairman of the American branch of the Irish Press Ltd, wrote to the bondholders to put forward the case for the reassignment of their bonds. In his circular, Walsh appealed to them to make their money available a second time 'to break the stranglehold imposed on the Irish people by an alien press'. According to Walsh, many bondholders had already informed de Valera that on receipt of their checks, they would 'immediately endorse them and turn them in to his account, so as to be available for the establishment of the needed Irish newspaper'. While the funds were being solicited by way of donation, de Valera would not 'derive personally any profit from them'. Indeed, according to Walsh, de Valera would ensure that the subscribers who would by Justice Peter's decision 'receive only a part of the monies originally subscribed by them' would not 'ultimately suffer'. He could not 'conceive of any Irish national government worthy of the name refusing or neglecting to make good to the subscribers the monies that were advanced by them and used in the national effort from 1919 to 1921'.[46] In later years, de Valera would indeed 'make good' the promises of the 1919 Irish government by repaying all of the money due on the bonds, the proceeds of which would not go to the original subscribers, but to the *Irish Press*. Recipients of Walsh's circular were invited to sign a power of attorney form, which invited bondholders to 'sell, assign, transfer and set over unto Eamon de Valera, his executors, administrators and assigns, all my right, title and interest in and to the Bond Certificate(s) . . . and all sums of money, both principal and interest now due on, or hereafter to become due on . . . said Bond Certificate(s)'.[47] Since the holders of most of the bonds were supporters of de Valera and the republican movement, instead of reclaiming their money, many assigned the bonds to him to finance the *Irish Press*. In any event, only about one third of the bondholders applied for a refund in the wake of the repayment decision, with the majority of bondholders either disregarding the value of the bonds or signing them over to de Valera.[48] The campaign to get bondholders to assign their bonds to de Valera caused much controversy in Ireland, with Cumann na nGaedheal deputies later claiming that the bondholders were 'swindled'.[49] In a memo to President William Cosgrave, however, a finance department secretary expressed the view that the repayment by the receivers of fifty-eight per cent of the value of the bonds had received so much publicity that the bondholders could not 'be regarded as being unaware of the value of the bonds'. According to the secretary, if they transferred their bonds to de Valera, they were 'doing so with their eyes open, as far as the question of parting with valuable consideration' was concerned.[50]

When the reassigned bonds began to arrive, Conbey wrote to Walsh expressing his surprise 'that a large number of bonds in favour of Mr de Valera' had been filed with the receivers. Conbey did not know anything about them and presumed that Walsh was 'familiar with them'.[51] Walsh replied immediately, pleading with Conbey to play along with the scheme and again represent de Valera at the hearings that the receivers had organised. According to Walsh, because he was 'appearing before the receivers in the above matters representing the bondholders', he had already taken an 'opportunity of expressing the opinion that the form of assignment, assigning bond certificates to Mr de Valera was in every way correct'. He now believed that the assignments would 'not be questioned'. Nonetheless, Walsh thought it prudent that Conbey stay on as de Valera's attorney. According to Walsh, should the assignments to de Valera be questioned in any way, the opinion that he had already expressed would stand for what it was worth and not be weakened by him also having to appear on de Valera's behalf.[52] The assignment of bonds so preoccupied de Valera's mind that on Christmas Eve 1928 he cabled Conbey and instructed him to 'file claim with receivers immediately as my attorney for all bond certificates assigned to me'.[53] Conbey replied that such a direct claim was unnecessary as there had been a number of meetings between himself, the attorney for the receivers and the judge appointed to referee the claims. The outcome of these negotiations had seen the judge recognise the legality of the ordinary assignments – those bonds assigned to de Valera by the individuals in whose name the bonds stood. There were, however, a number of assignments from the next of kin of deceased bondholders, and Conbey foresaw 'some difficulty in convincing the referee that these should be allowed in the absence of proof of the devolution of title'.[54] While the exact number of bonds converted has never been made public, the money de Valera received from the transfer was crucial as start-up capital for the *Irish Press*. Ironically, William Martin Murphy, founder of the Independent Newspapers legacy, had also bought a Dáil Bond Certificate to the value of ten pounds. He also received a power of attorney form to turn the bond over to de Valera but, needless to say, he did not turn over his bond to help fund the *Irish Press*.[55]

In March 1927, Fianna Fáil launched its first party publication, a weekly newspaper called *The Nation*. The paper was established by Fianna Fáil TD Sean T. O'Kelly and was the direct precursor to the *Irish Press*. The paper which 'stood for the freedom for which the men and women of 1916 and the years succeeding fought and died' was extremely nationalist and gave extensive coverage to de Valera's 1927 America trip.[56] *The Nation* was edited by O'Kelly until 1929, when Frank Gallagher (who later became founding editor of the *Irish Press*) took over. This position allowed Gallagher to experiment with various populist themes and tones that would later be mirrored in the *Irish Press*. From its genesis, *The Nation* attempted to win the support of the lower and rural classes by adopting a populist anti-imperialistic outlook. With headlines like 'Irish Labour Party Stands for Imperialism' and 'Cumann na nGaedheal's Subterfuge Fails' the paper successfully branded the parties as imperialists responsible for the economic malaise afflicting the country. In contrast, the paper highlighted the virtues of Fianna Fáil's policy of protectionism and also published the party's election material during the two 1927 elections, during which, faced with the hostility of the existing press, the party won forty-four seats in the June election and fifty-seven seats in the September election. Although *The Nation* played a central role in allowing Fianna Fáil and Frank Gallagher to experiment with various political themes and policies, the paper's circulation peaked at ten thousand copies per issue and did not meet the party's need to combat the negative coverage of the *Irish Independent* and the *Irish Times*. As a party publication it was merely preaching to the converted and it was clear that a more professional newspaper was needed. This, of course, meant raising capital, and de Valera's Association for the Recognition of the Irish Republic proved invaluable by providing the organisational structure needed to form fund raising committees around America.

In early 1928, de Valera and Gallagher again spent almost two months touring America. This tour, again organised by Frank Walsh and Martin Conbey, included Boston, New York, Washington, San Francisco, Chicago and Los Angeles. It saw de Valera use an anti-British ideology to appeal to Irish-American sentimentalities and entice donations. According to de Valera, in Ireland 'it was impossible to raise our million dollars for our paper from our people because of the money taken from the Irish people and not used to build up Irish enterprise'. Fianna Fáil was thus seeking to raise 'half the money at home and to get half from our friends in the United States'. The Irish people had 'subscribed half a million dollars within six weeks' simply because the new paper was 'something they wanted'.[57] Again trying to harness the financial support of the Irish-American community, de Valera wrote to Joseph McGarrity shortly before leaving Ireland, stating that the total capital required was £250,000 or roughly $1,250,000. Of this sum £100,000 was 'being sought in Ireland by way of subscriptions in advance of the prospectus for blocks of shares of value £100 and over and in America for blocks of shares of $500 and over'. De Valera therefore wanted '1000 people in the United States' who would 'invest at least $500 in the enterprise'. He reassured McGarrity that as the proposition was 'purely a business one' he did not expect it would be 'difficult to get them'.[58] But both Clan na nGael and McGarrity were as cold to this attempt by de Valera to found a newspaper as they had been to his plans to purchase the *Freeman's Journal*. Thus the organisation of fund raising fell to de Valera's own

Irish-American organisation, the AARIR. At one meeting of Irish-American businessmen held in January 1928 on the roof New York's Waldorf Astoria hotel, de Valera secured twenty-four individual subscriptions of $500, a total of $12,000 for the new paper.[59]

The AARIR was also particularly strong in California, where it was led by prominent Irish-American businessman, Andrew Gallagher. De Valera arrived in San Francisco on 20 January 1928, having given Gallagher only three days' notice. At that stage, all Gallagher could do was publicise the visit by word of mouth. As a result only thirty people showed up to hear de Valera's speech and very few offered subscriptions.[60] De Valera also visited Los Angles and Chicago. Although the visit was not as financially rewarding as previous visits, from an organisational point of view it was highly successful because de Valera augmented the AARIR with the establishment of the American Promotions Committee. This New York based body was handed the unenviable task of identifying one thousand wealthy individuals and convincing them to invest five hundred dollars each in de Valera's newspaper. Both the AARIR and the APC worked closely together. While the APC co-ordinated the fund raising on a national basis, the AARIR instructed its state branches to establish committees in each major city to search out and approach potential investors. To generate interest among the Irish-American community, the APC circulated a paper written by Frank Gallagher. The circular, entitled *The Need for a National Daily Newspaper in Ireland*, noted that there was no real 'national daily newspaper in Ireland' because the existing press was 'consistently pro-British and imperialistic in its outlook'. As a result, 'disgust with the present Irish daily press' had resulted in 'a rapid increase in the circulation of English newspapers in Ireland'. There was, according to Gallagher, only one remedy; to 'establish a great daily newspaper' that would 'faithfully interpret Irish thought and foster Irish culture and courageously champion the right of the Irish people'. That, according to Gallagher, was the 'purpose of the Irish Press Limited'.[61] The circular also made the concept of the *Irish Press* a viable business proposition by noting that in the 1927 election, 411,000 first preference votes went to Fianna Fáil candidates who had no daily newspaper to represent their views. The circular claimed that if such a feat could be repeated in sales of the paper, it was sure to be a financial success. In addition to this, the circular noted that many other potential readers were 'opposed to the anti-national attitude of the present daily press' and would instead buy the *Irish Press*.[62] Despite all this activity throughout

America, the AARIR found it hard to attract investors. Investment was not very forthcoming and in May 1928, the national committee of the APC was forced to reduce the minimum subscription from five hundred dollars to fifty dollars. It was later forced to again reduce the minimum rate to five dollars.[63]

De Valera returned to Ireland in February 1928, and the following September incorporated the Irish Press Ltd, even though the American quota of half a million dollars had not yet been fully subscribed. To encourage further American donations, he sent copies of the company's share prospectus to the APC. He also dispatched Frank Aiken and Ernie O'Malley to co-ordinate the American fundraising effort. Before Aiken left for America, de Valera provided him with explicit instructions. Aiken was to 'get the AARIR in all cases to accept the American Promotions Committee as the duly constituted authority so far as the newspaper is concerned'. He was also instructed to seek help from the Ancient Order of Hibernians, the Knights of Columbus and from 'any IRA organisations that may exist in the principal cities'.[64] The issue of how control over the American subscriptions was to be achieved was also explicitly spelled out to Aiken:

> You understand that the American subscriptions are all to be pooled and that I am to apply *in my own name* for the equivalent number of shares at Five Dollars to the Pound. A single certificate will then be issued by the company in my name for the whole amount pooled. This will give me the voting strength of the whole of the American shares. I am to take such steps as will secure the capital and interest rights of the individual subscribers. I shall write the lawyers especially about this matter and will send you a copy. You must be careful not to suggest that the American subscribers will get shares or certificates for shares *directly from the company*. What they are likely to get will be 'Participation Certificates' from an American Trust Company if this can be arranged without too much expense. Of course, if any large subscribers make it an absolute *condition* that they should get shares directly from the company, that can be arranged.[65]

Both Aiken and O'Malley arrived in New York in October 1928 and concentrated on contacting prominent individuals associated with the previous bond drive. They also visited Irish-American communities in Boston, Philadelphia and Chicago, encouraging past members of the AARIR to rejoin and help the latest cause. In particular, they concentrated on the de Valera stronghold of California, with Aiken arriving in San Francisco in late November 1928 to address a meeting of the state's APC at the Whitcomb Hotel. His speech concentrated on the discrepancy between the speed of the Irish and American collections and warned that the venture could not proceed until the American quota had been subscribed. He also described the miserable social and political conditions of the Free State – the unemployment, emigration, and poverty – and emphasised that the *Irish Press* would give Ireland the freedom and prosperity of a republic. According to Aiken, the 'sacrifices of those' who had 'struggled for the freedom of Ireland' were 'as yet without fruit . . . because the daily papers in Ireland helped the enemy'. Freedom would only be achieved when Ireland had 'a national daily press' that would 'sustain the courage of the people in a hard struggle and give a fair representation to the views' of those who knew how best to 'shake off England's political and economic domination'. Aiken told them that the 'proposed paper' would do this.[66] He then launched a reinvigorated drive within the state by visiting and cajoling *Irish Press* committees in Sacramento, Stockton and Los Angeles. In that city, door-to-door collections in Irish-American parts of the city proved highly successful. By December 1928, San Francisco and Los Angeles had collected fifteen thousand dollars. By the end of January 1929, the twenty thousand dollar mark was surpassed.[67] The issue of the American subscriptions was never far from de Valera's mind as he urged Aiken to 'move heaven and earth to get our people to realise that if we fail in getting the American quota before May, we will have received the biggest blow we have got since the Cease Fire'.[68] In April 1929, satisfied that he had done as much as he could, Aiken returned home. O'Malley remained behind and began to write for Vanguard Press in New York. During Aiken's time in America, the issue of Irish-Americans making prepaid yearly subscriptions to the *Irish Press* was brought to his attention many times. When he suggested the idea to de Valera, the latter rejected it because it would 'run across the effort to secure share capital'.[69] But despite the success of the Aiken and O'Malley visit, in the following months the economic situation in America deteriorated as the great depression took hold. Totally oblivious to the economic hardship suffered by Irish-Americans, de Valera persisted in his demands for reaching the quota as quickly as possible.

In a letter to William Lyndon, secretary of the AARIR, de Valera bluntly stated that when he started to organise the paper, he expected that the 'securing of the American quota would be the least of difficulties to be faced'. In contrast, America had been a 'sore disappointment' despite the fact that his every appeal had 'been to make the securing of this capital the main activity of those' who desired to advance Ireland's cause. The successful establishment of the paper was necessary to create a 'right national spirit' and 'counter the present efforts at Anglicisation'. On the other hand, failure to secure the necessary funding would mean 'failure of far more than the establishment of the newspaper'. According to de Valera, the 'capacity of Fianna Fáil as a party' would 'be judged by it and the reaction on our credit in the popular mind may postpone for a considerable period the day when control of affairs is entrusted to a national government'.[70] Such letters often prompted a gentle rebuff from the representatives of the Irish-American community who, given the economic conditions, were doing as much as they could for the new newspaper. According to one correspondent, if de Valera really knew what condition America was in he 'would not be surprised at the slow progress . . . in raising money for the new newspaper. . . . Hundreds of thousands of men were out of work' and it was 'hard to interest them in anything outside purely American affairs'. An extension of time was necessary, as the AARIR 'got no help from anyone but the working class and they require time to make money on dances and picnics and all such things'.[71] Incensed at Clan na nGael's attitude towards the *Irish Press*, de Valera accused them of 'hostility'.[72] Indeed, the Clan, and in particular Joseph McGarrity, were aghast at de Valera for splitting with Sinn Féin and had no faith in the constitutional path that both he and Fianna Fáil had embarked upon. According to McGarrity, the 'Clan as an organisation' was 'cold to the proposition' of a newspaper. It considered it as 'a part of the political effort' in which the Clan had 'no faith whatever'. Nonetheless, McGarrity noted that 'things in a business way' were bad and many former supporters were avoiding gatherings where subscriptions were likely to be asked.[73]

De Valera returned to America one last time in December 1929, 'for the purpose of making a last ditch effort to fill the American quota' to use the words of the AARIR publicity bulletin.[74] It was during a speech in San Francisco that de Valera uttered for the first time the phrase that was to become the motto of the *Irish Press*. According to de Valera, the only reason he was founding a newspaper was to provide the Irish with a paper that would 'give them the truth in the news, without attempting to colour it for party purposes'.[75] To drag out the last few subscriptions, a pack was put together for potential investors. Each recipient received a copy of

Frank Gallagher's *The Need for a National Newspaper in Ireland*, a cover letter from de Valera himself and an addressed envelope for the return of subscriptions. During his visit, de Valera used a statement by Free State government minister Ernest Blythe to the effect that the Free State was happy to be a member of the British Commonwealth to show how complacent the Irish people had become because of the absence of a truly national newspaper. According to de Valera, if Fianna Fáil had a daily paper, 'Blythe's statement could be used to waken up the nation'. The existing press had pretended that 'nothing vital' had been said. This, according to de Valera, was 'Britain's final victory over what remained of the Collins mentality and policy'.[76] It was thus of 'fundamental importance' that Ireland's 'old friends and active sympathisers' give their all to help bring the 'newspaper enterprise' to a quick 'successful issue'.[77] As well as fund raising, de Valera also acquired practical newspaper experience, spending over six months visiting American newspapers to study production techniques. According to Tim Pat Coogan, 'he criss-crossed the United States collecting money and called at newspapers to see how they were run. One of the most frequently asked questions by de Valera as he toured American newspaper offices was "How do you control it?"'[78] By this time, support for the paper in America had waned although several letters and telegrams of support and subscriptions for the new paper still arrived expressing 'great interest to the coming of the *Irish Press*'. The paper would, it was hoped, be 'superior to its competitors . . . on the grounds of truth and perspective' and would make a 'startling appearance in a field . . . long held by the English propaganda press'.[79]

Despite the depression, de Valera succeeded in raising a substantial sum of money in America and a corporation was formed in Delaware in May 1931 to invest this money in the newspaper. This entity represented a sizeable shareholding (believed to be forty-three per cent) in the newspaper company and control of it secured effective control of the Irish company.[80] Despite the fact that the American office of the *Irish Press* was based in New York, de Valera chose America's second smallest state Delaware as the location for what was to become known as the American Corporation. Comparable to Switzerland in its acceptance of money from anywhere and its obtuse state corporation legislation governing company formation, structure and existence, Delaware was unique among American states. The American Corporation held two types of shares. It held 60,000 non-voting 'A' shares financed and owned by the Irish-American investors. It also held 200 'B' shares that carried the voting rights.[81] These de

Valera himself acquired, establishing a separate holding trust that was administered by both himself and Fianna Fáil advocate and Irish diplomat Sean Nunan. Although de Valera adopted the role of trustee to the American investors, since he controlled the voting shares he also controlled the Corporation. Thus, the American Corporation ultimately achieved what it was established to do; maintain absolute control of the Press company for the de Valera family. It was de Valera more so than anyone else who benefited – politically and financially – from the establishment of the *Irish Press*. To many, such a share structure represented 'the most brazen concentration of power in the hands of one individual known to the newspaper industry anywhere in the Western world'.[82] According to de Valera, the motive behind the establishment of the American Corporation lay not in assuming control but in accommodating American shareholders. According to de Valera, 'the dividends on all the shares purchased with their money' were 'to be transferred under trust deed to them for division in America, amongst their own shareholders, for a very good reason, that in America, American Corporation Stock would be more readily transferable and more information could be obtained about it than Irish Stock'.[83] Conversely, in later years when Irish shareholders wanted to known more about the voting rights that control of the American Corporation carried, they often found that such information was unattainable. Such a set-up also alienated American shareholders, who had to depend on de Valera for information about the company. Thus instead of the American Corporation being 'an act of representation of the assignees, an act taken for their own defence, for their own protection and in their own interests',[84] in essence it was established by de Valera to ensure that ultimate control of the company remained within the family.

In Ireland, fund raising was hampered by the fact that both the *Irish Independent* and the *Irish Times* refused to carry advertisements soliciting investment for the new paper. Upon his return from America in February 1928, de Valera and former director of publicity for Sinn Féin, Bob Brennan, toured Ireland to encourage local branches or cumann of Fianna Fáil to canvass local supporters for subscriptions and organise door-to-door collections. Indeed, de Valera modelled his method of fund raising on that of Daniel O'Connell, valuing even the smallest contribution as a guarantee of a sense of belonging to the great enterprise.[85] Frank Gallagher again penned several circulars for distribution to potential business investors. According to Gallagher, while the imported British press was 'markedly hostile to Irish thought, culture and philosophy', the existing Irish newspapers were

'British in sympathy and outlook' and coloured 'both home and foreign news to suit imperial policy'. The Irish people longed for 'a paper that would express their own thoughts and portray their own feelings'. This desire would make 'the success of the proposed journal almost a certainty'. The new paper would not, however, be 'a propagandist sheet or a mere party organ'; it would be 'an Irish national newspaper in the broadest sense championing the full rights and the people of Ireland'. Proof of this lay in the fact that 'the policy of the paper' would be 'under the control of Mr de Valera'.[86] The Fianna Fáil weekly publication, *The Nation*, was also utilised to appeal to the party faithful for financial support. Indeed, the illusion of shared ownership of the party publication seemed too attractive an opportunity for most party faithful to turn down. A prospectus soliciting share investment of £200,000 in one pound ordinary shares was published, encouraging party faithful to contribute. This figure was the bare minimum needed. It was, as de Valera put it, a 'figure cut to the bone'.[87] The objective of the company, according to the prospectus, was to provide what was 'generally admitted to be a national necessity, an up-to-date morning, evening and weekly Press that would be characteristic of the nation, thoroughly Irish in every respect, and unlike the present press strictly fair to all parties'.[88]

A competition for a name for the new paper attracted many replies, including some from America. Writing to de Valera, one entrant suggested calling the new paper *The National Compass* 'because like the compass, north, south, east and west are Ireland's cardinal points and she has 32 counties, which corresponds to the 32 points of the Mariners' compass'. The analogy was perfect; 'with a compass and a captain like the man this letter is sent to, Ireland would soon be on the true course'.[89] An Irish name was also suggested and rejected; a close friend of de Valera, Aodh de Blacam, who later wrote for the *Irish Press*, 'pleaded with de Valera to name the *Irish Press* newspaper in Irish, "Sceala Éireann" or something similar, but de Valera the hard businessman, never permitted romantic Irish proclivities to interfere with financial or political reality'.[90] Instead de Valera decided on the title of Joseph McGarrity's Irish-American newspaper founded in Philadelphia for Irish emigrants in 1918, that of *Irish Press*. The ethos of de Valera's *Irish Press* also mirrored the aspirations of the Philadelphian newspaper. In its first edition, the Philadelphian *Irish Press* claimed that it was 'a journal of Irish news, Irish opinions and Irish literature published in the interests of an independent Ireland'.[91] De Valera's *Irish Press* also followed such a path, with its primary emphasis being local news, nationalist opinion, the Irish language and Irish literature. In essence, de Valera aimed to create a newspaper that would 'be as Irish as the *London Times* is English'.[92]

It was de Valera himself who drew up the company's carefully drafted articles of association, securing for himself the most powerful position on the board – that of controlling director – and allowing him to keep the post for as long as he saw fit. The position was not subject to re-election and on the death, resignation or incapacity of the controlling director, the director to whom he chose to transfer his powers automatically became controlling director. It was in this way that the de Valera stranglehold of the Press company was cast in stone. As the position of controlling director also incorporated the powerful positions of editor-in-chief and managing director, it meant that de Valera had complete control of the editorial content of the paper as well as over the appointment of all staff. In effect, the controlling director had 'sole and absolute control of the public and political policy of the company and of the editorial management thereof and of all newspapers, pamphlets or other writings which may be from time to time owned, published, circulated or printed by the said company'. In addition, the controlling director could 'appoint and at his discretion remove or suspend all editors, sub-editors, reporters, writers, contributors of news or information and all such other persons as may be employed in or connected with the editorial department and may determine their duties and fix their salaries and or emoluments'.[93] Such powers were, however, at odds with the power associated with being a shareholder as outlined in a letter sent by de Valera to the eight thousand applicants who had replied to the advertisement seeking shareholders. According to de Valera, each shareholder was 'a proprietor' of the paper and each shareholder was to 'show his pride in it and uphold it in his district by word and by deed'. De Valera also noted that the first six months would be 'the most critical period for the enterprise'. That was the period when those who were against the new paper would be most active, and it was during this time that 'co-operation by the shareholders with management' would be of 'especial value'.[94] De Valera's assertion that the co-operation needed to make the newspaper successful was in the form of 'co-operation by the shareholders with the management' as opposed to co-operation between shareholders and management, implied that for the paper to be a success, shareholders had to comply with what the directors instructed them to do. Such a paternal attitude was to become the hallmark of the management/shareholder relationship during the life of the Press newspapers. To a certain extent, this was borne out further in the letter when de Valera gave examples of how shareholders could promote the newspaper. These included reserving the newspaper in local shops and giving advertising business to the paper. De Valera also revealed that since an evening paper was 'the more profitable branch of a daily newspaper enterprise' and a weekly paper was 'necessary to render in full, the national service we require', he proposed 'to produce an evening and also a weekly' once the company had 'proved itself capable of successfully handling the morning edition'.[95] In spite of, or perhaps because of, the illusion of shared ownership, the Fianna Fáil faithful rallied to finance de Valera's new enterprise. Besides door-to-door collections, investors could also avail of a gradual system of purchase through the Munster and Leinster Bank. Upon application, investors were required to pay two shillings per share. Upon allotment, a charge of five shillings per share was payable. Two months after allotment, another five shillings per share was due. Six months after allotment another four shillings per share was due. A final payment of four shillings per share was due no later than nine months after allotment. Quite a few investors partook in this system. By February 1929, 124,679 shares were allotted, while cash receipts stood at only half that at £64,824. Over the following months applications for shares flooded in. By December 1929, a total of 125,579 shares had been sold. In May and June of 1931, over 27,367 shares were recorded in the names of Australian shareholders. Indeed, in the three months after publication it sold 469 shares. Most Irish shareholders bought one, two or five shares although a few bought twenty, fifty and at most one hundred shares. Those who purchased the shares came from all walks of life and are recorded as such in the company's original shareholders register. The occupations listed included shop assistant, tailor, painter, nurse, grocer, barmaid, clerk, farmer, builder and baker.[96]

In March 1929, the Press company 'acquired a magnificent site' at Burgh Quay, Dublin. It had 'historical associations too, having been originally the famous Conciliation Hall' from which Daniel O'Connell had led the Repeal Movement.[97] The Young Ireland Movement had also been based there, so the building had a firm historical base for the headquarters of the new republican minded newspaper. In latter years, the building had housed the Tivoli music hall. This proved to be a source of amusement for several generations of staff members, who held that the music and drama must have been ingrained in the walls, since seldom a day went by without some sort of theatrical event livening up the lives of those who worked there. Secondhand printing presses were purchased and the conversion of the building began in August 1930, with the launch date set for July 1931. The work came to a halt shortly afterwards however, in the first industrial dispute to affect Burgh Quay. A Dublin builders' strike brought conversion of the building and the installation of the printing presses to a standstill for several months. At this stage most of the staff had been recruited and were already on the payroll, and the company's funds began to dwindle as the strike dragged on. It took the personal intervention of de Valera to convince the builders to return to work and finish the building at their old rate of pay. As a result of the strike, the launch of the *Irish Press* was delayed two months until September 1931 and the company's capital suffered a severe dent. In the interim, the staff already recruited continued with the preparations for the launch of 'the truth in the news'.

CHAPTER TWO

The Launch of the 'Truth in the News'

> Our paper is the people's paper. It has no interest to serve but theirs . . . It is pledged to be an honest paper and to give them the truth in its news columns without colour or bias. It is pledged to strive through its editorial policy to unite them, to make the necessary effort to bring back the former glory of our nation, to make it independent, self-reliant and as self-supporting as possible, to build up native industries so that Irishmen may be given an opportunity of earning a decent livelihood in their own land.[1]
>
> *Eamon de Valera at the first Irish Press AGM*

The advertisements for staff attracted numerous replies, especially from the party faithful, with many either emphasising their allegiance to the party or enclosing references from their local Fianna Fáil TD. One such reference from Sean MacEntee concluded that one individual's family had 'a good record since 1916, in which both his brothers were out'. They had 'served all through the Black and Tan war' and had 'remained Republican'.[2] Others emphasised their own involvement in the republican struggle and their malevolence towards the Irish Free State. One individual reminded de Valera that he was 'one of your own sixteen men at Boland's Company III from 1915–21'. He also informed de Valera that he hadn't qualified for 'a pension from the Free State' and was sure he would 'die singing a hymn of hate to that breed'.[3] Others tried a more personal approach, including Maire Devane, a sister of Thomas Ashe, whose son had applied for a job as a reporter. Devane wrote a heart rendering letter to de Valera, pleading with him to save her son from emigration by securing him a position at the *Irish Press*. She hoped that as 'Thomas's sister', he would do her 'this favour'. According to Devane, her son, whose 'appearance and manner' was 'Thomas all over again', was 'secretary to the Fianna Fáil Comhairle Ceanntar Cumann' and already had his passage ticket for America. Could de Valera 'save him from such a fate?'[4] In reply, de Valera instructed Devane to get her son to send his application to the company secretary, 'stating in particular the extent of his knowledge of the Irish language'.[5] Of course, not all party supporters could secure jobs in the new paper, and most received a standard reply stating that 'the directors of the Irish Press Ltd have placed on the heads of the different departments the responsibility for the selection of the best staff possible', an answer that elicited many bitter replies to de Valera, especially from those who knew him personally.[6] One such indignant individual retorted that 'as an honourable Republican soldier and one of your constituents' he had 'expected a personal reply'. Since this had not been forthcoming, he was certain that he and his friends would 'decline to listen to belated explanations at election time'.[7] Indeed, de Valera came under such pressure over the allocation of positions that he felt compelled to write back to another complainant stating that there were 'no favourites and no other form of hand-picking'. According to de Valera, the point in the one or two complaints that he had had received seemed to be precisely this – 'that some form of favouritism' had not been shown.[8]

Frank Gallagher, once described as 'a fanatical supporter of Fianna Fáil [who] worshipped de Valera' was appointed editor-in-chief.[9] As his letter of application for the position pointed out, he was vastly experienced in the field of journalism. He had joined the proofreading department of the *Cork Free Press* as a teenager, and less than a year later had been promoted to junior reporter. In 1913, he had been dispatched to London as parliamentary correspondent and reported on the Home Rule Debates. Returning home in 1917, he had worked first with Desmond Fitzgerald producing the Sinn Féin newspaper, the *Irish Bulletin*, and then as assistant editor under Erskine Childers at *Poblacht na h-Éireann*. He had also edited *The Nation* and was the Irish correspondent for newspapers in Australia, America and South Africa. In his application, Gallagher requested a four-year contract at a salary of £1,000 rising by £50 per annum to a maximum of £1,200. The requested salary obviously shocked de Valera who, despite having the power to appoint an editor directly, sidestepped the issue by instructing Gallagher to write to the board of directors officially seeking the position without reference to their discussions.[10] Negotiations continued between the two, however, with Gallagher eventually telling de Valera that 'the question of salary should be left entirely in your hands having regard to your view that it should begin at £850 and go in a stated period to £1000'. Indeed, he would consent for it 'to come down for the first year to £800 . . . in pursuit of a principle rather that as an estimate of the position or of its worth'. In its reply to Gallagher's application, the board approved his appointment as editor-in-chief for a period of one year from March 1931 at a salary of £850 per annum.[11]

Gallagher, who was highly principled and intensely loyal to his staff, was also a meticulous organiser who worked from 11.30am to 3.00am each day. Despite having canvassed the financial support of the business community, to Gallagher the republican ethos of the paper always came before commercial concerns. Indeed, according to one director of the company, Gallagher was primarily responsible for the distinctly pro-Irish tone of the paper, as it was under his editorship that 'the paper established itself as a trustworthy and reliable journal, bright without being cheap, cultured without being ponderous, and above all, Irish through and through in the things that mattered'.[12] In a circular, Gallagher informed his sub-editors that 'Ireland matters most to the *Irish Press*'. They were always to 'give the Irish angle in the headlines' and be on their guard 'against the habits of British and foreign news agencies who look at the world mainly through imperialist eyes'. With regard to partition, Gallagher reminded his staff that 'the Free State is not Ireland and Northern Ireland is not either Northern Ireland or Ulster – it is the Six Counties'.[13] In a letter to the news distributor British United Press, Gallagher outlined the type of stories that the *Irish Press* would be interested in. In essence, the list outlined the ethos and identity of the new paper. According to Gallagher, the *Irish Press* would be interested in receiving stories regarding:

> Movements for national independence anywhere, particularly those in the British empire . . . Irish groups in other countries . . . Political situations in all big nations with particular reference to foreign comments on British policy abroad . . . Events in Catholic nations, European and South American and Catholic events and the actions of Catholic parties in other countries . . . All reference to Protection and Tariffs, both industrial and agricultural with particular reference to new tariffs . . . We would be interested for instance, in a statement giving the protectionist's viewpoint in the U.S. – the only data we are getting in the British press is the criticism of protectionism . . . Definite news from Russia (facts rather than propaganda). Details of the work of the Five Year Plan etc . . . The progress of Gandhi's movement in India . . . the national movement in Palestine, the Frontier Movement in India, and also all secessionist movements in Canada, Australia and South Africa.[14]

Such topics mirrored exactly the subject matter covered by *The Nation* when Gallagher had been editor, and in reality the *Irish Press* was a continuation of that paper; its last edition had stated that its purpose and aims would 'be fulfilled by the appearance of the *Irish Press*'.[15]

The staff appointed to write for the *Irish Press* came mainly from a republican background – so much so that northern unionist politicians nicknamed the paper the 'gunman's gazette'. Most of those employed in the early years were 'republican retainers – people who had fought for or with de Valera during the war of independence and civil war'.[16] The general manager, Bob Brennan, was a former director of publicity for Sinn Féin, while assistant editor Paddy Kirwan had written for *An Phoblacht*. Leader writer John Moynihan had written for *The Nation* and would later become government secretary for Fianna Fáil after the 1932 election. Night town reporter Paddy Clare had previously worked for both *An Phoblacht* and *The Nation*. He stayed with the *Irish Press* for well over fifty years, with the exception of a sabbatical to fight with the International Brigade in the Spanish Civil War. Agricultural reporter Maurice Liston had fought in the war of independence and was a founder member of the National Union of Journalists in Ireland. Another founder member of the Irish branch of the NUJ was *Irish Press* reporter Brendan Malin who later went on to have a very distinguished career with the *Boston Globe*. The paper made a special emphasis to recruit female writers and was the first newspaper in Ireland to appoint a woman's page editor. This position went to Anna Kelly, who had once been Michael Collins' secretary and who had also worked for the *Irish Bulletin*. Kathleen Brennan, sister of 1916 Rising leader Eamon Ceannt, joined as a reporter, as did Maíre Comerford, who had been Frank Aiken's driver during the war of independence. Another veteran republican, Dorothy MacArdle, was appointed as the paper's drama critic. The Press company later published her seminal account of the war of independence, *The Irish Republic* with a foreword by de Valera in 1951. The feminist Hanna Sheehy Skeffington also contributed drama reviews. Other notable republicans then employed by the *Irish Press* included circulation managers Padraig O'Criogáin and Liam Pedlar, as well as Sean MacBride, who had worked with the *Morning Post* in London. Even the sport reporters were republican. Paddy Devlin and Mitchel Cogley had previously written for *Sinn Féin* and *An Phoblacht* respectively. The sports editor and deputy editor were, however, less familiar with Gaelic games. Joe Sherwood and Herbert Moxley were both Englishmen more used to reporting on soccer, rugby and racing.

The *Irish Press* also boasted a fine literary tradition, with the historian and biographer M. J. MacManus being appointed literary editor. Along with Aodh de Blacam, he later recruited Patrick Kavanagh, Brian Nolan (alias Myles na gCopaleen), Lennox Robinson, Máirtín Ó Cadhain and Brendan Behan as regular contributors. Indeed, a compendium of Behan's celebrated column was later published by the Press company. The book, *Hold Your Hour and Have Another*, published in 1963, was a collection of Behan's anecdotal articles on Dublin's pub life that had first appeared in the *Irish Press*.

In Belfast a young reporter, James Kelly, then working for the *Irish News* applied for a position in de Valera's new paper and received two replies. The first came from editor Frank Gallagher and informed him that no staff vacancies existed. The second reply came from news editor Bob Egan who invited him to Dublin for an interview. Kelly was subsequently appointed as the paper's first northern staff reporter. Leaving Burgh Quay after the interview, Egan admitted to Kelly that amid all the preparations for the paper's launch, they had forgotten to appoint any local correspondents in the north. Kelly subsequently supplied the names of all the *Irish News*' local correspondents to Egan, who promptly posted letters of appointment and books of press telegraph passes to the bemused journalists, many of whom later boasted of being appointed to de Valera's new paper without even applying.[17] Another Belfast man, Geoffrey Coulter, secured a position of sub-editor and later played a central role in organising the paper's NUJ chapel. A trainee barrister, Cearbhall O'Dálaigh, who later became President of Ireland, was appointed as Irish editor. Another future president, Erskine Childers, was appointed assistant advertising editor and used his extensive business contacts to attract crucial advertising for the new paper. Another advertising executive, Jack Dempsey, joined the paper well before the launch and later became general manager in 1948. A Claremorris reporter, Joseph Dennigan, was appointed as chief political reporter while Bill Sweetman was appointed London editor, then a junior position, as London affairs were regarded as less significant than Irish affairs. Others who joined the *Irish Press* in its infant years included its first news editor Bob Egan; his deputy Jack Grealish; features writer Liam MacGabhann; newsroom chief Bill Redmond and Joe Walsh, who would edit the paper during the 1960s. But while the paper attracted such big names to work for it, 'most of the established journalists wanted nothing to do with the Press because there was no job security. Some of the staff hired as journalists were not up to it, but the *Irish Press* was innovative, progressive and finely produced.'[18]

Indeed, according to Frank Gallagher himself, the *Irish Press* was staffed by what he himself called 'the most mixed elements, trained, partly trained and untrained . . . men who for the most part were schooled in a journalism wholly foreign to the democratic and republican outlook' that was the 'essential mark' of the newspaper and on which 'its appeal to the people' was based.[19] The working conditions at Burgh Quay were not much better and would be a source of grievance for generations of Press workers.

Contrary to popular opinion, national publicity announcing the launch of the new paper was not a major problem for the company. Although the *Irish Independent* ignored its impending arrival, the *Irish Times* published several advertisements publicising the new paper. Under the headline of 'A National Hope Realised', one such advert announced that the *Irish Press* would not be 'a party organ or a political paper'. Instead, it promised to be 'truly national in its contents, its vision and its appeal'.[20] According to another such advert, nothing was 'so evident as the people's desire' for a newspaper that would 'reflect the thoughts of the nation'.[21] Provincial newspapers and word of mouth publicity directed through the Fianna Fáil cumann network also helped to promote the new paper. Nonetheless, the only national paper to write an appraisal of the newspaper venture was the British-owned *Sunday Times*. The paper's Irish correspondent, John Keane, described by Gallagher as 'no friend of the Irish Ireland movement' seemed impressed by the plans.[22] The paper reported that Fianna Fáil was to 'start a daily newspaper' and commented that the board was 'certainly impressive' and seemed to support the statement that the project was 'not too rigidly one of party'.[23] Keane was under this impression because, with the exception of de Valera, all the directors were successful businessmen. However, such impartiality on the part of the directors was illusionary. Despite *The Nation* having proclaimed that the board was 'selected for its commercial capabilities rather than its political persuasions',[24] the original directors of the Press company were businessmen who had vested interests in promoting Fianna Fáil's policy of protectionism and self-sufficiency and who advertised their goods and services in the *Irish Press*. The board consisted of de Valera and seven businessmen – James Dowdall from Cork, Stephen O'Mara from Limerick, Philip Pierce from Wexford, Edmund Williams from Offaly and Dublin businessmen Henry Gallagher, James Stirling and John Hughes. All were directors of their own companies that produced tea, butter, iron, chocolate and bacon for the Irish market. All bought five hundred shares with the exception of Pierce and Hughes who bought one thousand each.[25] Indeed, the protectionism later implemented under the guise of the Control of Manufacturers Act of 1932, was influenced by ministers meeting delegations of manufacturers, the members of which on at least one occasion included the directors of the Irish Press Ltd.[26] Nonetheless, the *Sunday Times* noted that the project had 'every prospect of success' and opined that if its circulation were 'to bear any relation to the party vote it ought to be considerable'. There was, the paper noted, 'ample scope for three daily papers' so therefore the 'project ought to be generally welcome'.[27] In reality, though, after its launch the *Irish Press* encountered severe hostility from many quarters.

The first weekend in September 1931 was set as the launch date for the new paper, chosen because of the All-Ireland hurling final held that weekend.[28] The button to start the printing presses for the final trial run was pressed by Margaret Pearse, mother of Padraig Pearse, and the twelve-page first edition of 200,000 copies carried a front-page picture of the ceremony. Inevitably, the launch was laden with republican symbolism. Many regarded Mrs Pearse as a 'Mother Ireland' figure, who, after losing two sons in the 1916 Rising, voted against the Anglo-Irish Treaty which she argued would ruin Ireland. Indeed, in a symbolic link with the patriots of the rising, the editorial objective of the *Irish Press* 'Do cum Gloire De Agus Onora na hEireann' (for the glory of God and the honour of Ireland) restated Joseph Plunkett's reason for participating in the rising. A special first edition souvenir copy of the paper was printed specially for those involved in the American fund raising drive and carried a note of thanks from de Valera to the Irish-American community. This special edition was 'dedicated to the friends of Ireland in America' whose support had made the 'enterprise possible'.[29] Such were the festivities surrounding the launch that the paper missed the newspaper train for the south with the result that many readers did not receive their first edition until well into the afternoon. Determined to be different, the paper was the first Irish national daily newspaper to carry current affairs news on its front page, an idea spotted by de Valera while in America. Oblivious to this initiative, the other national titles continued to reserve their front page for advertisements and government notices.

Frank Gallagher spent hours writing and rewriting the paper's first editorial in the knowledge that it was not very often that someone had the opportunity to write the first editorial of a new national newspaper. In his first editorial entitled 'Our Purpose', Gallagher stated the paper's intention 'to be the voice of the people, to speak for them, to give utterance to their ideals, to defend them against slander and false witness'.[30] The *Irish Press* would not be 'the organ of an individual or a group or a party', although it would support Fianna Fáil, 'but only because the philosophy and aspirations of the party' were 'identical with its own philosophy and aspirations'.[31] The paper would adhere to its motto of 'the truth in the news', even if that news exposed either a 'shortcoming in the policies' the paper supported or 'a criticism of individuals' with whom it was associated. The paper also promised to give particular attention to Irish affairs. With the appearance of the *Irish Press*, other nations now had a 'means of knowing that Irish opinion' was not 'merely an indistinct echo of the opinion of sections of the British press'.[32] Indeed, the paper succeeded in expressing the sense of nation that had not been previously articulated; the *Irish Press* 'captured the time and mood of the nation. It had its finger on the pulse of the nation but still had a common touch and was reader friendly.'[33] Much of its success lay in the fact that it set out to give 'ordinary people' a voice:

> The *Irish Press* was set up to reflect a different type of Irish life; to cover rural life, the Irish language and Irish sporting life. The *Irish Press* set out to circulate everywhere. It made itself available in every village and crossroads in the country. Previous to this, people had to go to the nearest big town to buy a paper, but every hamlet that had a small shop would have a few copies of the *Irish Press*. It was a costly process carried out with military precision but it was successful and the *Irish Independent* soon began to copy us. Back then the *Irish Times* was inescapably Anglo-Irish and Protestant. The *Irish Independent* was Catholic but commercial; it was the paper of auctioneers, big farmers and doctors. So the ordinary man was not getting his paper – one paper was the wrong religion and the other was aimed at people with money. This was the perception. The personality of the *Irish Press* stemmed from its founding ethos, which was to celebrate the life of the plain people of Ireland. It was a journal of frugality, of simple life and plain values. And the new paper, being the creature of Eamon de Valera, was going to make all these plain, decent people supporters of Fianna Fáil.[34]

In line with Fianna Fáil's aim of restoring the Irish language, the first edition carried a 'Message to the Nation' by Douglas Hyde urging people to 'Speak the Irish'. It also carried an agricultural column entitled 'The Lure of Grass' that propagated Fianna Fáil's preference of tillage over grazing, as well as a stinging criticism (attributed to the Labour Party) of the government's failure to provide jobs. The sport's page was also imbued with the nationalist tone that was to become typical of the paper. 'The Inspiration is Patriotism' screamed the headline over the story of 'the secret of South Africa's rugby triumphs and British defeats'. Even the advertisements had a patriotic ring to them, as the New Ireland Assurance Ltd wished success to the new enterprise from 'another Irish enterprise that has earned success'. As one may expect, there were many letters wishing the paper well, with one Dublin letter-writer stating that it was 'better for a newspaper to have a soul and be propagandist than to have no soul and still be propagandist' as was the case with the existing press. The Irish people had been 'a long time waiting for a newspaper' that had 'a proper sense of news values and a fixed Irish-Ireland outlook'.[35] There was, however, one small *faux pas*, the fault for which lay squarely at the feet of the sports editor and deputy editor. Joe Sherwood and Herbert Moxley were both Englishmen more used to reporting on soccer. Hence their infamous misprint in their report of the GAA All-Ireland hurling final in the first edition of the paper. They reported the 'kick-off' time as 3.15pm. However, Gaelic hurling and football, unlike soccer, begin not with a 'kick-off', but with a 'throw-in'. Both men put it down to experience and 'from the very beginning the *Irish Press* gave Gaelic games more coverage than anyone had ever done and forced everyone else to follow'.[36] Besides the previously unseen GAA coverage and trade union notes, the novel features of the paper included 'The Turf Cutter's Children', a serial aimed at young readers, and Aodh de Blacam's infamous 'Roddy the Rover' column. De Blacam was the paper's roving reporter, going from town to town and writing a piece on each. This had a double appeal – it took readers on a different journey every day and it thrilled people to see their small village mentioned in a national newspaper. After the launch, several county councils and GAA county boards passed motions of congratulations and sent telegrams of support to the paper. Northern nationalists also greeted the new arrival with enthusiasm. In Belfast, Douglas Gageby, then a teenager, but who would later go on to edit the *Evening Press*, lay ill in bed. He was roused from his sleep by his father bursting into the room, throwing a newspaper on the bed and proclaiming that 'de Valera had brought out a new newspaper in Dublin'.[37]

But whatever about the reaction north of the border, the reaction in the south was certainly more muted – in certain quarters at least. The *Irish Times* again published an advert announcing the arrival of the new paper,[38] but instead of a review, under the headline of 'Looking to the New Paper', the paper reported on a speech given by Fianna Fáil's P. J. Ruttledge at a party meeting in Ballinrobe.

According to the report, Ruttledge had declared that Fianna Fáil would 'no longer be misrepresented to the public' because a new national newspaper had taken the place of 'an alien and pro-English press'.[39] In contrast, the *Irish Independent* totally ignored the new arrival and instead launched an extensive outdoor advertising campaign. The only nationally distributed paper to review the new publication was the British-owned *Tribune*. It was impressed with what it saw and noted that the general tone was 'above the level of journalism' then present in Ireland. The new paper was 'entirely moderate in its political references and though intended to be the organ of the Fianna Fáil party, it might more justly claim to be called independent than papers who proudly use the title'.[40] Indeed, at the 1931 Fianna Fáil ard fheis, de Valera demanded that the paper be free from party political influence. According to de Valera, the paper should not be 'tied to any party . . . it was established for a definite national purpose, in order that the people of Ireland might get the news that was necessary for them to have to form a correct judgement upon current affairs'.[41] In later years, de Valera's son Vivion carried a copy of this speech to every shareholders' meeting and frequently used it to counter criticism that the paper was not friendly enough to Fianna Fáil.[42]

Not everyone was happy with the new paper, however. In his autobiography, *Against the Tide*, Noel Browne stated his belief that the Press newspapers 'influenced a substantial number of the Irish people and created and kept unchallenged the awesome charisma of Eamon de Valera. They also contributed to the formation of the unique Fianna Fáil ethos of Irish republicanism, particularly in rural areas.'[43] As Fianna Fáil's main political target, Cumann na nGaedheal disliked the tone of the paper. When the issue of the new publication and its editorial tone was raised in the Dáil, the party's leader, William Cosgrave, accused the paper of an unrelenting campaign of innuendo against the Free State establishment. According to Cosgrave, there was 'a publication in this country called the *Irish Press*' which postured as 'an impartial journal' but which made 'every possible attempt' to 'belittle the institutions of this State'.[44] To cries of 'suppress it', Cosgrave replied, 'it would be a pity to suppress it' because it would eventually 'suppress itself'.[45] Whatever the verbal reaction of Cumann na nGaedheal deputies to the establishment of the *Irish Press*, the party's official written reaction is lost forever, due to a fire at the party's Hume Street headquarters in the 1950s which virtually destroyed all of its archives. Nonetheless, the surviving archives suggest that while the party saw fit to condemn Fianna Fáil's use of a newspaper to recruit support, it knew full well the power of the press. At one meeting of the party's standing committee, 'the propaganda sub-committee was requested to keep in the closest co-operation with the election and policy sub-committee' so that the party's 'weekly organ may be used to the greatest advantage to expound the findings of these bodies'.[46] Indeed, Cumann na nGaedheal and its successor Fine Gael had very mixed fortunes in setting up a newspaper to combat the presence of the *Irish Press*. Several titles including *An Realt* (*The Star*), *United Irishman* and *United Ireland* were published intermittently with the expense for the most part being borne by the party's deputies. Eventually, the party gave up its attempts to publish a paper, noting that 'the results scarcely justified the expense'.[47]

Six months after the paper's launch, the Free State government prosecuted editor Frank Gallagher before a military tribunal for seditious libel. The summons was ill-timed as an election was due and the action was viewed by many as an attempt to stifle free speech. During January and February 1932, the *Irish Press* had published several statements by prisoners who claimed to have been beaten up while in custody. The paper had publicly embarrassed the government by calling on 'those in charge of the forces of the law to exercise the most scrupulous supervision and impose upon individuals the most stern restraints'[48] as 'the beating of prisoners appeared to be becoming part of the system of government'.[49] The paper also took the opportunity to jibe at the jurisdiction of the Free State by stating that it had 'no hostility to any of the forces of the Free State Government'. They were, after all, 'composed of brother Irishmen' who someday would 'be members of one free community'.[50] The government responded by charging the *Irish Press* with publishing articles that were intended to 'bring the administration of the law into disrepute and to scandalise and vilify the government and the Garda Siochana'.[51] Such a reaction showed how effective the *Irish Press* was in undermining the confidence of Cumann na nGaedheal, and the show trial designed to demonstrate the party's commitment to law and order instead demonstrated its preoccupation with avoiding criticism of the economic malaise afflicting the country. Gallagher was summoned to appear before the tribunal on 5 February 1932, eleven days before polling day. He argued that the articles were fair and accurate and the evidence given by the majority of witnesses backed up his claims. Ironically, the judgement was delivered after polling day. The *Irish Press* was fined a paltry £100, but the paper's readers responded by sending £500 in contributions to help pay the fines.

The whole saga ultimately helped raise the public profile of the paper and it soon built up a reputation as the best paper in the country for hard accurate news, with its circulation being boosted by the publicity surrounding the tribunal.

Alongside the political hostility, the paper also had to deal with commercial opposition that hit its advertising base. While the first edition was successful, for subsequent editions adverts were hard to come by. Many British-owned firms were reluctant to advertise in the new paper, given its republican ideals and support for self-sufficiency. According to one editor, 'the excuses as relayed to the paper's advertising representatives were many and varied but seldom true'. The excuses given included the assertions that the 'readers of that paper hadn't got the purchasing power', it was 'only read by penniless rapparees' and its policy was not 'in the best interests of the consumers'. Such refusals were manifestations of a 'pro-British snobbish attitude . . . towards those who dared to question the treaty or to use the treaty to end our economic dependence on Britain'.[52] The situation had its lighter moments, however. When the British tyre firm Dunlop cancelled its advertising contract with the *Irish Press*, Erskine Childers was despatched to London to try to salvage the deal. At the subsequent meeting, the company's managing director, Sir George Harrod, asked Childers whether or not he was related to the author of the same name who had written his favourite novel, the famous spy yarn, *The Riddle of the Sands*. When Childers replied that his father had written the book, the advertising contract was promptly restored.[53] Larger Irish businesses also seemed reluctant to use the paper as an advertising medium, helped in no small way by the fact that in 1928 Independent Newspapers had offered £200,000 in shares to the public. Most had been purchased by business people such as auctioneers, newsagents, solicitors and undertakers who had a vested interest in advertising in the company's newspapers. In an attempt to build up business, adverts were lifted from other papers and planted in the *Irish Press*. On one occasion, the paper lifted a death notice with the rather common name of Murphy from the *Irish Independent*. The Murphy in question was, however, a member of the Murphy family who owned Independent Newspapers and Gallagher had to make a personal apology.[54] Such actions incurred much indignation from Independent Newspapers and the feud between both companies ran deep and bitter for many years. So deep was the mutual antipathy, that freelance journalists working for Independent Newspapers were allowed to work for English papers but not for the *Irish Press*. The feud also affected the distribution of the new newspaper.

From almost the very beginning, the *Irish Press* was excluded from the special train that distributed newspapers throughout the country. The irony that William Lombard Murphy, chairman of Independent Newspapers, was also a director of the Great Southern Railway Company was not lost on anyone involved in the *Irish Press*. By a contract agreed before the *Irish Press* was actually published but after its proposed issue was announced, the GSRC undertook to give Independent Newspapers and the *Irish Times* exclusive use of the 3.55am train on weekdays from Dublin's Kingsbridge station to Cork, with various bus connections for provincial towns along the way. Under the agreement, no other newspapers were to be conveyed on the train but the GSRC retained the right to use it for passengers and other types of traffic. When the *Irish Press* applied to use the train, permission was refused but it was offered a later train at a cost of £24,200 per year. The *Irish Press* objected and claimed that the exclusive arrangement was prejudicial to its interests and gave its competitors an undue preference. It thus applied to the Railway Tribunal to have the arrangement for the other papers set aside on the grounds that it was a violation of Section 2 of the Railway and Canal Traffic Act 1854.[55] According to the company's complaint, the GSRC had refused to give a quote for the conveyance of the *Irish Press* on the special newspaper train on the grounds that the train was run under contract for Independent Newspapers and the *Irish Times*. It also complained that the company's subsequent quotation for a similar service for the *Irish Press* alone was in excess of the charge made to the other papers. Consequently, the Press company sought a declaration from the tribunal that 'the services and facilities to other papers and the refusal of the same to the *Irish Press* constituted an undue or unreasonable preference or advantage in favour of those other Dublin newspapers'.[56] It also sought an injunction restraining the railway company from 'persisting in its refusal to afford to the applicants the services and facilities afforded to the other Dublin newspapers'.[57] While the Railway Tribunal investigated the complaint, it issued an interim decision in July 1931 that ordered the railway company to supply the *Irish Press* at reasonable rates 'facilities for the carriage' of the newspaper 'equal to those enjoyed by the other two Dublin newspapers'.[58] In response to this decision, the railway company emphasised that the respondent companies had the 'exclusive rights of conveyance of newspapers by the 3.55am train' and that the *Irish Press* was 'not entitled to avail of this particular service'.[59] The company had offered to supply a similar train with a later departure time, but held that 'having regard to the respective volumes of traffic, the *Irish Press* was not entitled to identical rates' and it denied that any preference was given to the other two newspapers.[60] In preparation for the case, the GSRC was joined by Independent Newspapers and the Irish Times Ltd as co-respondents.

When the case proper began in March 1932, the GSRC stated that an atmosphere had been introduced into the proceedings to make it seem that the company was antagonistic towards the *Irish Press*. According to the GSRC, it was merely standing over the contract that it had made with the other papers. The *Irish Press*, it claimed, had turned the case into a political issue. Counsel for the respondents, Frank Fitzgerald, held that the evidence of *Irish Press* general manager, Bob Brennan, contained a veiled charge that the object of the GSRC entering into the agreement with the respondent newspapers was to block the *Irish Press* when it came into circulation. Fitzgerald also stated that a veiled remark had been made in the court that William Lombard Murphy was a director of both the GSRC and Independent Newspapers. He questioned what the object of that comment was, if not to suggest that the dual directorship of Murphy had been used in some way to obtain the agreement. For its part, the GSRC held that the charge was 'absolutely untrue'. The newspaper train was a special service and there was nothing in the Railway Acts to prevent the company from entering into a special agreement. The GSRC held that from 4 May 1931, it had carried under agreement with the respondent newspapers all their traffic on the special train which otherwise would not have run. This exclusive arrangement was provisional for a year with an option of renewal for a further four years.

According to the GSRC, up to 1 July 1930, all the traffic of the respondent newspapers had been carried on ordinary trains, but during that month a dispute arose between the management and employees of the GSRC that disrupted the distribution of the papers. The newspaper companies had resented this and hired a distribution company to distribute the papers by truck until January 1931. The GSRC thought that it had lost the newspaper business, and alarmed by the loss of such revenue, it approached the newspaper companies to reach a new distribution deal. Negotiations began in February 1931 between the GSRC, Independent Newspapers and the Irish Times Ltd, then the only two Dublin newspapers engaged in distribution outside Dublin. After prolonged discussion, a contract was reached in March 1931, whereby a special newspaper train would run exclusively for them. According to the GSRC, during the negotiations nothing was said by either the GSRC or the newspapers to deliberately set up a barrier against the *Irish Press*, which was not circulating at the time. The agreement was not made with that object in mind. It was a fair trading agreement to get the newspapers on the market as early as possible. The attitude of the *Irish Press* in claiming that it was entitled to use the train and interfere with a contract was an impossible one to accept, especially since it had been offered similar services at a reasonable sum. Before the respondents entered into the agreement with the GSRC, they had an exclusive lorry service and it could not be suggested that the *Irish Press* be entitled to participate in that service.[61]

Putting forward the case for the *Irish Press,* its counsel Gavan Duffy stated that the dispute was the worst case of boycott on record. According to Duffy, the object of the Independent Group was to bar the access of the *Irish Press* to the 'breakfast table'. Its co-conspirator was the GSRC, which was guilty of aiding and abetting 'in that scheme by ceding the monopoly of its valuable services'. If allowed to continue, the scheme would give direct, deliberate and overwhelming advantages to the competitors of the *Irish Press*. This was compounded by the suggestion by the GSRC of a four year contract, 'doubtless in the hope that in that time the *Irish Press* would be dead and buried'. According to Duffy, a daily newspaper was such a peculiar commodity that the granting of an exclusive service by the GSRC to two daily newspapers precluded it from being able to give equal treatment to any other competitor. In theory, the railway company was meant to be a public utility service, whereas in fact the agreement amounted to a boycott of the *Irish Press*. The gross disproportion between the charges made to the respondents and those proposed for the *Irish Press* highlighted this. Never in the history of railways, Duffy contended, had there been so audacious a coup or unscrupulous a contract.[62] In evidence, *Irish Press* general manager, Bob Brennan, claimed that anything short of the paper being carried on the 3.55am train would give undue preference to its competitors. With respect to a duplication of the service for the *Irish Press*, with the paper leaving Dublin either half-an-hour before or after the 3.55am train, Brennan stated that if the *Irish Press* had to leave half-an-hour earlier, it would have to go to press earlier and would be compelled to travel without a large section of news that would seriously affect the value of the paper. If it had to leave half-an-hour later, it would arrive at destinations later than the respondent newspapers with consequent loss of sales. According to Brennan, simultaneous delivery of all newspapers was the fairest solution.[63]

The final decision of the Railway Tribunal went against the *Irish Press*. The tribunal stated that for the *Irish Press* to establish boycott, it needed to demonstrate a refusal on the part of the GSRC to deal or associate with the *Irish Press*. In the eyes of the tribunal, this had not been established. Likewise, with respect to the issue of monopoly, this had been negated by the willingness of the GSRC to offer the paper a duplicate service. In the wake of the judgement, Gavan Duffy applied to have the injunction continued pending an application to the Supreme Court to appeal the tribunal's decision. All of the respondents objected and the application was refused. In response, Duffy said he would make an immediate application to the Supreme Court to appeal this decision. In the interim, he requested that the respondents consent to allow the *Irish Press* use the train. After consideration, they replied that they would consent to this over the weekend, so as not 'to see the *Irish Press* in the lurch'. Later that day, leave to appeal the decision of the tribunal was granted by the Supreme Court, but the injunction was discontinued.[64] Sensing that the tide was turning against it, the paper withdrew from a costly Supreme Court appeal of the Railway Tribunal's decision.[65] The judgement was both a psychological and financial blow to the *Irish Press*. Psychologically, 'being put off the train led to a siege mentality and paranoia'.[66] While the paper initially responded by using the old IRA network to distribute the paper, the company was eventually forced to hire its own train at an annual cost of £30,000. It was not until 1937 that the *Irish Press* was again allowed to use the newspaper train. In an attempt to mislead its competitors, the company bought a van and photographed it in a different town every day, giving the impression that the company was building up a huge distribution fleet of its own.[67] In the end, the Great Southern Railway Company backed down and allowed the *Irish Press* access to the newspaper train. In reality, however, the paper was critically short of cash, a fact acknowledged by de Valera, who noted that 'considerable risks were taken in starting the paper with less than the estimated minimum capital. The alternative was however, to abandon the enterprise altogether and return the money collected.' The financial position of the paper had, however, 'never ceased to be critical' and it had 'never ceased consequently to be a source of very great anxiety'. According to de Valera, the following year would 'determine definitely the paper's future'.[68] Indeed, the financial position of the company was very grave. A significant percentage of the original share capital was not paid up as several hundred shareholders who had made initial deposits failed to complete the payments. This, coupled with the cost of the building strike and the cost of being put off the newspaper train, made deep dents into the company's cash reserves.[69]

But despite the concerted opposition of its political and media opponents, the *Irish Press* survived. Circulation rose from an average of 56,821 for the last three months of 1931 to an average of 86,825 for the second quarter of 1932, and eventually settled down at a circulation of around 90,000.[70] For those 'who had endured the total hostility of the national press for many years, it provided a welcome antidote to their political poison' and was to become 'an inspiration and powerful morale booster for the republican cause'.[71] The paper played a crucial role in the development of the Fianna Fáil party in its early days, and augmented the party's robust opposition to Cumann na nGaedheal, which up to then had dominated the political arena. According to one party activist, the paper:

> gave an added impetus to the already considerable growth of Fianna Fáil all over the country. While it adhered firmly to its motto of 'Truth in the News', it was nevertheless frankly a party paper and as such, was zealous in spreading the gospel of Fianna Fáil in its daily issues. It was the necessary coping stone to all the speeches, lectures and propaganda of the movement . . . The result of the combined efforts of the party and the daily *Irish Press* was soon to be seen.[72]

For the first year of its life, the *Irish Press* was especially radical. It voiced a radical populist critique of the society that had developed in Ireland since independence and delivered sharp criticism of issues such as the prevailing high levels of unemployment and emigration, as well as promoting the policies of protectionism and self-sufficiency. It condemned Cumann na nGaedheal's subservience to British imperialism, such as the paying of the land annuities and its export market orientated agricultural policy that was narrowly focused on Britain and ever increased Ireland's economic dependence on its former imperial ruler. The *Irish Press*' populist tone succeeded in identifying Fianna Fáil with the mass of the people while simultaneously portraying Cumann na nGaedheal as an imperial-friendly party. It covered India's struggle for independence, criticised international capitalism for causing the great depression and promoted Fianna Fáil's call for an independent banking system for

Ireland. When the paper launched a campaign against the threat to native industry by the dumping of foreign goods on the Irish market, Fianna Fáil supported the move and stated that it would 'resort to an absolute embargo if tariffs were not sufficient'.[73] In November 1931, when Britain imposed trade tariffs and Ireland was left behind, the *Irish Press* highlighted Britain's self-interest as opposed to Cumann na nGaedheal's fatal hesitation. The paper's subsequent 'Buy Irish' campaign, supported by Fianna Fáil, won for both the support of indigenous industry and businessmen. Thus while Fianna Fáil and the *Irish Press* became associated with self-sufficiency and Irishness, Cumann na nGaedheal was portrayed as being an ally of the capitalist, free trade, imperialist system. Fianna Fáil's intention to retain the land annuities and its plans for economic and social reform based on the development and protection of indigenous industry were all actively supported and propagated to the masses by the *Irish Press*. The paper also urged the ruralisation of industry while the urban concentration of industry was castigated for dehumanising the population: 'it drew the people from their closeness to nature and then cooped them up amongst bricks and mortar'.[74] According to the paper, the varied life of a rural setting 'would be the source of a culture and happiness for the people which concentration in the cities must always deny them'.[75] But to achieve this, the paper rejected the ideology of class struggle in favour of all classes working together to achieve social and economic progress. Even as far back as 1931, the *Irish Press* was preaching the doctrine of social partnership. According to the paper, it was in the 'absolute principle of social relations that alone we can find the solution for the world's miseries'.[76] Thus by appealing to various interest groups that suffered from the economic policies of the Cumann na nGaedheal government, such as smaller farmers, small businessmen, the urban working class and trade unionists, the *Irish Press* succeeded in uniting a cross-class spectrum of support for Fianna Fáil's policies, the level of which was tested in the 1932 general election. Indeed, the paper was to play 'a dominant role in the success of the election campaign which was to bring Fianna Fáil to power'.[77]

The election battle was fought chiefly between Cumann na nGaedheal, which concentrated on law and order issues and raised the spectre of communist rule under Fianna Fáil, and the latter, which concentrated on cutting the remaining links with Britain and gave special emphasis to political, economic and social reform. During the election campaign, the *Irish Independent* (whose sales had dropped from 150,000 to 120,000 following the launch of the *Irish Press*) sided with Cumann na nGaedheal while the *Irish Press* propagated the Fianna Fáil viewpoint. The paper would later accuse the outgoing government of using the 'most offensive propaganda ever known in a general election', but would also admit that 'during the election campaign, the *Irish Press* in its news columns, reported all sides fairly, but threw the whole weight of its editorial policy behind the Fianna Fáil Party'.[78] The *Irish Independent*, for its part, sought to dismiss Fianna Fáil's extensive programme for government on the grounds that 'no facade of pretended economic policies' could 'obscure the fact that it would be inherently impossible to attend to the economic interests of the people during the intense political agitation and unrest which would follow a Fianna Fáil victory'.[79] Ironically, the paper also reminded its readers that Cumann na nGaedheal had the unqualified support of both the unionist party and the British government.

Using red scare tactics, the *Irish Independent* raised the prospect of communist style rule under a Fianna Fáil government. Through a process of association, the paper continually likened the policies of Fianna Fáil to those espoused by communists. With headlines like 'The Introduction of Russian Methods' and 'A Tonic for Moscow', it also dismissed Fianna Fáil's policies of state promoted rural industrialisation, protectionism and self-sufficiency, and accused the party of adopting the policy of the 'soviet system'. The paper dismissed the party's assertion that 'countless thousands of extra hands would be employed' by stating that this could only be done 'if the reaping were to be done as of old, by means of hooks'. According to the paper, 'protection on an intolerable scale would be applied and if that proved inadequate, the state would establish and promote industries. In other words, the soviet system would be applied.'[80] In an attempt to scare the business community, the paper maintained that Fianna Fáil was 'prepared to set down an arbitrary limit of self-sufficiency and to enforce it by a process of state socialism'. This authoritarian state would then 'through its government machinery or through boards which it creates, determine the ownership of every natural resource, control its utilisation, fix wages, prices and production and take over the management of industry'.[81] In response, the *Irish Press* stated that Fianna Fáil's policy was the opposite of socialism. According to the paper, the rights of the individual and family to own private property would be recognised while the government would provide work for the unemployed by establishing rural industries. Such a social policy, the paper argued, was not socialism, but was in fact advocated by Pope Pius XI in the papal encyclical *Quadragesimo Anno* that denounced the reduction of society to slavery at the hands of capitalism. A week before the election, the *Irish Press* published the Fianna Fáil manifesto that promised to remove the oath of allegiance; an oath that was described as 'standing in the way of national unity'.[82]

According to the manifesto, the party would 'organise systematically, the establishment of the industries required to meet the needs of the community in manufactured goods'. The aim was to make Ireland 'as independent of foreign imports as possible'. Thus, 'suitable fiscal laws would be passed to give the protection necessary against unfair foreign competition'. The party also pledged to 'never cease to protest against the iniquity of the partition' of Ireland which was 'ruthlessly cut in two against the wishes of the people'. The party would 'by every peaceful means strive to bring it to an end'. In reply to the allegations made by the *Irish Independent*, the party stated that it had 'no leaning towards communism and no belief in communist doctrines' and pleaded with the electorate 'not to allow themselves to be deceived by the misrepresentations' of the party's opponents.[83] During the election campaign, the *Irish Press* published several half-page advertisements for Fianna Fáil in which the declines in tillage, exports and population, coupled with the rise in emigration and unemployment, were highlighted. The adverts also criticised Cumann na nGaedheal for having concentrated on export legislation and neglecting the protection of the home market against foreign competition. They also quoted the Minister for Industry and Commerce, Patrick McGilligan, as having said that it was not the 'business of this Dáil to provide work'.[84] As election day approached, both the *Irish Press* and Fianna Fáil hammered home these points. On the eve of election day the paper noted that 'along the whole range of political affairs' there was 'an almost complete conflict of views between the two principle parties'. Nowhere was this 'more marked than in their social and economic policies'. While Fianna Fáil believed that it was 'the duty of the state to provide work', Cumann na nGaedheal did not.[85] Indeed, on election day itself, the paper noted that 'finding work for the workless' was 'a determining factor in that swing of public opinion' that had been noted.[86] That same day the *Irish Times* warned that now was the time for 'all unionists and imperialists to do their duty' by not voting for Fianna Fáil.[87] Despite this, the party received a healthy endorsement from the electorate, winning seventy-two seats to Cumann na nGaedheal's fifty-seven. The Labour Party won seven seats, the Farmers Party three seats and the Independents fourteen seats. With the support of the Labour Party, Fianna Fáil formed its first ever administration. The party's support was drawn from small farmers and businessmen, attracted by the protectionist policies, as well as trade unionists and much of the urban working class attracted to Fianna Fáil via the radical social views of the *Irish Press*. In a move that was to return to haunt him in later decades, when appointing his first cabinet de Valera announced that to maintain its impartiality all its members would relinquish their company directorships. When appointed Minister for Posts and Telegraphs, *Irish Press* director Joseph Connolly resigned from the board apparently unaware that while de Valera had resigned the position of board chairman, he had retained the position of controlling director. After the election, de Valera acknowledged the importance of the *Irish Press* in helping bring Fianna Fáil to power. In a letter in 1932 to Archbishop Daniel Mannix of Melbourne, de Valera expressed his belief that 'had the risk not been taken', he doubted if the 'present government would be in power today'.[88] Even after de Valera came to power, the *Irish Press* was the only daily paper to lend support to the new government. Indeed, as de Valera himself noted, 'if the paper were to disappear, the government would disappear with it'.[89]

Shortly after assuming power, Fianna Fáil turned its attention to the abolition of the oath of allegiance, supported wholeheartedly by the *Irish Press*. According to the paper, the oath condemned the Irish people to 'an unrepresentative assembly'. It 'reserved representative government' for those who 'were willing to take an oath of allegiance either as an effective oath or as an empty formula' and 'excluded from any share in government that large body of Irish public opinion' that would 'never give even titular allegiance to an outside authority'.[90] When the oath was eventually abolished the paper noted that there was 'never any genuine cause of doubt as to what the view of the people was'. At election time, the Irish people had 'called on Fianna Fáil to assert themselves and claim their rights'. They had 'voted for oath abolition, for the removal of a hateful test which for ten years had wrought frustration on the whole community'. According to the paper, the abolition of the oath was 'as momentous as anything that had happened in Irish politics for many years'. It lifted 'a stigma' from the nation and ended 'any sign of voluntary submission by the people's representatives to an over lordship' that was 'galling to Irish nationalism'. Thus, the paper concluded, the Irish nation 'owed such gratitude' as was 'not easy to express' to Fianna Fáil.[91] Having abolished the oath, de Valera turned his attention towards abolishing or at least downgrading the position of Governor-General. Both the government and the *Irish Press* completely ignored the existence of the King's representative in Ireland. This had the effect of reducing the position to one of complete impotence. Eventually de Valera succeeded in having his own nominee appointed to the position. The new Governor-General was Domhnall Ó Buachalla, a hardware store owner and 1916 veteran from Maynooth. Significantly, Ó Buachalla refused to take up residence in the Viceregal Lodge and never appeared in public. The position gradually faded from public consciousness and was eventually abolished in 1937.

With the party finally in office, attention at the *Irish Press* turned towards the publication of an evening title. The very first edition of the *Evening Press*, edited by Bob Egan, was published on 3 June 1932 to cover the Eucharistic Congress of that year and received a welcome reception from readers. At a board meeting ten days later, however, it was decided to change the name to the *Evening Telegraph and Evening Press*. The change came into effect on 17 June and attracted the wrath of Independent Newspapers. It owned the *Evening Telegraph* title that had formerly been the evening newspaper of the *Freeman's Journal*. The company succeeded in obtaining an interim injunction preventing the Press company from using the title, and in the actual court case it sought a permanent court order to restrain the company from 'printing, publishing, selling and passing off a newspaper entitled . . . the *Evening Telegraph* so as to induce members of the public to purchase, or to publish advertisements in that paper in the belief that the said newspaper was the *Evening Telegraph*, previously the property of and published by the *Freeman's Journal*'.[92] Since the demise of the *Evening Telegraph*, the circulation of the *Evening Herald* had increased by 46,000 and Independent Newspapers claimed that the action of the Press company was a 'deliberate attempt . . . to lead the public to believe that the new publication has something to do with the old *Evening Telegraph*, which we bought, and in so doing, to take profits from us'.[93] According to *Irish Press* general manager, Bob Brennan, the decision to change the name was taken for several reasons. These included to avoid the *Evening Press* being confused with the *Irish Press*, because Independent Newspapers was not using the name, and because the name was not associated with that company. Most of the case was taken up by legal arguments over the copyright of newspaper names and the transfer of goodwill – the advantage a good quality or well-known name brings to a business.[94]

Although the court held that Independent Newspapers' action was 'formally maintainable', it did not grant the order because the company had failed to prove that damage to its titles had occurred.[95] However, the court advised that another injunction could be sought if the company could 'prove actual damage or an imminent risk of damage'.[96] Although counsel for Independent Newspapers indicated that they would appeal to the Supreme Court, the Press company again titled the paper as the *Evening Telegraph and Evening Press* from the day after the judgement was delivered in July 1932. A second court case was avoided, however, after a strike by Dublin's newsboys abruptly ended the paper's life. A picket on the *Irish Press* offices by badly paid newsboys won the support of the dispatch department workers and brought the distribution of the evening paper to a halt. Sean MacBride, then a journalist with the *Irish Press*, tried to convince the National Union of Journalists to support the strike, but to no avail. In the 1930s, the NUJ consisted of a 'Dublin Branch Committee' composed of representatives from all the Dublin newspapers. This committee met once a month and was affiliated to the National Executive Council of NUJ headquarters in London. The first attempt to unionise the journalists at the *Irish Press* occurred during July 1932, and one of the first disputes concerned the employment 'of a civil servant to the detriment to working journalists'. The *Irish Press* chapel (branch) of the NUJ wrote to editor Frank Gallagher bringing the matter to his attention and he agreed to investigate the complaint. Following further representations by the chapel to Gallagher, regarding 'the employment of a civil servant on sporting assignments', it subsequently reported that 'the abuse' complained of 'ceased a few weeks later'.[97] In any event, to prevent further industrial unrest within the company and avoid a second legal action by Independent Newspapers, management simply abandoned the evening newspaper in October 1932. Such an abrupt approach by management to staff and production problems was to become commonplace at the Press company over the coming decades.

In keeping its election pledge to retain the land annuities for Irish governmental use, in July 1932 the Fianna Fáil administration announced that it was withholding the payment of £1.5 million then due to be paid to the British exchequer. As before, the *Irish Press* again lent the government its support. The paper supported de Valera's call for independent international arbitration to resolve the issue as opposed to the British proposal of a commonwealth commission that the paper stated would be chosen from 'a restricted personnel in an area where the British view was likely to be predominant'. The paper noted that although the 'settlement of international disputes by international arbitration' was 'supposed to be one of the planks of British foreign policy throughout the world', Ireland was 'excluded from any benefits' that this was calculated to bring. Instead, Ireland belonged to 'a special and lower class' where disputes with Britain were to be decided as Britain thought fit. According to the paper, no true Irish person would 'approve submission' to what was 'an irrational as well as an unjust demand'. The stance taken by Fianna Fáil was 'unquestionably fair and open'. Britain had 'no legal or moral right' to the annuities and the government was 'ready to prove this before any impartial court and to abide by that court's decision'. In contrast, the British response was 'to try to win its case by threats'. This only served 'to unite the Irish people in defence of a right which they are asserting in all courtesy and fairness against a truculent and court fearing imperialism'.[98] When the British government responded by imposing a twenty per cent duty on Irish imports, the paper retorted that 'the British decision to tax Irish produce rather than wait for arbitration' displayed 'sheer anti-Irish prejudice and anxiety to wound the Irish people'. While the British government had 'conducted this dispute like a pack of uncouth school boys', the Irish people were 'manly enough to stand by the Fianna Fáil government and assist it to defeat one of the stupidest pieces of injustice of which Britain has been guilty'.[99] Fianna Fáil's response was to impose duties on imports of British coal, cement, sugar, iron and steel.

Although the subsequent economic war hit Irish exporters hard, it allowed Fianna Fáil to consolidate its support base by disguising protectionism as patriotism. Indeed, 'the beauty of the economic war was that frugal fare could be depicted as the economic price for political freedom'.[100] In January 1933 de Valera called a snap election to test the national mood as regards support for his government's action. Although the *Irish Press* published full and half-page advertisements for Fianna Fáil, its daily editorials were the main weapon of the paper's arsenal. The paper was particularly vocal in denouncing Cumann na nGaedheal's opposition to de Valera's economic reforms as unpatriotic and strong editorials sought to reinforce this view. According to the *Irish Press*, the British government had 'delayed a settlement of the land annuities dispute' because it had 'the illusion created by the reckless campaign of unpatriotic groups at home, that by exercising pressure on the Irish people' it could 'force them to replace Fianna Fáil by a government . . . more compliant to British wishes'.[101] Ever since Fianna Fáil had been elected, Britain's Irish policy had 'been directed to one end only – the removal of Mr de Valera from office'. According to the paper:

> this attack on the fundamental rights of the Irish people was carried on in conjunction with the opposition parties in the Free State. Every speech Mr Cosgrave and his associates made here heartened and was probably meant to hearten the British in their interference in our domestic policies. Alternatively, every British statement against Mr de Valera's policy was used by Cumann na nGaedheal to shake the government's authority.[102]

The editorials also castigated Cumann na nGaedheal's election promise of ending the economic war and giving the farmers back their markets within three days of taking office as a sign of 'a close alliance between Downing Street and Cumann na nGaedheal headquarters'.[103] In a snide reference to the Boundary Commission that copper-fastened partition, the paper mocked William Cosgrave's past record of negotiating with the British government and concluded that 'were he to return to power today, Britain might make some agreement with him . . . but it would be an agreement in which Britain as always in the past, would make an appearance of giving while in fact receiving back more than she parted with'.[104] The paper also resented the British government's attempts to influence who should rule Ireland, and noted that 'in ten months Fianna Fáil created the situation in which Britain had to yield something'. According to the paper, 'to escape any real surrender', Britain wanted 'the Cosgrave administration back'. Fianna Fáil, on the other hand, had made a 'gallant effort to redeem its pledges to the electorate'.[105] The paper thus called on the electorate 'to resent this effort of Downing Street to dictate to them whom they shall choose as their rulers'.[106] It should choose 'their own government . . . a strong government . . . and an Irish government'.[107] The titles of Independent Newspapers again supported Cumann na nGaedheal and this attracted the wrath of the *Irish Press*. According to the latter, 'the latest electioneering method of the evening edition of the paper which is tied to no party' was to 'imply that Free State Ministers have come back from the country in despair at the apathy of the electorate for Fianna Fáil'. The paper retorted that 'like most inventions from that quarter' it was 'stupid'. One could not 'go into the street these days without feeling at once the optimism of Republicans'. There was 'a general consensus of opinion that on polling day' Fianna Fáil was 'going to win the most remarkable electoral victory since 1918'. The 'gloomy picture drawn by the Cumann na nGaedheal press' was the mere 'product of despondent minds'.[108]

The English publications available in Ireland also attracted criticism from the *Irish Press*; they had used 'the influence they have been allowed to get here, to interfere in politics and under the thin disguise of selective news, wage a campaign for the opposition'. Immediate action should thus 'be taken with regard to the British press' to counter its 'discreditable journalism'.[109] Despite the hardship that the economic war had so far caused, Fianna Fáil won an overall majority, winning seventy-seven seats to Cumann na nGaedheal's forty-eight. The result in effect gave the party a national mandate to continue the economic war and effectively disarmed the threat of Cumann na nGaedheal. The *Irish Press* triumphantly declared the victory as proof that Britain was 'ignorant as always of the public opinion of nations struggling to be free, contemptuous as always of the idealisms which strengthens that opinion'.[110] The paper also declared the result a humiliation for Cumann na nGaedheal. The party had gone 'deliberately into this fight against their own people. Throwing aside all considerations of patriotism, they refused to accept the majority vote of February last and in a matter of external affairs, when common sense and common decency should have combined to make them support their own state against the aggression of another, they played the outsider's game.' According to the paper, the only object the party had had 'in this unfortunate policy was to climb back into office'.[111]

The responses to the Fianna Fáil victory in the English press did nothing to restore the confidence of the *Irish Press* in it. Instead, the paper denounced the English publications as anti-Irish and called for a tax to be levied on foreign newspapers. Referring to a *Daily Mail* editorial that had been critical of the election result, the *Irish Press* held that the paper 'like most of its contemporaries' was 'angry with Irish voters for so completely ignoring its fantastic prophecies of a Cumann na nGaedheal romp home'. The fact that the paper 'should declare that as a result of the election, the tariff war should not only be maintained but perhaps even increased' was 'something of which notice must be taken'. The *Irish Press* then expressed the view that the new government would 'fail in its duty' if it did 'not tackle this matter at once and tax heavily those newspapers, which have advocated economic sabotage against Ireland for their own political purposes'.[112] The *Irish Press* did not have long to wait. In the spring of 1933, Fianna Fáil introduced its second budget, the Finance Act 1933, details of which appeared in the *Irish Press* before they were announced in the Dáil. The act included the provision of a duty on daily newspapers imported into the state. The value of such imports subsequently dropped from £216,000 in 1932 to £134,000 in 1933 and £99,000 in 1934.[113] The new tax benefited the *Irish Independent* and *Irish Press* more so than the *Irish Times* which was still perceived as a Protestant and unionist orientated paper. As a result of the new tax, sales of the *Irish Independent* gradually rose from 123,000 in 1935 to 134,000 in 1937 and 140,000 in 1939. Sales of the *Irish Press* rose from 95,000 in 1935 to 100,000 in 1937 and 110,000 in 1939.[114] There was, however, a high price to pay for such success.

CHAPTER THREE

De Valera Rule at the Irish Press

> It was established in order to put the Republican position before the people, in order to keep the Republican flag flying, in order to put a Republican Government in this Dáil and in order to give a Republican Constitution to the people of Ireland.[1]
>
> *Sean MacEntee on the founding of the* Irish Press

Although the year 1933 started on a high note with the opening of a brand new rotary printing press by Sean T. O'Kelly, by summer the tension at Burgh Quay had reached fever pitch. Indeed, the troubled industrial relations that contributed to the collapse of the Press Group in 1995 began in the early 1930s. The years 1933 to 1938 were littered with resignations, sackings, claims of wrongful dismissal, suspicions, intrigue and a culture of what Frank Gallagher termed as 'the half-spoken innuendo' that seemed 'to blast more than any charge' that could 'be met and answered'.[2] An acute shortage of capital, scarce resources, low pay and poor working conditions all contributed to the sense of unease that was forever present at the paper.[3] In fact, the rates of pay for *Irish Press* journalists were markedly below those paid to journalists at the other national papers.[4] Penury was very much the norm at the *Irish Press*. On frequent occasions, the company secretary Frank Ridgeway had to empty the cash register at the front advertisement office to pay impatient creditors waiting in his office. On other occasions he had to leave by the works entrance to avoid meeting creditors waiting for him at the front door.[5] The shortage of capital was a result of the failure of shareholders to subscribe in full for the shares allocated to them and this left the paper critically short of cash as it fought to maintain its niche in the market.

However, the culture of appalling industrial relations that forever haunted the Press Group began with the treatment meted out to the paper's founding editor, Frank Gallagher. After the paper had established itself in the marketplace, the de Valera family moved to reassert its control. De Valera's son Vivion was appointed as an unpaid director of the company in 1932 and soon immersed himself in the day-to-day running of the paper. Vivion would always be remembered for being perpetually paranoid about the finances of the company.[6] That same year, de Valera senior appointed an efficiency expert in the form of John J. Harrington, a journalism and business graduate from New York. While de Valera claimed that Harrington was appointed at the behest of the American shareholders, in reality he was appointed to bolster de Valera's control at the paper. When Harrington arrived as general manager in the summer of 1933, Gallagher was initially 'anxious to cooperate with him in every way' and personally introduced him to the various heads of departments.[7] In contrast, the adverse employment conditions and mediocre pay ensured the staff's resentment of Harrington, who despite calling for cost saving measures stayed for a while in a city-centre hotel at the expense of the company. Rumours of planned redundancies saw the NUJ forbid its members from cooperating with him in any way. Shortly after his arrival, Harrington began to stray outside his remit and, according to Gallagher, his arrival caused a degree of panic among the staff because 'it began to be stated freely throughout the *Irish Press* commercial offices that the existing staff were greatly to be reduced by dismissals. These rumours became intensified in August 1933 and in the next month of September, members of the staff began to join the union.'[8] Harrington's appointment also led to some very lively board meetings during which he and Gallagher constantly clashed.

On one occasion, Harrington ordered the night editor to carry out work that was not part of his duties and 'spoke to him in a grossly insulting way' in front of his subordinates until 'vigorously checked' by Gallagher. At a subsequent board meeting, Harrington criticised the employee as incompetent and having no knowledge of newspapers. When challenged by Gallagher, Harrington declared that this was the opinion of the overseer and quoted the latter as saying that the night editor was the worst he had ever known. Gallagher then accused him of discussing editorial staff and their weaknesses with subordinates and accepting their biased opinion without even consulting the editor.[9] At another board meeting Harrington produced material that had been submitted by the woman's page editor, Anna Kelly, claiming that it was agency copy. Harrington concluded although she was drawing a wage, Kelly had not done any original work and should be immediately dismissed. It later transpired that Kelly had prepared the copy in advance of her holidays to save the cash-starved newspaper from the expense of hiring a substitute.[10] Indeed, the chronic lack of resources had already forced Gallagher to reorganise the editorial staff. Dissatisfaction with wage levels was so bad that when one sub-editor resigned, Gallagher suggested to the board that rather than hiring a replacement, the saved wage should be divided among the remaining nine sub-editors.[11]

The situation was particularly stressful for Gallagher who felt he had to 'continually fight for recognition' from the board. Alongside Harrington, Vivion de Valera had also begun to make his presence felt around the *Irish Press*, concentrating particularly on the company finances. All three men were wary of each other and were in perpetual dispute over finance and authority. According to Gallagher, such a situation distracted him from his editorial duties and harmed the paper.[12] Despite the latter's protests, Harrington was given a free reign and Gallagher resorted to writing letters to de Valera senior urging him to resolve the situation. In one letter, Gallagher expressed the view that Harrington was 'the worst possible man to handle staffs' and would have the *Irish Press* 'in turmoil if he had executive authority'. He had 'the American view of workers – that they must be shown who is the boss and the best way to show them this is to sack somebody important'. According to Gallagher, if Harrington were in control he would produce 'a smart looking paper on the model of the Paris edition of the *Chicago Tribune*, but there would be very little of the spirit of what we have stood for in that paper'. Gallagher also protested against the culture of penury, expressing the view that 'to press on heads of departments not to spend' was acceptable, but 'if driven too far' it would 'kill initiative'. There were times when a paper could not 'afford to make a poor mouth'.[13] In another letter, Gallagher quoted a printer as having told him that the innovations suggested by Harrington 'had been abandoned in the Irish offices thirty years ago and were only found now in the worst provincial papers'. The latter related to an incident in the print room, when against the advice of the works manager and technicians 'the Linotypes were changed to places marked with chalk on the floor by Mr Harrington'. That night a 'serious delay was caused in publication by the discovery that two of the machines had been screwed down so close to obstructions that they could not be used'. As a result, the printers 'became angry at his interference' and Harrington was barred from the caseroom. It was, according to Gallagher, 'common talk on the floor that Mr Harrington did not know anything about the printing business'.[14]

Gallagher's patience was stretched to its limits when the board of directors decided in July 1933 to reject his recommendation that a reporter relocating to London be given £5 in expenses (the equivalent expenses allowed by Independent Newspapers was £25) on the grounds that it constituted 'extravagance'. Despite the fact that Gallagher was running the *Irish Press* with ten per cent fewer staff and £50 less in wages than its competitor the *Irish Independent*, the board harshly accused Gallagher of being 'unmindful of the need for care in spending'.[15] In response to the board's outlandish claim, Gallagher criticised both the acute lack of resources available and the lack of faith that the board had in him, and in effect tendered his resignation. Indeed, Gallagher's conflict with the board demonstrated the conflict over editorial expenditure, financial rectitude and scarce resources that was to mar industrial relations at the *Irish Press* for the rest of its life. According to Gallagher, for some months he had not been 'receiving the board's confidence'. This had been made 'increasingly clear at successive meetings'. Such was the 'wholly inadequate staff' levels that he was 'doing personally, work that could have been delegated' leaving him 'free to scrutinise the accounts . . . and save expenses'. But every appeal he had made 'for nearly a year to the board for extra help was denied', even though he had demonstrated that he 'was trying to do with two young men and Ms Clyde what the rival paper was doing with more than twice that number of senior journalists'. The board's only response was that he was 'foolish and should have delegated' his work 'to a staff that did not exist . . . and look after the monetary end of editorship'. The success of the paper would not have been achieved if he had 'taken the casual view' of his duties as 'indicated in the board's criticism'. In contrast, the board had implicitly expressed the view that if he had overworked himself 'in creating and directing a new national daily journal', he had shown 'a species of incompetence'. This, according to Gallagher, had been 'their attitude for some months past'. He thus warned the board that he would not 'remain for one moment further' in his position until he had 'their full confidence as editor-in-chief and their full recognition of all that position involves'.[16]

That same month, de Valera introduced legislation in the Dáil 'to make provision for the redemption of the outstanding balances of the loans floated by public subscription' in what was now a depression ridden America.[17] Explaining his reason for the repayment, he stated that 'a good many of the people who subscribed at the time would be very glad to have it now because they are not as affluent – a number of them – as they were at the time'.[18] By de Valera's repayment scheme, one dollar twenty-five cents was to be repaid to those subscribers who had not applied for a refund in 1927. For each subscriber who had received the sixty-seven cents refund in 1927, an additional fifty-eight cents was payable. Although claiming to have the welfare of the bondholders at heart, de Valera had an ulterior motive. Since some of the bonds had been signed over to de Valera to fund the *Irish Press*, he, or at least the newspaper, stood to reap a very substantial financial dividend from the repayment scheme. When the *Irish Independent* brought this fact into the public domain, the *Irish Press* accused it of trying 'to convict Mr de Valera of tricking with public funds . . . by giving sufficient twist to plain facts to make them the basis for false suggestions'.[19] Cumann na nGaedheal strenuously opposed the bill and pointed out that in 1927, de Valera had contested the assertion that the Free State Dáil was heir to the assets and liabilities of the bond drive. Now that he was in power, he had changed his mind when the cash-strapped *Irish Press* was to benefit. The party also contended that since it was de Valera and not the exchequer that had received the money from the bonds, the state had no obligation to pay the dividend.

Not so, stated the *Irish Press*, which strongly defended de Valera's bill. According to the paper, in 1924 the Cosgrave government had acknowledged its liability to repay the debt, and in 1926 had promised to 'take immediate steps to repay'.[20] This decision to repay 'was repeated in July 1928, after it was known that thousands of bondholders in the US had assigned their interest to Mr de Valera as trustee'. But the Cumann na nGaedheal ministers 'could not bring themselves to introduce legislation by which a truly national newspaper might be benefited'. It was these facts that were 'being twisted by the *Irish Independent* into a charge of dishonest use of public money by Mr de Valera'. The paper claimed that the real dishonesty was 'surely on the part of those who altered their reaffirmed financial policy and dishonoured their pledges to gratify a party prejudice and prevent money, with which investors desired to found a national journal, from going to that purpose'. It was, the paper noted, 'the fear of this newspaper, its appeal and its power' that had 'inspired the contemptible charges now being made against the head of the government'.[21] Defending Cumann na nGaedheal's delay in repayment, deputy Desmond FitzGerald stated that the party 'did not want the people to be swindled'.[22] The debate on de Valera's legislation was extremely bitter, with the opposition strenuously opposed to the diversion of taxpayer's money to the *Irish Press*. In reply to allegations that he would benefit financially from the repayment scheme, de Valera stated that he had invested the bond money 'in the *Irish Press* on conditions which meant that every single cent of dividend on it would go to the American Corporation to be distributed' and any beneficiary interest that he had in the *Irish Press* would 'similarly go for distribution'.[23] Although the bill was defended in terms of helping the original subscribers to the Dáil Loan who were now suffering the effects of the great depression, the fact that the *Irish Press* was to receive some money incensed Cumann na nGaedheal. Deputy James FitzGerald-Kenny pointed out that the 'money was subscribed for the most part by persons of meagre means', but under the repayment scheme proposed by de Valera, a 'very considerable portion' of the repayment money was 'going to be invested in shares in the *Irish Press*'. According to FitzGerald-Kenny, 'no matter how hard up they may be, out of work and starving, walking the streets' the subscribers would not receive any money and would have to await a company dividend 'to have a number of cents posted to them in America'.[24]

The well-known, unsound financial position of the *Irish Press* led other Cumann na nGaedheal deputies to accuse Fianna Fáil of underhand motives for introducing the bill at that time. Deputy Paddy Hogan claimed that what was 'biting' the Fianna Fáil party was that there was 'another far more successful paper in the country' that was 'beating their paper to the ropes as a business proposition'. According to Hogan, the *Irish Press* had 'lost almost £1,000 a week since it was started' and was by then 'in an extremely shaky financial position'.[25] In response, Michael Cleary of Fianna Fáil stated that 'anybody listening to the hysterical speech of Deputy Cosgrave' could see that he still felt 'very sore because the *Irish Press*, it must be admitted played a big part in removing Deputy Cosgrave across the floor of the house'. If on the other hand, the *Irish Press* collapsed then 'the *Irish Independent* could go ahead and tell any lies that the Cumann na nGaedheal party wanted covered up'.[26] James FitzGerald-Kenny of Cumann na nGaedheal retorted that if one left out 'the sporting news and the racing news and all that type of news and . . . the very small quantity of advertisements' that it received, then the *Irish Press* was 'a political pamphlet, pure and simple'. To call it 'a paper representing the Irish people' was 'a flight of rhetoric which required a considerable amount of courage to embark upon'.[27] De Valera, however, defended the newspaper and stated that it was not 'a party newspaper in the sense of a party controlled organ'. The party did 'not own it or control it'. It was, according to de Valera, 'owned by the shareholders'. The only case where he would 'intervene actively' would be 'if the policy of the paper were to depart from that of supporting the movement for Irish independence and supporting the policy of economic independence also'.[28]

Although Cumann na nGaedheal eventually agreed with the concept of repayment, an amendment to ensure that the money would go directly to the original subscribers (and not to whoever held the bonds, i.e. de Valera and the *Irish Press*), was rejected by Fianna Fáil. Arguing that the money should be given to the original subscribers, deputy Desmond Fitzgerald stated that 'it should be put to them and not thrown into a bankrupt concern'. If they so wished they could then 'pitch it into the *Irish Press*', if they felt that 'the *Irish Press* having produced this government and an economic war and other things' was a paper they wanted. This, observed Fitzgerald, would 'keep the *Irish Press* going for another year or so, or until the next general election'.[29] In a lengthy reply, de Valera pointed out that the opposition wanted the legal assignment compromised simply because it did 'not like the fact that American people chose to put their interest in these bonds in the form of subscriptions to the capital' of the paper. The money, according to de Valera, was 'lawfully and legally due to the *Irish Press*'.[30] He also accused the opposition of 'abusing privileges of this house to sabotage an Irish industry . . . of 333 employees'.[31] De Valera further explained that despite the fact that they were enduring the worst days of the great depression, the bondholders who had assigned their bonds to him would be entitled to extra shares in the American Corporation for future dividend on the stock. He also spoke of the national obligation of repayment and stated that he regarded his control of the bonds and of the *Irish Press* as part of a sacred 'trust' to safeguard the values of the Irish people.[32] Indeed, the 'great respect in which people held de Valera, combined with the use of the word trust not only in the debate but on many subsequent occasions, coupled with his disclaimers about directors fees misled many people into thinking that the *Irish Press* was run on non-profit-making lines'.[33]

In a hard-hitting editorial, the paper castigated the behaviour of both Cumann na nGaedheal and the *Irish Independent* and accused both of conspiring in an 'unnatural hatred' of de Valera to bring down the paper. It accused Cumann na nGaedheal of 'shamefully endeavouring to convict him of dishonest action' and of abusing its 'privileged position in an attempt to destroy' the newspaper. According to the paper, the debate was a revelation of the 'intimate association' that existed 'between the Cumann na nGaedheal party and the *Irish Independent*'. It had shown that the newspaper that had 'attacked every patriot leader since it was founded' had 'at that same work today, the heads of the Cumann na nGaedheal organisation'. It had also shown that 'no depths' were 'so low for them to sink to in a vain effort to restrain' the *Irish Press*' 'influence in reshaping the rebuilding of this nation'.[34] Eventually, Fianna Fáil's majority ensured that the bill was passed. A few days previously at the Press company's annual general meeting, no balance sheet had been provided to the assembled shareholders. Accounts circulated at the meeting, however, showed that most of the £200,000 capital raised to finance the founding of the company had been spent. Initial start-up spending had cost £109,000, while outgoings had reached £115,137. Thus the £100,000 due to the *Irish Press* by the bond repayment scheme was crucial to its survival.[35]

Industrial relations at the *Irish Press* were just as bad as its financial situation. In September 1933, Frank Gallagher again offered to resign after the efficiency expert John Harrington convinced the board to hire an architect to 'remodel the entire editorial section . . . to prevent the congregating of sports casuals and to eliminate the smell of drink'. Incensed at this interference, Gallagher claimed that although he was editor, the board sought and received 'its advice on the editorial dept elsewhere . . . advice not sound or to the benefit of the paper'.[36] His offer to resign was, of course, turned down. To add to Gallagher's problems, the paper's chief political reporter, Joseph Dennigan, became embroiled in a case of alleged political victimisation during which the issue of government information passing from Fianna Fáil to the *Irish Press* was raised. Following its severe defeat in the 1933 election, Cumann na nGaedheal had merged along with all the other opposition parties in the Dáil (with the exception of the Labour Party) to form Fine Gael. In response, the *Irish Press* accused the parties of 'cynically uniting in a last effort to divide' the cohesive 'national strength' that Fianna Fáil had created. In their old forms, the various parties had been 'dedicated to Britain's triumph' but had decayed due to 'their own chronic political failure'. To the *Irish Press*, therefore, the new party was still 'Britain's ally in the perpetuation of the war'.[37] The new party had the expressed support of the Young Ireland Association, more commonly known as the Blueshirts, the banning of which in December 1933 led to allegations of collusion between Fianna Fáil and the *Irish Press*. That same month, Dennigan was summoned to appear before a military tribunal where an army commandant, E. J. Cronin, was charged of membership of an illegal organisation – the Young Ireland Association. Dennigan was summoned by Cronin's defence team and, in reply to questions, he refused to divulge his source of information for a story relating to the proclaiming of the Young Ireland Association as an illegal organisation. During questioning, the defence handed Dennigan a copy of the *Irish Press* with the relevant report. He confirmed that the by-line of political correspondent belonged to him, that he had written that it was 'proposed to allow a short period to members of the organisation so as to provide an opportunity of ceasing membership' and confirmed that it was in reference to the banning of the Young Ireland Association. When asked whether he had received this information from an official source, Dennigan claimed it was initially his own 'speculation' since that had been the practice on every other occasion that organisations were banned, but that he 'took steps to confirm it afterwards from official sources'. He had asked official sources if he would be right in 'assuming this' and had received a positive answer. He confirmed that all this had happened prior to publication.[38] When asked to identify the official sources he claimed privilege, a claim that was disallowed by the president of the court. Dennigan than stated he could not name his source without the joint permission of his source and his editor. The defence then suggested that rather than having to reveal his source publicly, he could write down the name. Dennigan again replied that he needed the above permission. He stated that the privilege of the press was involved in the case and that his editor had asked him to 'take a certain line of action'. The president of the court then adjourned to allow Dennigan to consult both Gallagher and his source. In calling Dennigan as a witness, the defence tried to convince the court that the accused was being persecuted simply because he had not read the *Irish Press*, which, as the official organ of the Fianna Fáil government, had published a statement to the effect that the political correspondent understood that it was proposed to allow a short period to members of the banned organisation to terminate their membership. The defence argued that since the information had come from official sources and had only appeared in the *Irish Press*, those who did not and would not read de Valera's paper were at a distinct disadvantage. On resuming, Dennigan told the court that he had rung Gallagher who agreed with him that it would be a breach of confidence to give the information to anyone. He was then jailed for one month for contempt of court and taken into military custody.[39] Despite the best efforts of the NUJ, his appeal the following month was also rejected.

In any event, the final straw for Gallagher came in July 1934 in the aftermath of an administrative strike at the paper. When the strike ended, Harrington transferred one employee, Kevin Whelan, from the accounts department to the labour intensive despatch department. Reflecting later on his decision to resign as editor, Gallagher explained that the persistent arguing between himself, Harrington and Vivion de Valera had led to:

> a clash arising out of their anxiety for finances and mine, least economics make us unfitted to hold the lead we had gained. That clash uncovered another and deeper still, one of personalities. Finally and inevitably there was a clash of principle – though not an editorial matter – yet found us unbridgeably apart. Out of that – it arose from a dismissal which to me was unjust – came my resignation.[40]

It was the premeditated and gradual sacking of Kevin Whelan that forced Gallagher to finally cut his ties with the *Irish Press*. Whelan had worked as manager of *The Nation* until it ceased publication and transferred automatically to the *Irish Press*. He worked as a wages clerk and in this capacity got caught up in an administration (ITGWU) workers strike of July 1934. Although Whelan was a member of the union, he had not attended the meeting that had decided on strike action and he was still on his honeymoon when the strike began. When he returned, the strike committee asked him to compile a list of clerks and their respective wages. He refused and the committee compiled their own list by questioning individuals. When asked to confirm the accuracy of the list, Whelan corrected some mistakes but refused to disclose any other information. The list was subsequently published in support of the strike. When Whelan returned to work with the rest of the clerical staff, Harrington informed him that a new policy of interchanging members of the commercial department had been agreed upon before the strike. As a result, he was transferred to the position of collector, a position that involved travelling around businesses collecting adverts and money owned to paper. In February 1935, another collector was appointed to the city centre and Whelan was transferred to the suburbs. At the beginning of June 1935 he was again transferred, this time to the dispatch department. This position entailed not only manual work but also permanent night work. Finally, in March 1936, he and fifteen others were let go ‘owing to re-organisation’. Even though Harrington promised to rehire the men when he began his forthcoming circulation promotion, none of the sixteen men was ever rehired. Although he had already resigned and left Burgh Quay, when Gallagher heard that Whelan had finally been made redundant, he described the whole process as 'the half-spoken innuendo' that was typical of the work culture of the *Irish Press*.[41] Indeed, Gallagher had offered a verbal account for his resignation at the board meeting of October 1934, giving the required six months' notice of his intention to quit. Several letters to company secretary Frank Ridgeway 'advising him of the need for an appointment' were ignored by the board. According to the chairman, Gallagher's 'appointment as editor was a political nomination by Mr de Valera and that therefore they could not take cognisance' of his resignation. Gallagher refused to alter his decision 'though pressed many times by Mr de Valera to do so'.[42] Finally, sensing that Gallagher was determined to go and with only one day to go before his notice expired, the board requested that he stay until a suitable successor was found. Presented with the choice of going and leaving the paper he had built in the hands of Harrington or staying until a proper successor was appointed, Gallagher stayed on as editor until June 1935.

The news of Gallagher's eventual departure shocked all those left behind at the *Irish Press*. He left without any formal ceremony, even leaving his personal effects and files in his office. He later wrote to his secretary Maureen Kennedy to remove these for him. The first many learned of his departure was when his successor was introduced to the staff at a 'childish conference'.[43] Literary editor M. J. MacManus returned from holidays to find the *Irish Press* a place of 'desolation, gloom, suspicion and intrigue' and 'a young man of no experience occupying the editorial chair'.[44] Indeed, it was assistant editor Paddy Kirwan who kept the paper afloat during the editorial vacuum that followed Gallagher's departure. So high was Gallagher's reputation among his staff that many wrote pleading with him to reconsider his decision. Among these was Aodh de Blacam, who held that Gallagher's departure was a 'disaster'. His unique editorials had 'saved the country and the cause' and his 'versatility, energy, vision and knowledge' were 'irreplaceable'.[45] Another journalist expressed the view that without Gallagher, the *Irish Press* would become 'a colourless news-sheet, lacking character and the soul' that was 'the lifeblood of a real newspaper'.[46] M. J. MacManus wrote expressing his hope that 'some industrial action would have been taken by the editorial staff and the workers generally'. No strike ever emerged, although Anna Kelly resigned over the treatment of Gallagher and 'the manner of his departure laid the foundations of what would become a seemingly impregnable wall of distrust between the management and staff'.[47]

A letter from Maureen Kennedy, castigating the role of the de Valera family in the affair, was characteristic of the staff's thoughts on the treatment of Gallagher; 'I can't and won't forgive de Valera, he let you down badly, and as for Vivion, he is despicable – all that underhand, furtive dealing and never to say a word'.[48]

There was also much sympathy within Fianna Fáil for Gallagher's plight. According to Fianna Fáil minister Joseph Connolly, it was 'a tragedy not only for the paper but for the country when Gallagher ceased to be editor. From that time the whole tone of the paper gradually deteriorated. A new and undesirable streak crept into its columns'.[49] Replacing Gallagher proved to be a difficult task and the paper went through several editors during the mid-1930s. Such were the difficulties that de Valera consulted Gallagher on the best candidate to succeed him. The choice was between Bill Sweetman, then the paper's leader writer, or its chief sub-editor Patrick O'Reilly who knew 'Ireland extraordinarily well'. This was 'essential for a chief sub-editor' and O'Reilly 'would be very difficult to replace without loss to the general coverage of news'. Gallagher thus suggested Sweetman, whom he described as having 'great strength of character'. He would neither 'be influenced from an instructed course nor driven mad by pinpricks', he had 'the power to command' and could 'quietly compel obedience'. In addition, Gallagher noted that he would 'much prefer to mould Sweetman' whom he noted was 'practically moulded already'.[50] The de Valera curse struck again, however, and Gallagher was replaced not by Sweetman but by John O'Sullivan, a former *Irish Times* reporter who had worked under Gallagher for eighteen months as a sub-editor. Shortly afterwards, a rather curious article appeared in the *Roscommon Herald* that blamed Gallagher for the *Irish Press*' partisanship towards Fianna Fáil. The article suggested that now that Gallagher was no longer editor, a new less partisan editorial policy would be established. According to the article, the 'political policy of the *Irish Press*' had been 'seriously considered by the board of directors'. As a result, it had 'urged that the *Irish Press* should aim first of all at being a newspaper rather than concentrate on the propagation of political views'. Thus in 'political matters' the paper was to be 'less partisan that in the past'.[51] The article was, however, co-written at an hour-long conference by general manager John Harrington, the new editor John O'Sullivan and the chief political reporter Joseph Dennigan, the day after O'Sullivan had been appointed. In response, Gallagher received many letters from friends in other counties telling him of its appearance in most of the country's provincial papers. Gallagher himself wrote to de Valera, complaining that while the article was 'the explanation of the board's attitude' towards him, the paper itself was 'let down in the quotation'.[52] Despite the new start promised in the article, according to Gallagher's memoirs, he was continually 'pressed by Mr de Valera to return, pressed earnestly and anxiously'.[53] De Valera subsequently appointed Gallagher as deputy director of Radio Éireann, and although he never returned as editor, he continued to write for the paper under the pseudonym David Hogan and reviewed M. J. MacManus' 1944 biography of de Valera for the paper. Gallagher also had his seminal work on the war of independence *The Four Glorious Years* serialised in the *Sunday Press* in the 1950s. But his sudden departure from Burgh Quay left a wide vacuum that was not to be filled until the late 1930s.

In spite of the editorial vacuum that existed, the support of the *Irish Press* was crucial to the survival of the government. Even after de Valera assumed power in 1932, the *Irish Press* was the only daily paper to give any semblance of credibility to the Fianna Fáil administration. As a result of this, the paper, having originally been founded to articulate a radical populist discourse, became an organ of defence for the party. For example, when Fianna Fáil had been in opposition, the *Irish Press* had expressed sympathy for the Spanish Republic. However, after the outbreak of the Spanish Civil War in 1936, the paper did not stand by its previously expressed view, supporting instead de Valera's policy of impartiality. On the other hand, given the strength of the Catholic Church's support for Franco, a non-interventionist stance by de Valera and the *Irish Press* was very independent minded. Indeed, the paper's non-coverage of the war annoyed the Church, with one cleric recalling that 'alone among the metropolitan dailies' the *Irish Independent* 'gave the Irish public the full facts about the persecution of the church and the atrocities committed against priests and nuns'.[54] The *Irish Press*' insular editorial ethos of non-coverage also allowed the *Irish Independent* to increase its circulation. While the *Irish Press* barely mentioned the war (despite the fact that its night town reporter Paddy Clare took sabbatical leave to fight with the International Brigade), the *Irish Independent* stole the limelight with its daily half-page column 'In War Torn Spain'. This had dramatic results and according to one reviewer:

> in the Spanish War the *Irish Press* did not particularly favour either side; the *Irish Independent*'s policy was pro-Franco and the means by which policy was expressed was sensational. From the beginning of

> that war, the *Independent*'s sales, previously falling, climbed and its competitor paid the price of impartiality with a flattening out of its rapid rising circulation graph.[55]

The following year (1937) brought mixed fortunes for the party and the paper. The publication of de Valera's constitution for public scrutiny in May led to much debate at the paper and within the party itself. While Articles 2 and 3, which claimed jurisdiction over Northern Ireland, appeased the many nationalists working at the paper, it was Article 41, which stated that women should not 'be obliged by economic necessity to engage in labour to the neglect of their duties in the home'[56] that caused consternation within the *Irish Press*. Amid allegations of 'alleged political victimisation', the renowned feminist Hanna Sheehy Skeffington wrote to the paper's NUJ chapel stating that she would have to resign her membership since the paper had decided not to accept any more work from her because of her agitation concerning the clauses affecting the status of women. The chapel decided to investigate the claims and agreed that if substantiated, it would write to the editor and de Valera himself to point out that 'it was not usual to penalise journalists for the expression of political views in their private capacity and that failing a satisfactory adjustment, the facts would be published'. Knowing how important the *Irish Press* would be in securing a positive vote for the constitution and how this could be damaged by industrial action or the row becoming public, the paper's then editor, John Herlihy, backed down and the chapel reported that Sheehy Skeffington's 'grievance against the *Irish Press* had been adjusted through the NUJ's intervention'.[57] In the 1970s, Sheehy Skeffington's nephew, Conor Cruise O'Brien, would harbour a bigger grievance against the *Irish Press* that would not be resolved as easily.

When de Valera's constitution was passed by referendum in July 1937, the paper noted that the occasion was 'an epoch' in Irish history that was worth 'rejoicing'.[58] The provision of a territorial claim over the north within the constitution was not enough for some party members, however. In his address to that year's ard fheis, Valera ruled out force as a means to end partition because 'force would defeat itself' and the party 'would not get that basis of co-operation between all the people' that was most essential for 'national unity'.[59] In response, Kathleen Clarke, a member of the party's national executive and widow of Thomas Clarke, one of the signatories of the 1916 proclamation of independence, accused the party hierarchy of 'slipping, slipping' into political complacency.[60] According to Clarke, 'partition and the Irish language were the first things they [Fianna Fáil] were going to tackle when they became the government, but nothing was being done about either and many other members of the organisation were asking why'.[61] The *Irish Press* immediately defended de Valera and commented that while Clarke's speech was intended to be a 'severe and damaging criticism of the government', it turned out to be mere 'taunts about the backsliding of Mr de Valera and his colleagues'.[62] Clarke's criticism was nothing more than 'vague insinuations, sheer misstatements of facts and an absurd travesty of recent events in this country', while her phrase 'slipping, slipping' apparently 'meant nothing except to suggest that the government had proved false to their professions without adducing a particle of proof to substantiate what she had said'.[63] However, the disillusionment felt by Kathleen Clarke and other nationalists within the party 'became quite strong as the original impetus faltered' and would manifest itself again in 1946 in the shape of Clann na Poblachta.[64]

Despite towing the party line, the second person to succeed Frank Gallagher as editor of the *Irish Press*, John Herlihy, had a tough time as editor. He presided over a cut in expenses allowed to reporters – a move that incurred the wrath of the NUJ which reminded him that before the cutbacks, the expenses scale at the *Irish Press* 'had been worse than that of any other Irish daily'.[65] Herlihy also had to preside over a particularly embarrassing case of wrongful dismissal, much to the chagrin of de Valera. During the case, the appalling work conditions at the *Irish Press* were described in detail and in his evidence, Herlihy publicly stated that the paper had a 'well defined political policy'. The case centred on the dismissal of the paper's chief sub-editor Patrick O'Reilly, who had previously been considered by de Valera and Gallagher for the position of editor. He had joined the *Irish Press* in August 1931 as a sub-editor, was promoted to night editor in January 1932 and then to chief sub-editor in November 1933. Despite the promotions, his salary had stayed the same, even though he had applied for an increase. He was dismissed in June 1936 and subsequently sued for wrongful dismissal in the High Court. O'Reilly claimed that it was customary to give chief sub-editors six months' notice and so claimed six months' wages in lieu of notice. In contrast the Press company had informed him that it considered three months' notice as the norm and that it would forward a cheque to him for this period of notice. For the following fourteen weeks,

O'Reilly returned by registered post every cheque sent to him by the company. In evidence, O'Reilly stated that it had not been 'easy to work in the interests of the paper under the editorship' of Herlihy and the general management of Harrington. On several occasions he had written to Herlihy complaining that his staff was not sufficient and that some of them were not even qualified.

Describing his dismissal, O'Reilly stated that he had been met at the door of the public office by the company secretary, Frank Ridgeway, who handed him the notice terminating his employment. Ridgeway then informed him that the doormen would henceforth be given instructions to prevent him from entering the premises. After being contacted by O'Reilly's solicitor, Ridgeway claimed that the customary notice for sub-editors was three months. However, O'Reilly was a chief sub-editor and so claimed notice of six months. In reply, counsel for the *Irish Press*, Michael Maguire, examined O'Reilly's past experience with other newspapers. He had previously held the position of chief sub-editor of the *Evening Herald* and had been dismissed for 'neglect of duty' with only one month's notice in accordance with his contract. He had also worked for the *Enniscorthy Guardian* but had also been dismissed after six months for the same reason with only a fortnight's notice.[66] Since there was no precedent to go by, both sides called witnesses to testify as to what they thought was reasonable notice for a chief sub-editor. Previous *Irish Press* editors Frank Gallagher and John O'Sullivan testified that it was six months. John Anderson, editor of the *Evening Mail*, and Tom Quilty, former editor of the *Irish Independent*, also agreed that six months' notice was the norm. Robert Smyllie, editor of the *Irish Times* mischievously stated that while he had not heard of any definite custom governing the above, he had heard 'a lot of gossip in journalistic circles on the subject'.[67] Giving evidence for the *Irish Press*, John Herlihy noted that every member of the staff was a member of the NUJ and proceeded to quote its regulations that provided for three months' notice for sub-editors. He conceded that the regulations did not deal with chief sub-editors but argued that three months' notice was reasonable. Continuing his evidence, Herlihy contended that each of the daily national newspapers had a 'well defined political policy'. The editor of each paper had to be in 'sympathy with the policy of the paper in order to carry it out' and it would be impossible for him to become editor of another Irish daily 'unless he did a somersault'. He stated that sub-editors had nothing to do with policy and so could move from one paper to another 'policy being no bar'.[68]

The court also heard evidence from Dermot Gallagher, the original chief sub-editor of the *Irish Press*, who had left in November 1933. Although he stated his opinion that the proper notice for a chief sub-editor was six months, he admitted he had asked Frank Gallagher to let him go as soon as he could be replaced and had suggested one month's notice. This was agreed to by mutual consent and he left at the end of the agreed notice. Counsel for the *Irish Press* then sought permission to recall Frank Gallagher to clarify whether or not he had advised the board of directors on the question of notice. Permission was refused, as was permission to enter the minutes of the relevant board meeting into evidence. Nonetheless, the *Irish Press* sought a dismissal of the action on the grounds that the only evidence put before the court was 'gossip and opinion' and no custom had been established by providing specific instances of its use. Summing up the case for O'Reilly, his counsel held that Herlihy's evidence was 'coloured in favour of the *Irish Press*'. Herlihy had admitted that sub-editors were entitled to three months' notice and so there could be no question but that the notice given to a chief sub-editor should be longer than that given to a sub-editor.[69] In his judgement, Justice Maguire found that while O'Reilly had failed to establish a custom of six months, the position of chief sub-editor was a very responsible one. The success or failure of a newspaper depended to a great extent upon the competence, judgement and taste of the chief sub-editor and the reason why there were so few instances of dismissals was that newspaper managers took extraordinary care to see that they got for this post those who were tried and experienced. The amount of responsibility placed on the shoulders of a chief sub-editor seemed to justify a distinction being made between that position and that of sub-editor. Three months' notice was inadequate and therefore O'Reilly had been entitled to six months' notice or payment in lieu. He was thus awarded £258 in damages plus costs.[70] Editorial stability eventually returned to the *Irish Press* in May 1938, when Bill Sweetman was finally appointed editor. The manner in which Sweetman was appointed demonstrated that an editor's toleration of Fianna Fáil was an essential qualification for the job. According to Sweetman:

> when appointed in 1938, de Valera called him to government buildings and delivered a long lecture on Fianna Fáil policy and philosophy. When he had finished, Sweetman remarked that there was nothing in that that was in conflict with his conscience. De Valera said he was very pleased to hear it, as it was vital for a newspaper editor to believe in the line he was taking.[71]

Indeed, Sweetman took over as editor in time to highlight the Anglo-Irish Agreement of 1938 that ended the economic war. In return for one lump sum payment of £10 million, the British government agreed to return the Treaty ports, while the trade tariffs imposed by both governments were also withdrawn. Under the headline 'British to Leave the Ports', the *Irish Press* described the agreement as a 'triumph of negotiation for de Valera', while the return of the Treaty ports was described as 'a recognition of the complete sovereignty of Éire over her present territory'.[72] The agreement would 'be hailed with joy and gratification by the Irish people' who would recognise that it was 'the very best that could have been obtained in the circumstances'. The paper also had words of comfort for those who had suffered during the economic war. In time, they would realise that the 'manly and patriotic stand which they took eventually brought with it for them an abundant and rich reward'.[73] Although the agreement necessitated a review of the existing tariffs to give British industry opportunity for 'reasonable competition', the paper sought to assure Irish industry that 'adequate protection' would still be maintained.[74] Despite complaints from a number of industrial sectors and opposition from small farmers, the paper exalted the benefits that future competition from British firms would bring. Noting that the 'era of spoonfeeding' was over, the paper declared that competition from Britain would encourage Irish industry to modernise and be efficient, for when 'the manufacturer sees what his rival can produce, it is an incentive and a goal for him to do better next time'.[75] In the subsequent election, the paper noted that 'the bigger the poll, the better for Fianna Fáil'. It was the 'party of the people, the real representatives of the ideals and traditions of the average Irishman and woman'. Therefore, a big poll was 'not only good democracy but good nationalism and therefore good for the only national party'. Fine Gael, on the other hand, 'did not possess even the shreds of an intelligible national policy'.[76] The choice therefore was between 'a position of stalemate and recurring elections and one of stable government and prolonged peace'. According to the paper, the stalemate position would be 'nothing short of a national disaster' and would 'hold up the business of government indefinitely'. Stable government could only be secured by 'voting for Fianna Fáil'.[77] On election day, the paper noted that Fianna Fáil 'was not merely the only possible government but the best possible government'.[78] In the wake of the overall majority of sixteen seats that the party achieved, the paper triumphantly proclaimed that the electorate had expressed a wish for 'a Fianna Fáil policy and a Fianna Fáil government'.[79]

As the Second World War loomed, the *Irish Press* took its role as the organ of the Fianna Fáil government very seriously. Editorials on topics such as 'National Discipline', 'National Honour', 'Tolerance' and 'Unity' helped reinforce Fianna Fáil's policy of neutrality. For the party, if not the paper, the radicalism of being in opposition had finally given way to the reality of being in government. While the paper's first editorials had spoken of the 'Irish people' and the 'Irish nation' and encouraged the electorate to unite and make the government listen to and act for it, as the war loomed the paper spoke down to the electorate effectively telling it what its duty was. The editorial of 4 September 1939 demonstrated most precisely the paper's ideological shift from radicalism populism to conservatism. Entitled 'A Testing Time', the editorial proclaimed that the electorate's 'responsibilities as citizens' were to ensure that 'no word or act' should extend beyond what the state had 'proclaimed the national purpose to be'.[80] The war years were particularly demanding ones for the Fianna Fáil government. Although many of the new factories set up during the 1930s were not geared to face the challenges presented by the war, they were crucial in ensuring the state's survival. Nonetheless, the government was forced to introduce drastic controls on both consumption and production of goods. Under the 1939 Emergency Powers Bill, Sean Lemass, as chief architect of Fianna Fáil's import-substitution policy, took charge of the new Department of Supplies that assumed responsibility for the supply and distribution of essential raw materials and foodstuffs. During the war, the Irish economy was virtually cut off from world markets, although the state-owned Irish Shipping Company was established in 1941 to secure a lifeline to whatever foreign supplies were available. During the war years, coal imports dropped by one third.[81] Oil imports dropped to a trickle and both producers and consumers resorted to burning bog peat. The output of gas dropped and its use for domestic heating was prohibited. Only doctors and clergymen were exempt from the prohibition on the use of private cars and public rail transport was drastically cut back to make way for freight. Although the government introduced compulsory tillage orders, agricultural output was hampered by the lack of artificial fertilisers. Rationing was introduced and while supplies of potatoes, eggs, sugar and meat were adequate, supplies of milk and butter were barely sufficient. On the other hand, tea and margarine were very scarce, while coffee and imported fruit were almost unobtainable. Not surprisingly, emigration levels soared. Between 1940–45, 136,000 travel permits or passports were issued to men and 62,000 to women, most of whom moved to Britain where the demand for labour was never higher.[82]

In early 1943, pleading special circumstances (the Emergency), de Valera introduced legislation seeking to extend the life of the Dáil but then withdrew it in the face of widespread opposition. During the subsequent election campaign, the *Irish Press* accused the opposition parties of having made it their 'sole business to see that the public are not allowed to forget for a moment even the very slightest of the minor inconveniences that they have suffered as a result of the war'.[83] Editorially, the paper queried what Fine Gael had done 'in all those critical years before the war . . . during which the present government was preparing the ground for the present emergency, preparing it both politically in order to make our neutrality possible, and economically so that we should be able to feed and clothe ourselves in the isolated conditions under which we live today'.[84] Turning its attention to the Labour Party, the paper held that while the party had begun its campaign by 'promising the moon with a planet or two thrown in', it was now 'keeping to carefully vague generalities'.[85] The *Irish Press* also dismissed the concept of a national government composed of representatives from all parties. According to the paper, the proponents of the concept 'seem to feel that they can emit cries of corrupt, incompetent, futile and dishonest at the majority leaders from one side of their mouths while from the other they plead "won't you please join us in governing the country" and that nobody will think it odd'.[86] Thus the choice was 'between Fianna Fáil or a melody of sectional groups; Fine Gael representing the conservatives, the Labour Party representing nobody in particular, certainly not the workers and even more certainly not the trade unionists, and other groups standing for a mixture of radicalism, fascism, cheap money, an end to democracy etc'.[87] It was 'not only folly but madness to suggest that at this moment of peril, the people should hand over the government to a bunch of squabbling groups whose speeches every day for the last six weeks have shown that they have not a glimmer of comprehension of the difficulties and dangers through which our people have been guided by Fianna Fáil'.[88] On election day, the paper expressed the view that it was 'inconceivable that a wise people could do other than choose a Fianna Fáil government in this election'.[89] Despite such partisan coverage, the party's support dropped by ten per cent and Fianna Fáil returned to minority government, holding just forty-eight per cent of Dáil seats. In response, the *Irish Press* held that 'the country's first reaction will be one of disappointment' because Fianna Fáil had had 'placed on it, the onus of forming a government without having received from the electorate the all over strength required to carry out effectively that grave responsibility'.[90]

During the war, both Fianna Fáil and the *Irish Press* exploited the American and British hostility to Irish neutrality by hyping the threat of invasion. It was, proclaimed the *Irish Press*, 'no time for a weak or a rickety government'.[91] It was also no time for a rickety press industry and so de Valera appointed former *Irish Press* editor Frank Gallagher as head of the Government Information Bureau in 1939. In close consultation with de Valera, Gallagher was, in effect, chief censor during the war years. Despite this, the *Irish Press* was treated to the same strict rules of censorship as the other daily newspapers. De Valera's neutrality was, however, 'a friendly neutrality to the Allies' and the *Irish Press* was seen as more pro-British than neutral.[92] The German embassy insisted that since the paper was 'looked upon as the organ of the government party' it should 'be pledged to particular care'.[93] Thus the paper had a rather precarious relationship with the press censor, former *Irish Independent* journalist Michael Knightly. As the war dragged on, *Irish Press* editor Bill Sweetman became convinced that Knightly, in order to prove the paper's impartiality, discriminated against it. Referring to a report that was censored in November 1943, he accused the censor of spiking the story because the version of the story as submitted by the *Irish Times* was unacceptable. According to Sweetman, the *Irish Press* version was spiked 'so that the press censorship, if questioned by the *Irish Times* could answer, but look what we have done to the *Irish Press*'.[94] In effect, the paper's reputation had 'on several occasions been injured for no better reason than that a censor was afraid of hurting the susceptibilities of another paper'.[95] Such were his feelings on the matter that Sweetman wrote directly to Frank Aiken who held the position of Minister for the Co-ordination of Defensive Measures, stating that it was 'clear that in taking care to be right with the other newspapers' the censor was 'careless as to the injury he may cause the *Irish Press*'.[96] As the war progressed, the German embassy also presented content analysis of the paper's war coverage that it regarded as being anti-German to Aiken who promised to have a word with Sweetman. Such bias was subsequently attributed by the Minister for Justice, Gerry Boland, to 'a kind of carelessness and negligence, the automatic publication of everything which comes to the newspaper from British News Agencies to which it subscribes, without any effort to avoid giving the impression of pro-British prejudice which the exercise of a little editorial care and ingenuity could easily prevent'.[97] Indeed, a series of *Daily Telegraph* articles that had been reprinted in the *Irish Press* prompted the Secretary of the Department of Foreign Affairs, Joe Walshe, to suggest to the German ambassador Edouard Hempel, 'that the Germans, as a counter, supply a series of articles favourable to Germany which could also be published in the *Irish Press*, the government organ'.[98] Such editorial sloppiness at the paper contrasted sharply with Frank Gallagher's initial instruction to sub-editors to be wary of the propaganda-spinning British news agencies. Indeed, several Fianna Fáil TDs also expressed dissatisfaction at what they regarded as the pro-British tone of the paper. In a letter to the editor that was stopped by the censor in June 1941, party TD Dan Breen claimed that the paper was 'more British than the British'.[99] He accused the paper of pandering to the 'rotten pro-British element' and of being 'guilty of crimes that would make Irishmen who gave their all for a free Ireland hang their heads in shame'.[100]

During the war years, the *Irish Press* London office was kept open. In 1946, Terry Ward became London editor and was later joined by Jim McGuinness, who became editor of the paper during the 1950s. The office junior was Donal Foley who played a major role in the reinvention of the *Irish Times* during the 1960s. As well as censorship, all of the nation's newspapers had to deal with shortages of newsprint and electricity. Brass and lead were constantly recycled and spare parts for the printing machines were hard to come by. Old animosities were forgotten as the newspaper train run by the Great Southern Railway Company was abandoned because of a lack of coal and the three newspaper companies pooled together to buy two lorries to replace it. All the newspapers shrank in size in 1940, as the price of newsprint soared from £15 a tonne to £25 a tonne in a matter of days. The *Sunday Independent*, then the only Irish Sunday newspaper, became a single sheet newspaper. During the war years (acknowledged only as The Emergency), the *Irish Press* shrank in size from sixteen pages an issue to a mere four pages. Later, William Sweetman was to observe that the quality of the paper had improved because 'all the padding that had filled out the pages of the *Irish Press* before the war fell away, leaving only quality articles'.[101] When the publishing restrictions were finally lifted in 1945, the *Irish Independent* criticised the severe censorship and accused the Fianna Fáil government of having displayed favouritism towards the *Irish Press*. According to the paper, the 'censorship was operated in a stupid, clumsy and unjust manner' and was 'frequently inspired not by national unity but by party political motives'. On several occasions it had been 'prohibited from publishing news which at the same time was allowed to appear in other Dublin newspapers'. Such contradictory decisions were 'capable of explanation only by the existence of a desire to judge whether or not publication at a particular time was capable of winning political advantage'.[102] Likewise, the *Irish Times* believed that it had been singled out for particular attention because it was 'pro-British' in as much as the paper 'believed . . . that the system of democracy' that existed 'throughout the British Commonwealth' represented 'for all its faults, the highest achievement that yet has been made by man as a political being'. The paper's 'sympathies from the start were with the opponents of tyranny and injustice'.[103] Under the headline, 'They Can Be Published Now', the paper later published all the major news photographs that had been banned during the war. In sharp contrast, however, the *Irish Press* felt it 'incumbent to pay a tribute to the sense and impartiality which characterised the very complex and difficult work which the censors were called upon to do'.[104] Disregarding its quarrels with the censor, the paper noted that 'in every case where news was suppressed, the reason was always a sound one; that its publication might have been dangerous to security'. According to the paper, the restrictions were never 'a case of suppressing the truth' since '90% of the news which came under the bar of the censor was fake'. This occurred because during the war, the news agencies of belligerent countries were 'not as much concerned with the truth as with making propaganda for their own side'.[105] The paper also reprinted in pamphlet form several thousand copies of de Valera's famous radio reply to Winston Churchill's attack on Irish neutrality. *Why Ireland was Neutral – Mr de Valera's Reply to Mr Churchill*, cost one penny and represented not only a commercial opportunity but also an opportunity to defend the party's policy of neutrality during the war.

The post-war years saw a number of new journalists join the *Irish Press*. One such individual was Benedict Kiely who was offered a job by literary editor M. J. MacManus. Kiely thus left his old job at the *Irish Times* and joined the *Irish Press* where he would later succeed MacManus as literary editor after the latter's sudden death. Another new arrival was Douglas Gageby, who had worked with Major Vivion de Valera at military intelligence during the war. Before the war, Gageby had contacted editor Bill Sweetman, suggesting that the paper establish a Trinity College correspondent. He was invited in to discuss his proposal with Sweetman but the column never materialised. Towards the end of the war, he again began to submit articles to the paper before joining its staff on 25 June 1945 – the day that Fianna Fáil's Sean T. O'Kelly was inaugurated as President. According to Gageby, as a barrister Sweetman could be quite a 'sardonic' editor. His assistant editor, Paddy Kirwan, was also a barrister and both were prone to summoning journalists to their editorial conferences to interview them on the accuracy of their articles. The journalist would have to read their article aloud, both Sweetman and Kirwan would listen and then 'the adversarial thing of two lawyers would emerge with both arguing against each other'. For their antics, Anna Kelly, who had by then rejoined the paper, nicknamed the pair 'lo and behold', although she never identified who exactly was who. Sweetman was, however, a confident editor. On one occasion he showed Gageby a letter of complaint from a Fianna Fáil cumann secretary complaining that for a second time its notes had been omitted. He also showed Gageby his reply that stated 'if you people would all buy the *Irish Press* instead of the *Independent*, we'd have more pages and more space to fit in your cumann notes'.[106] Indeed, according to Gageby, despite the prevailing view that the *Irish Press* was run by Catholics and Fianna Fáil hacks, the staff consisted of 'a very mixed crowd'. Along with Gageby, the Protestant religion was represented by Matt Chambers, later deputy editor of the *Irish Times*, and Donald Smyllie, brother of *Irish Times* editor Robert Smyllie. Alternative political views were represented by the presence of 'a lot of left wing republicans and people who didn't give a damn'.[107] The mid-1940s also saw the NUJ chapel and *Irish Press* management at loggerheads over changes in the sports department. The chapel expressed its displeasure at management signing a three-year contract with a professional attached to Portmarnock golf course. This, the chapel argued, was not in the interests of the sports staff or 'journalism in general'. The renegotiation of a freelance sport reporter's contract also caused some difficulty. Under the new contract, the reporter, William Madden, received less pay and less holidays. According to the chapel 'a vital principle was at stake that would undermine all the rights of the entire staff in every department'. It contemplated strike action and sought the appointment of Madden to the staff at the standard rate. The dispute and lengthy negotiations continued for a year until Madden reported that his position had 'improved generally'.[108] In 1947 the NUJ and the Dublin Newspapers Management Committee clashed over pay and conditions. Strike notice was to be served in May 1947, but through the intervention of the Labour Court, negotiations between the two sides restarted. The strike was averted and the revolutionary eight-hour day and minimum rates of pay were agreed upon.[109] That same year, a young American student who was studying in London but paying a quick visit to Dublin, dropped by the offices of the *Irish Press* to introduce himself. The paper's news editor Jack Grealish gave the visitor a tour of the plant and later escorted him to the next-door hostelry for refreshments. On returning to the paper, Grealish remarked that the young visitor, John Fitzgerald Kennedy, had a bright future ahead of him.[110]

The future was not so bright for Fianna Fáil, however. The late 1940s saw the popularity of the party decline considerably. Despite some major governmental initiatives in social policy such as the Children's Allowances Act of 1944 and the creation of two new government departments – Health and Social Welfare – on Christmas Eve 1946, after sixteen years in power, nine of which had been spent presiding over food and fuel rationing, low wages, high prices and public sector industrial disputes, Fianna Fáil looked as worn out as the country itself.[111] By the end of the war, the party had 'attained as much of their inaugural programme as seemed attainable' but 'the ending of partition, the party's other great objective was no nearer then before'. The green card had 'slipped from Fianna Fáil's grasp and was once more in the pack'.[112] The radical alternative to Fianna Fáil took the form of the Clann na Poblachta, a republican party built largely around former members of the IRA. The party was led by ex-*Irish Press* employee and former chief-of-staff of the IRA, Sean MacBride. In 1946, several ex-members of Fianna Fáil joined MacBride's new party. These included former Fianna Fáil national executive members Noel Hartnett, Aodh de Blacam and Kathleen Clarke. This group of disillusioned nationalists was disappointed that the radicalism that Fianna Fáil and the *Irish Press* had initially stood for had subsided. Promising a radical programme of political, economic and social reform, the new party won two by-elections in October 1947. Although the Fianna Fáil government still had eighteen months of its term to run, de Valera called a snap election for February 1948. As election tension grew, the *Irish Press* sought to defend Fianna Fáil's record during its sixteen-year period in office by casting doubts on the adverse economic conditions blamed for mass emigration. According to the paper, emigration was caused by 'various motives, amongst which economic pressure was not usually the most compelling'.[113] Likewise, Fianna Fáil's policy of restoring the Irish language was defended after one Clann na Poblachta candidate declared that 'compulsory Irish and teaching through Irish amounted to mental murder' and promised to abolish it. The paper responded by accusing the party of trying to 'catch a few West-British votes' and declared that thanks to Fianna Fáil 'tens of thousands of young people' had 'a working knowledge of Irish'. According to the paper, if not for the policy pursued by the party, they 'would not have been able to speak a word of the tongue of their forefathers'.[114]

The *Irish Press* also criticised Clann na Poblachta's call for a break with sterling by chastising those 'candidates eager to create the impression' that Fianna Fáil had displayed a 'supine subservience to England in financial matters'.[115] In addition, Clann na Poblachta's plan to allow Northern Ireland MPs to take seats in the Senate was dismissed by the paper as 'a stunt adopted without thought as to the consequences'. According to the paper, unity would not be secured by those who brought 'down the problem to the level of auctioneering by offering the electorate every flashy proposal' that entered their heads, but by those who took 'their duties to the nation and its lost province seriously'.[116] It was obvious that Clann na Poblachta's radical approach to partition disturbed Fianna Fáil and presented a formidable challenge to the party's position as the principal nationalist party. This fear led the *Irish Press* to comment that partition was 'not an issue in this election'. Despite this assertion, the paper castigated candidates who claimed 'that if the party to which they belong' was returned to power, it would 'produce a practicable, cut and dried plan to end partition'.[117] At an election rally in Dublin, Matt Feehan, later founding editor of the *Sunday Press*, declared that Fianna Fáil and de Valera was the best combination to achieve a thirty-two county Ireland. The people had a patriotic duty to vote for Fianna Fáil although 'they could, if they wished be renegade Irishmen and knife Eamon de Valera in the back'.[118] The extent to which the paper helped Fianna Fáil defend its hegemony and demonise its opposition was demonstrated by the results of an *Irish Independent* pre-election content analysis survey. It found that during the campaign, the *Irish Press* had devoted seventy-six per cent of its political column inches to Fianna Fáil, while Clann na Poblachta had received only six per cent.[119] Despite such an aggressive defence, however, Fianna Fáil was defeated when Fine Gael, Labour, Clann na Talmhan, National Labour and Clann na Poblachta united to form the first inter-party government – a concept disapproved of by the *Irish Press*. According to Clann na Poblachta's Noel Browne, in the 'negotiations leading to the formation of the coalition, an interesting piece of black propaganda appeared in de Valera's *Irish Press*. The paper issued a list of probable ministerial candidates for office were a Labour/Fine Gael coalition to be formed'.[120] The black propaganda element was the inclusion in the list of Labour TD Jim Larkin as Minister for Education. Larkin had previously stood for election as a member of the Communist Party. According to Browne, 'what the writer of the *Irish Press* article well knew was that the proposal of Larkin as Minister for Education would almost certainly scupper any possibility of the formation of a coalition government. A Communist in the Department of Education even today is unthinkable . . . Needless to say, the very experienced, widely acknowledged and talented Larkin . . . was not nominated . . . or elected by the party for a cabinet position'.[121] Such 'black propaganda' was to continue during the coalition's term of office as Fianna Fáil again turned its attention towards using the *Irish Press* to spread its message to the electorate.

In February 1948, at de Valera's invitation and following newspaper production training with the *Daily Mail*, Sean Lemass became managing director of the *Irish Press*. Although remembered as 'a good businessman and very practical', Lemass also immersed himself in the journalistic side of the business.[122] His official role in the paper was a managerial one, but a new weekly 'Political Commentary' column appeared in March 1948 and it quickly became evident that much of the commentary originated from Lemass. As Noel Browne pointed out, 'understandably he concentrated on the members of our cabinet, and all of us came under scrutiny'.[123] Indeed, when Lemass criticised the accuracy of an emigration report in the Dáil, the Labour leader and coalition Minister for Social Welfare, William Norton, retorted that Lemass' 'leading articles in the *Irish Press*' were not 'notable for their accuracy either'.[124] In a reply to a Dáil question on the accuracy of newspapers, i.e. misleading reports corrected by the Government Information Bureau, it emerged that for the year April 1948 to April 1949, while both the *Irish Independent* and the *Irish Times* had been corrected six times each, the *Irish Press* had been corrected twenty-six times. In reply, Lemass argued that the publication of a contradiction by the Government Information Bureau did not necessarily mean that the report published in the paper was incorrect.[125] In 1949, when Lemass delivered a critique of Norton in the *Irish Press*, the latter sued the paper for libel. During the case, Lemass spent a considerable amount of time in the witness box defending his article.

In evidence, Lemass admitted that it was he who decided on the weekly topic to be commented on and also admitted that he prepared notes on the topic before passing them on to the editor. The notes were then passed on to the political correspondent, Brendan Mailin, who composed the final article. Lemass admitted that he had written the notes for the Norton article, but as the notes had gone 'missing', he could not recall how much he or the political correspondent had contributed to the article. When pressed, Lemass conceded to having composed the 'general substance of the article'.[126] The article in question was a commentary appraising the abilities and oratorical style of members of the coalition, and according to Lemass, he had supplied the appraisal on Norton from opinion circulating within the Dáil. When asked if his comments and those of the *Irish Press* were always consistent, Lemass replied that he 'would hesitate to assert otherwise'. When questioned on a previous 'Political Commentary' column of November 1948, that had stated that 'news should be given objectively, with due regard to its importance and without reference to its political effect', Lemass replied that the statement 'referred to news given by Radio Éireann, not in a newspaper'. When asked whether he thought 'news given by Radio Éireann should be given in that way and news in the *Irish Press* should be in another form', Lemass replied that news given by Radio Éireann which was 'a public service, should be given without regard for its political effect'. According to Lemass, to 'lay down the same standard for a newspaper' was 'ridiculous'. Such a standard had, however, been promised by both de Valera and founding editor Frank Gallagher. In effect Lemass acknowledged that the *Irish Press* was a party newspaper, a claim repeatedly denied by de Valera. Confirming that he regarded the medium as the message, Lemass, when asked to comment on the standard of news in the paper, replied that they tried 'to give it objectively, with due regard to its importance and we have a close regard for its political effect'.[127] Such a statement was a direct contradiction to the assurances given by de Valera and Gallagher when fund raising for the paper. In any event, the jury found in favour of Norton but awarded him only £1 damages. The *Irish Press* was jubilant and from then on Fianna Fáil politicians constantly referred to Norton as 'Billy the Quid'. To add insult to injury, Norton's costs were awarded in proportion to damages received – a measly thirteen shillings and four pence.

Lemass also ran into difficulties with his plan to abolish the newspaper's practice of referring to former military men by their rank. Lemass held a particular dislike for Fine Gael's General Richard Mulcahy and felt that the paper stripping him of his rank would ease the situation. Lemass was forced to back down, however, when he realised that the ruling would also affect Major Vivion de Valera.[128] But despite such tribulations, Lemass also contributed to the paper's success, by helping to secure one of the biggest post-war scoops in the guise of features writer Liam MacGabhann and his serialisation of what became known as the Aga Muller saga. In 1948, the young girl and her father had decided to set sail from depression-ridden Germany. Tragedy struck and their small boat was shipwrecked off the coast of Liberia where her father died. Interest in her plight was worldwide and MacGabhann convinced Lemass to let him travel out to Liberia to interview the girl. With the help of Aer Lingus, MacGabhann brought Muller back to Dublin to write up the full story of her plight. For a full month the story of the adventures and tragedies of the Muller family were serialised in the paper and circulation soared.[129] It was, however, for the launch of the *Sunday Press* that Lemass would be most remembered.

CHAPTER FOUR

Expansion and Exposure

> The *Irish Press* was funded by one pound notes collected from rank and file republican supporters of the party. It was the intention that it should become a national newspaper and certainly not the political play thing and enormous financial asset of the de Valera family which it later became.[1]
>
> *Noel Browne on the financing of the* Irish Press

Under Sean Lemass' supervision, a new 'Superspeed' printing press was installed in Burgh Quay in March 1949. Capable of producing 100,000 copies per hour and boasting colour facilities, the press was officially put into service in a ceremony presided over by board chairman Edmund Williams.[2] Later that same year, along with general manager Jack Dempsey and other senior executives at the company, Lemass was centrally involved in the foundation of the *Sunday Press*, the plans for which were 'very delicate' because of wariness from the board of directors. As chairman of the board, Edmund Williams was strongly against the idea of a Sunday paper and argued that it would ruin the *Irish Press* financially.[3] Nonetheless, the paper went ahead with Douglas Gageby being appointed deputy editor. Lemass' plan was to build up a loyal readership first and then concentrate on attracting advertising. He thus looked to the large Fianna Fáil rural constituency as the target basis for the paper's initial readership. To beat the *Sunday Independent*, Lemass planned to have the *Sunday Press* on sale outside every church after first mass. The organisation of this feat rested on the shoulders of veteran republicans Liam Pedlar and Padraig O'Criogáin who ran the circulation department. A new distribution network based on the most recent ordnance survey maps was devised. To get the paper to the more remote countryside churches, parish priests who were also party supporters were recruited to collect the papers from the larger towns and deliver them on time for after the first mass. It was in this way that the enormous rural readership of the *Sunday Press* was built up. The paper was subsequently always more popular in rural rather than urban areas.

It was while these plans were being prepared that Gageby was 'suddenly told that Matt Feehan' had been appointed editor. Feehan, who had held the rank of Lieutenant Colonel during the Emergency, was a member of Fianna Fáil's national executive and was 'put in to be the voice of Fianna Fáil'. Feehan had 'never been in a newspaper office in his life' and initially confessed to Gageby that 'he knew nothing about newspapers but knew what he wanted'.[4] A staunch republican, Feehan had once stated that he would never cross the border 'unless at the head of a battalion of men'. Nonetheless, Feehan brought his considerable military organisational skills to the paper.[5] The *Irish Times* was again used to publicise the imminent arrival of the new paper. By this time, relations between the two companies had improved considerably, helped in no small part by 'the cross-fertilisation of staff from Burgh Quay to Westmoreland Street'.[6] With its emphasis on light, easily read material, the *Sunday Press* had an innovative make-up in that it divided itself into a news section, a magazine section and a sports section. The magazine section proved to be very successful with a woman's page, a weekly fashion competition, a crossword with a £750 prize as well as film, book and theatre reviews. The extensive sports section also added to the entertainment value of the paper. The paper featured a popular cartoon strip 'Éire Ar Agaidh' that told the story of the war of independence. One of the more popular features of the paper was the roving reporter 'On the Road' column by Terry O'Sullivan and photographer Dick Shakesphere.

Launched on the Sunday of the All-Ireland hurling final in 1949, the new arrival was ignored by its main rival, the *Sunday Independent,* which began an advertising campaign proclaiming itself to be 'Ireland's National Sunday Paper'. From its very birth the *Sunday Press* was characterised by a nationalist tone. Its first edition complained of how Irish readers were 'obliged to fall back for their weekend reading on imported Sunday newspapers' that were 'alien to the Irish temperament, the Irish character and the Irish way of life'.[7] There was a wide market for a native journal that would not be 'inferior to the imported article in news or entertainment value while surpassing it as an organ of thought and culture'. While the paper's policy would be 'in keeping with the nationalist tradition of a century and a half, the policy that was given its first ringing utterance by Theobald Wolfe Tone' and was 'embodied forever in the Proclamation of Easter Week', it would strive for 'democratic government based on

Christian principles over every inch of Irish soil'.[8] The first issue was a massive success and, ironically, the first winner of the crossword prize was a Kerry-born and Dublin-based Garda by the name of Michael Collins! The following day, the *Irish Press* noted that sales of the *Sunday Press* had exceeded all expectations and had sold particularly well in the 'unconquered north'.[9] Subsequent editions of the paper were equally successful, due to its journalistic flair and its crosswords and fashion competitions that paid substantial prizes. By the mid 1950s, with a circulation of 379,000, the paper was offering prizes such as a trip for two to New York and a Volkswagen car. Eventually 'the *Sunday Press* became a licence to print money. In 1967–68 people were literally queuing up to advertise in it.'[10] Indeed, the paper attracted advertising simply because advertising agencies were glad that their dependence on the *Sunday Independent* had been lessened. By the mid 1960s, the *Sunday Press* had achieved a circulation of over 400,000, at that time the highest ever circulation for an Irish Sunday newspaper. However, with stories headlined as 'The Curse of Cromwell', 'IRA Commander Speaks' and 'IRA Raid by Ernie O'Malley' the paper's strong nationalist tone gave rise to some concern: 'the *Sunday Press* was violently political and its profoundly "green" approach may have helped inspire the 1950s IRA activities'.[11] Indeed, according to Tim Pat Coogan, 'it is a historical fact that in the mid 1950s, some of the new generation IRA in their inexperience, deduced from de Valera's position with the *Irish Press* and the fact that the *Sunday Press* editor, Colonel Matthew Feehan, was a member of the Fianna Fáil National Executive, that a blind eye would be turned to their activities'.[12] Its letters page was equally nationalist, with one reader going so far as to suggest that the Post Office should frank all post with anti-partition slogans.

The launch of the new paper could not have been timed better, as Ireland took advantage of the American European Recovery Programme (more commonly known as the Marshall Plan) and received forty-seven million dollars over a three-year period. The inter-party government also established the Industrial Development Authority that offered state aid to indigenous industry.[13] The coalition held on to power until April 1951 when it collapsed amid much acrimony. The previous year, the Minister for Health, Noel Browne, had tried to introduce a scheme whereby mothers and children would get free health care, but encountered opposition from the Catholic bishops and the Irish Medical Association, both of which feared losing control over the social issue of health care. These objections, combined with the cost involved, ensured Fine Gael's and Clann na Poblachta's opposition to the scheme. The subsequent infighting within the coalition ensured its downfall when Browne resigned. In an editorial, the *Irish Press* observed that 'the inevitable' had happened. The coalition had 'collapsed not because of any attacks made upon it from without, but because of the rottenness within'. According to the paper, the coalition had 'not come into being through the will of the people . . . nor as a result of the natural coming together of forces moving in the same direction' but because of the 'backstairs intrigue between parties who had nothing in common save their determination to prevent, by hook or by crook, Fianna Fáil from forming a government'. Now the coalition had collapsed 'under a load of ignominy' leaving behind it 'a legacy of broken promises and reckless dealings'.[14] To disarm the threat of another coalition depriving Fianna Fáil of power, the *Irish Press* attempted to demonise the very concept of coalition government, which it labelled as a 'negation of democratic government'. According to the paper, such governments could not 'come into existence without bargaining', the nature of which was 'always carefully concealed from the public'. In the allocation of ministerial appointments, it was always 'the numerical strength of the parties' that was 'the deciding factor, and not personal fitness or ability'. Whatever 'facade of unity' was presented to the public, behind the scenes there was 'always jealously, cross purposes, squabbling and intrigue'. In coalition government, the 'interests of the parties' that composed it always came 'before the interests of the people as a whole'. There was a 'constant bidding for popularity' although very little could be done 'with the different groups pulling in different directions'. The workings of government were sooner rather than later 'overcome by a sort of creeping paralysis'.[15] The paper was particularly critical of the Labour Party. It had entered coalition 'for the sake of office' and had been reduced 'to a position of virtual impotence'.[16] Combined with the finger pointing and acrimony that had caused the collapse of the coalition, the partisan coverage from the Press titles helped Fianna Fáil form a minority government, supported ironically by the now independent deputy Noel Browne. When Sean Lemass returned to cabinet, Vivion de Valera turned down the offer of a ministerial post from his father and opted to remain on the backbenches and succeed Lemass as managing director of the Press Group.[17]

But while the *Irish Press* had vigorously defended the party's hegemony and original aims during the 1940s, by the middle of the

1950s the party had all the appearance of a spent force. There was, however, a 'certain appreciation of the new social policies of the post-war era in Europe and of the need for ideological repositioning within the newly emerging welfarist justice model that was reaching the status of an orthodoxy elsewhere'.[18] It was Sean Lemass who first articulated a new attitude towards the central problems of the north and the economy by linking national unity with economic development. In advocating cooperation with Northern Ireland on economic matters, Lemass as Minister for Industry and Commerce declared that the mutual benefits 'would hasten the day of unity'.[19] This statement was highly significant in regard to Fianna Fáil policy. Not only did it suggest the south should accept the reality of the border, but it also emphasised the benefits that would accrue from adopting a free trade rather than a protectionist mentality. Although the change suggested by Lemass represented a major new departure, it was subtly disguised in nationalist rhetoric to make the change look like a development of existing policy rather than a complete u-turn. This approach of disguising such change as policy progression rather than policy regression was to become more common during the late 1950s as Fianna Fáil struggled to repeal the policy of protectionism without making it look as if the party had been wrong to adopt such a policy. Although Lemass was the main architect of this approach that sought to turn fundamental party policy on its head without alienating the party faithful, he was still only de Valera's heir-apparent and was not yet solely in charge of formulating or directing party policy. The non-development of the economy along the lines hoped for resulted in much in-party debate during the mid 1950s. With the limits of import substitution industrialisation having been reached, the question of how to further develop the economy occupied the mind, heart and very soul of the Fianna Fáil party. While de Valera had concentrated his energy on building a 'rural arcadia . . . other of his lieutenants had other notions however, although they were to keep rather quite about it until the late 1950s, when they finally emerged into the political limelight with a programme of outright modernisation and detraditionalisation'.[20] The different opinions within the party clearly manifested themselves in the shape of Sean Lemass and the Minister for Finance Sean MacEntee, the latter having decreed that not only was it natural that a pool of unemployed people serve the whims of the marketplace but that the sole role of the state was to ensure 'the operation of the free play of forces' in the market.[21] This was a far cry from his stated position in 1932, when he publicly proclaimed that it was a government's responsibility to find jobs for the unemployed. While MacEntee still advocated non-interventionism, Lemass advocated state-led investment to kick-start the economy. Whatever the solution, a further problem faced the party. Self-sufficiency was a cornerstone philosophy of the party and had been since its foundation. How could the party possibly change to free trade without losing face? The solution lay in Lemass' approach. Thus the Fianna Fáil government of 1951–54 began experimenting on how to safely change from protectionism to free trade. While not abandoning protectionism altogether, the party and the *Irish Press* actively encouraged an export mentality. With headlines such as 'Free Trade Gives More Low-Price Goods' and 'Bid to Win Bigger US Market For Our Goods',[22] the *Irish Press* tried to gradually sell the idea of free trade to Irish industry. But after two by-election defeats in March 1954, de Valera called a general election. Since the party's return to government depended on maximising its rural support, it reverted to preaching a policy of protectionism and ruralism to appease supporters from the agricultural and small business community. As a result, during the 1950s the party was 'deeply schizophrenic'. It was 'charged with modernising a backward country while relying on the more traditionally minded elements of the country for the core of its political support' and so the 'ambiguous public posture of the party reflected its need to mediate between these two ideological tendencies'.[23] The risk of losing the election was too high – thus the party's propensity to defer economic reform and revert to its traditional position.

Comparing the economic policies of the two main parties, the *Irish Press* held that under Fianna Fáil, agriculture had 'done remarkably well'. Prices were good and the volume of production had 'substantially increased'. Fine Gael, on the other hand, had adopted 'a cityman's approach' and displayed 'hostility to the farmer'.[24] The above was in reference to the free trade debate also ranging within Fine Gael. While Fianna Fáil had successfully disguised its free trade discussion and experiment, Fine Gael had openly advocated a switch to free trade, thus allowing Fianna Fáil and the *Irish Press* to castigate the party as unpatriotic. According to the paper, if the nation were to attain 'national security, steady employment in factories and in farms and a better standard of living', the Irish people had to 'smash once and for all the Fine Gael link with nineteenth century British economic policy'.[25] The paper proclaimed that Fine Gael's free trade policy was 'the subject of criticism by thoughtful farmers' who pointed out that the party did 'not expect the farmers of England and

America, or any other country to be subjected to the competition of dumped surplus foods in their own home market'. These thoughtful farmers had only one question for Fine Gael – why did the party 'expect the Irish farmer alone of all farmers in the world to be deprived of protection?'[26] Not forgetting the threat of coalition government, the paper also highlighted the contrast between the 'firmness and coherence of Fianna Fáil' and the 'utter confusion and lack of purpose of the opposition parties' that proposed to merge to defeat Fianna Fáil and form another inter-party government. According to the paper, the opposition speakers had 'lapsed into incoherence' and did 'not pause to consider if they contradicted each other'. It noted that while Fine Gael had 'started off by promising cuts in food and drink prices', the party leader, John A. Costello, had 'ended up by denying practically everything the party's spokesmen were saying at the outset'. The paper also highlighted the fact that although at the start of the campaign the Labour Party had stated that it would 'nationalise the banks', towards the end of the campaign Costello was 'indignantly' denying such an occurrence. While the opposition had 'started out believing that a few slogans about food prices and taxes were enough', eventually their bluff had been called and 'the hollowness of their claims' brought to light the fatal 'cracks in the coalition'.[27] But despite such partisan coverage, Fianna Fáil was defeated at the polls and the second inter-party government assumed office with John A. Costello as Taoiseach. Fianna Fáil's brief flirtation with free trade and swift return to protectionism had done little to alleviate the acute unemployment and emigration and cost the party the election. Putting its own spin on the defeat, the *Irish Press* observed that 'by refusing to make facile promises, Fianna Fáil deliberately followed a harder path and it was a measure of the public confidence in the party that except in some urban constituencies it held its ground'.[28] In reality, however, the party held its lowest number of seats since 1932. During the campaign, Fianna Fáil's uncertainty on economic policy, glossed over by the *Irish Press*, was exploited by the opposition parties. But while the party had not decided which policy to follow, it was clear that two distinct strands of thought were now present in the party. While de Valera and Sean MacEntee had little or no time for state intervention in the economy, the leader in waiting, Sean Lemass, had been converted to the philosophy of state-led investment. Fundamental change, however disguised, was only a matter of time.

Change had, however, already occurred at Burgh Quay. In 1951, after Vivion de Valera had succeeded Sean Lemass as managing director of the company, Bill Sweetman had resigned as editor of the *Irish Press*. His replacement was Fianna Fáil party stalwart Jim McGuinness, who had a short but tough term as editor. In 1952, a printers' strike halted production of all Dublin titles for most of July and August, while the re-election of the inter-party coalition in 1954 resulted in severe pressure being placed on the *Irish Press* to promote Fianna Fáil and demonise the government. One new reporter to Burgh Quay at this time well remembered the hostility of Fine Gael and Labour deputies towards *Irish Press* reporters:

> Nobody was asked their political allegiances when they joined the *Irish Press* although it was possibly assumed that you were friendly to Fianna Fáil since you were joining the *Irish Press* and not the *Irish Independent*. When I tried to meet with Fine Gael government minister James Dillon, he replied that he had never met and never intended to meet with reporters from the *Irish Press*. Once I asked Tommy Mullins, general secretary of Fianna Fáil which papers he read. He replied that he read the *Irish Independent* and the *Irish Times*. When I asked why he didn't read the *Irish Press* he replied, 'I don't need to buy the *Irish Press*. I know what's in it'.[29]

During the inter-party years the 'party expected the paper to be pro-Fianna Fáil almost to the point of being propagandist. If de Valera made a speech it was reported verbatim but if the Taoiseach made a speech and paragraphs were cut nobody noticed.'[30] Indeed, accompanying de Valera on the campaign trail was a well-recognised occupational hazard for Burgh Quay journalists. This job usually fell to the person then regarded as the political correspondent of the *Irish Press*, Sean Cryan, who was regularly given the task of accompanying de Valera to various speechmaking ceremonies. Not only was Cryan the paper's fastest shorthand taker but he could also translate the Irish parts of de Valera's speeches into shorthand:

> Cryan accompanied de Valera on most of his trips and de Valera would tend to go off the script or not have a script at all, so it was critical to have him verbatim. The chief was very conscious of that. If you got a quote wrong there would be inquiries all the way down. In those days, all copy would be bagged for a period, day-by-day, week-by-week, big envelopes full of copy used to stretch all around the walls of the newsroom. So if anyone were pulled on anything, they would go back to the copy, see who subbed it and find out who made the mistake – whether it was the reporter or the sub-editor or both. Then you'd have inquiries coming down the line from the likes of

managing editor, Bill Redmond asking 'How was it that you got this quote wrong?'[31]

The persistent and repetitive attacks on the coalition made for very heavy reading and circulation gradually began to fall. The *Sunday Press* also managed to embroil itself in controversy by publishing an unauthorised aerial photograph of the new jet runways at Baldonnel Aerodrome in September 1954. The previous May, while still in office, Fianna Fáil had passed the 1954 Defence Act, Section 268 of which made it an offence to photograph, draw, sketch or paint any property belonging to the Department of Defence without prior permission.[32] However, the legislation did not come into force until January 1955 and it was this loophole that allowed the *Sunday Press* to outwit and infuriate the inter-party government. In August 1954, the paper's editor, Matt Feehan, instructed a photographer to fly over the aerodrome and take the picture. Only then did he seek permission from the Department of Defence to photograph the runways. Since the department had 'an accepted practice of not permitting the taking or publication of photographs of military installations', permission was refused.[33] When this was conveyed to Feehan, he 'displayed considerable annoyance and intimated that as he already had the photograph, he proposed to publish it'. According to government records, however, he 'subsequently realised that the photograph was procured through somewhat irregular circumstances' and informed military intelligence that 'he would not now publish or otherwise use the photograph'.[34] It is possible that this was a mere tactic to avoid an injunction as a fortnight later the *Sunday Press* published the photograph as a follow-up to a story about the Aer Corps' new jets that it had covered the previous month. The Taoiseach, John A. Costello, who was also acting Minister for Defence, was furious and a file on the matter was sent to the chief state solicitor's office to be forwarded to the attorney general Patrick McGilligan for 'whatever action he may consider desirable having regard to the provisions of the Official Secrets Act'.[35] After consulting with the attorney general, the chief state solicitor held that while the *Sunday Press* had 'acted quite improperly' and that Feehan's 'lack of co-operation with the military authorities' was to be 'deplored', the paper should not be prosecuted.[36] Since the 1954 Defence Act was not yet law, the only law applicable was the Official Secrets Act. This legislation held that 'the act complained of should be done for any purpose prejudicial to the safety or interest of the state' and

McGilligan believed that the facts did not 'warrant a prosecution'.[37] It was therefore 'not in the public interest to launch a prosecution under the Official Secrets Act' because it was 'likely to fail'. While 'prima facie, an offence had occurred', he did not have 'confidence in the likelihood of there being a conviction'.[38]

But despite such tribulations, in 1954 Burgh Quay had 'the most spectacular success of all with the launch of the *Evening Press*'.[39] The planning for the new title followed the same careful path of meticulous planning as that adopted for the *Sunday Press*. Both Vivion de Valera and general manager Jack Dempsey were determined to make the venture a success. At this stage, Dempsey had become a central authority figure at Burgh Quay. He was, remembered one colleague, 'the great rock there, a very powerful figure who ran the place well. He was tough but knew the advertising business well and knew how to get the money in.'[40] Indeed, Dempsey was intensely loyal to the Press Group at a time when the feud between itself and Independent Newspapers still ran deep. On one occasion at a meeting of the Dublin Newspaper Management Committee, Dempsey and the then manager of the *Irish Independent*, John Donovan, clashed over the contentious issue of paper imports. Inevitably, Dempsey lost his temper, 'stood up, banged the table and said, "you've always been against us, from the beginning you've tried to kill the *Irish Press*, you haven't succeeded and you never bloody will" and stormed out of the meeting'.[41]

Douglas Gageby, who had left the *Sunday Press* to work for the coalition's ill-fated Irish News Agency, returned to Burgh Quay in 1954 under the guise of managing editor. His supposed role was to liaise between the editors of the daily and Sunday titles, but in reality he had been appointed editor of the forthcoming evening title and devoted his time and energy to organising its launch. While most others at Burgh Quay perceived Vivion de Valera as a strict authoritarian figure, Gageby found him to be a 'good newspaper man, very fair in his dealings'. He was, however, intent on remaining in charge. When Gageby eventually received his contract, it stated that while he had been appointed editor of the *Evening Press*, Vivion remained as editor-in-chief. When Gageby questioned the terminology, Vivion insisted that Gageby 'would run the paper' while all he would do was 'provide the necessary resources'.[42] Gageby's news editor was Jack Smyth who had formally worked as a war correspondent with Reuters News Agency. The position of chief sub-editor fell to John O'Donovan who had a severe aversion to smoking and quickly developed a habit of running up and down the offices opening the windows in all weather.[43] Also recruited to work for the new paper were future editor of the *Irish Press* Tim Pat Coogan who started as a copy boy, Cathal O'Shannon who reviewed books, and the innovative reporter John Healy who would later have a distinguished career with the *Irish Times*. The night reporter was the much celebrated Terry O'Sullivan who was provided with a car and chauffeur at the expense of the paper. The *Irish Press*' original sports editor, Joe Sherwood, also made a return with his controversial sports column 'In the Soup'. A nature column, 'Wild Wisdom', that featured readers' pets every Saturday proved to be extremely popular, as did 'Prince Valiant', the paper's back-page colour adventure series – the first in Irish newspaper history. The establishment of an evening paper had several motives. It was established primarily to attract a more urban readership – a readership thought to be lacking for the other two Press titles. Such a readership, it was thought, would attract more advertising to the company. The *Evening Press* also set out to appeal to a female readership. It was thought that both the daily and Sunday titles concentrated on politics and sport – topics that at that time could possibly have alienated female readers. Indeed, Vivion de Valera made it explicitly clear to Gageby that there was to be 'no politics in the evening paper'. Instead, he was to 'leave the politics to the morning paper' because 'that was what it was for':[44]

> When giving these instructions of no politics, Vivion pulled open a deep drawer in his desk and said to me 'I've never shown you these'. He lifted out a big pile of letters from the likes of Sean MacEntee, all to the tune of 'what's that bloody editor of yours doing – I made a speech last night that contained the heart and soul of the party and not a line appeared in your paper'. There were dozens and dozens of them. Vivion rather enjoyed that – he was the boss slapping down ministers.[45]

Thus the *Evening Press* had no political correspondent. As a result, it was never perceived as being close to Fianna Fáil and was always regarded as the fun newspaper of the group. September 1954 was chosen as the launch date, but as was the norm, the news did not become official until the company's annual general meeting two months before the launch. The *Evening Press* hit the streets for the first time on 1 September 1954, amid a 'very clever commercial launch'.[46] Indeed, the *Evening Press* was 'one of the most outstanding publishing successes of the second half of the century and the day it was launched is still talked about today'.[47] To publicise the paper, boats festooned with flags sailed up and down the Liffey while the ITGWU brass band and elephants from the city zoo paraded up and down O'Connell Street. With such an innovative launch, the paper sold out within hours. The paper was the first to take the concept of recruiting small advertisers and selling small classified advertisement space seriously. In an aggressive marketing campaign organised by Jim Furlong, scores of teenagers were employed in Dublin to canvass door-to-door for advertisements from householders. Vacant premises were rented at strategic points around the city to act as depots for people to drop in advertisements and it was in this way that the *Evening Press* built up its reputation as the best small advert medium. There was a massive surplus of small ads for the first few editions and the paper warned readers that it would 'take some time to update'.[48] Unlike the first editions of the other two Press titles, the *Evening Press* carried no statement as to what it stood for, bar the statement that the paper believed in giving its readers 'as much news as possible'.[49] Indeed, 'what set up the *Evening Press* was its news-ness. Its rival, the *Evening Mail* carried obituaries on page one and was already beginning to fade.'[50] Alongside its news, the paper also contained more entertainment than the other two Press titles put together. With five pages of news, two centre pages of features including puzzles, a detective story, a nature series for children, radio listings, theatre, book and cinema reviews and a comprehensive sports section, the first issue totally sold out and achieved 'the highest sales ever recorded for an evening newspaper in Ireland'.[51] All this despite a technical hitch when the telegraph wires broke down, forcing the sports staff to go to the local betting office to get the day's racing results. Indeed, the *Evening Mail* wished its newest competition well but also noted that the launch was 'an act of real courage on the part of its parents, for in these days of costly production including paper at £50 a ton, the possibilities of disaster are colossal and the expectations of success not too substantial'.[52] In contrast, the *Evening Herald* ignored the new arrival and instead launched an advertising campaign that proclaimed that because of its 'complete local and world-wide news and pictorial coverage', it was 'the complete and unexcelled evening newspaper'.[53] Unexcelled that is, until the arrival of the *Evening Press*. But the new arrival had a tough few first weeks and was initially distributed free of charge in working class areas of Dublin. According to Douglas Gageby, two months after its launch, Vivion told him that although the board was having second thoughts, he was determined to hold out until the paper was a success.[54]

It was not until it helped solve the mystery of the missing Berrigan, Browne and Ashmore babies that the *Evening Press* finally established a niche for itself in the evening market. The scoop that the missing babies saga gave the paper was one of the most intriguing and tragic newspaper stories of the 1950s. At approximately 5pm on Saturday 18 December 1954, shoppers in Dublin's Henry Street were startled by the cries of twenty-one year old Teresa Berrigan. She had momentarily left her nine-month old son Patrick unattended in his pram outside a shop while she had been inside buying him a teddy bear. When she came out of the shop both the baby and the pram were gone. The Gardaí were alerted and an extensive search got underway within five minutes of the snatch. One hour later, the empty pram was found near Thomas Street.[55] Amid reports that a couple with a baby had been spotted hurrying from a taxi at Heuston station, the Saturday evening Dublin to Cork train was halted and searched at Thurles. The mail boat at Dun Laoghaire and a ferry that sailed from the North Wall to Liverpool were also searched but to no avail. With no sign of the baby being found, the *Evening Press* headline 'Kidnap Scare Hits City' captured the public's mood succinctly.[56] In its original report of the kidnapping, however, the paper got the child's surname wrong, calling him Bergin instead of Berrigan. This oversight was overlooked in the light of subsequent events involving the paper and the Berrigan family, who hailed from Moore Street. Over the next few days, the nation waited with baited breath for developments in the case. All Garda leave was cancelled and the story filled every available column inch of the nation's newspapers. Finally a witness came forward. Louise Doherty, a Castlebar-born woman who worked in Belfast, had caught the 6.35pm Dublin to Belfast train on the evening of the kidnapping. She told Gardaí that she had seen an exhausted woman carrying a baby wearing only one shoe and one sock boarding the train. The description of the baby fitted perfectly, since in the haste of the kidnapping the other shoe and sock came off the baby's foot and fell on the ground beside the pram. When shown a photograph of the missing baby, she confirmed it as the baby that had travelled on the train. On 21 December, the Press Association in London wired a news release to its associate newspapers informing them that the Berrigan baby had been found in Belfast – a claim denied by the RUC and subsequently withdrawn by the Press Association.[57] The following day, however, the *Evening Press* reported that a baby had been taken to police headquarters.[58] While this story was being written, the Berrigans travelled to Belfast in a Press Group staff car. On 23 December, with the banner headline 'Baby Comes Homes' over a photograph of the reunited family, the paper finally broke the happy news to the Irish public.[59] To maintain the exclusiveness of the story, the paper that usually went to print at 2pm was held back until 3.45pm to prevent the *Evening Herald* and *Evening Mail* from printing the story in their later editions.

The baby's kidnapper was forty-years old Barbara McGeehan. She had given birth to two children over the previous two years – both of whom had tragically died. In a bizarre twist to the saga, however, detectives then discovered that the other child in the house, four-year old Bernadette McGeehan, was in fact Elizabeth Browne, who at the tender age of three months had also been snatched from a pram in Dublin's Henry Street in November 1950. Browne's real parents were immediately driven to Belfast for an emotional reunion with their long lost daughter.[60] It later transpired that Barbara McGeehan had feigned pregnancy before snatching Elizabeth Browne and had given birth to a stillborn infant shortly before she had snatched Patrick Berrigan. Sadly, her husband was totally unaware that neither child was his and the whole country was gripped by the emotional trauma endured by all three couples as Barbara McGeehan was tried and sentenced to two years' imprisonment. Everyone thought that this marked the end of the missing babies saga. However, one baby, Pauline Ashmore, remained missing. She had been snatched from her pram outside a furniture store on Dublin's Camden Street on 19 October 1954. While the Berrigan and Browne children had been reunited with their parents, there was still no sign of the Ashmore child and the Garda investigation had come to a standstill. At the end of January 1955, however, an anonymous phone call came through to the *Evening Press*' news editor Jack Smyth. The caller told him that a woman who lived at Bridgefont Street Flats had had a baby at the Coome Hospital on the date the Ashmore baby had been snatched and had now just given birth to another baby – a mere three months later. Smyth immediately dispatched reporter Jim Flanagan and photographer Harry Stephens to the address supplied.

They sought permission to photograph the October baby and amazingly permission was granted. They immediately returned to Burgh Quay, developed the photograph and showed it to the mother of the missing child, Margaret Ashmore, who positively identified her daughter. Shortly afterwards, the Gardaí raided the flat and the Ashmore family was reunited.[61] Although the anonymous caller rang the paper to congratulate it, he refused to reveal his identity or accept a reward. To do so, he told Smyth, would cost him his job. In what was perhaps the newspaper scoop of the 1950s, the paper got all three mothers and their babies to pose for its front page and the manner in which the *Evening Press* helped solve the cases of the three missing babies met with national approval and established it as the premier national evening newspaper.

The great delivery innovation of the paper was the use of scooters. These delivered it to the suburbs of Dublin before the other two evening papers, both of which it soon began to outsell. The use of the 'Bush System' that enabled local news to be printed onto blank columns of the paper at local centres throughout the country, was another new innovation that made the paper more relevant than its rivals to provincial readers. The country edition of the paper was printed at noon with about a quarter of a page left blank. These newspapers were then driven in lorries to the paper's regional offices, where they were run through a stencil machine that printed local news and obituaries onto the blank space. The *Evening Press* was thus both a national and local paper and this made it enormously popular and successful. By 1959, the paper totally eclipsed the *Evening Herald* and *Evening Mail* by achieving a circulation of over 100,000. So stiff was the competition, that the latter paper finally ceased publication in July 1962.

In another scoop, the *Evening Press* was the first Irish newspaper to print the news of the assassination of John Fitzgerald Kennedy in November 1963. Confirmation of the killing was received at teatime over the newsroom radio that was tuned to the American Armed Forces Network. The staff of the *Evening Press* had all gone home and the following day's *Irish Press* was nowhere near ready to print. Since the metal plates of that day's *Evening Press* were still on the printing machines it was decided to print a special late edition of 20,000 copies for the city. A new front page was made up and soon afterwards the paper hit the streets and broke the sad news to the Irish public. It was only five months since Kennedy had visited Ireland as President of the United States and many journalists fondly remembered his visit as a student to the paper in 1947. There was, remembered one journalist, many a tear shed at Burgh Quay that night.[62] In an ironic twist of fate, shortly before Kennedy's death, a tree that he had planted with de Valera at Aras an Uachtarach had died. The Press titles were, however, forbidden to print this fact.[63] Despite the success of the papers, industrial relations at Burgh Quay still boarded on the medieval. The persistent refusal of management to meet union representatives over the employment of a non-union photographer was resented as 'a threat to the NUJ as a representative body'. Staff also complained of being overworked. A lack of staff meant that management had 'only one staff for all the papers' and the NUJ recorded numerous 'complaints of unfair treatment' towards members of the *Irish Press* regarding Saturday night work for the *Sunday Press*.[64]

But while the journalists of Burgh Quay may have been overworked, the members of the Fianna Fáil parliamentary party had plenty of time to ponder their future. With the party occupying the opposition benches, the leader in waiting, Sean Lemass, attempted to formulate a strategy to gradually remove protectionism and move towards free trade. The proposal for change emanating from the party and articulated in the *Irish Press* was, however, disguised as a continuation of existing policy rather than a radical new departure. The process of recruiting support for a change in policy began long before it was made public what that specific change was going to be. The legitimacy of this as yet unfound policy was justified by the party stating that it would be broadly based on principles already in existence and accepted by the party and the electorate. Thus in a major speech to the party in 1955, Lemass proclaimed that 'subject to the preservation of the party's aims as defined in the *Coru* of Fianna Fáil, every aspect of policy was open to question'.[65] To disarm concern about a break from the past, Lemass greatly emphasised the element of continuity. Any new developments would continue the party's policy of 'formulating and applying a long-term policy based on fundamental principles'. Seeking to assure the party faithful, Lemass proclaimed that while change was coming, it would 'enlarge the fruits of past efforts, not destroy them'. Fianna Fáil had always sought to 'conform to the deep rooted sentiments and hopes' of the Irish people, and the 'new programme' (yet to be revealed) would also be 'inspired by the same sentiments and hopes'.[66] But it was not just anyone who could successfully implement such change. According to Lemass, the change that would 'help to restore health to the national economy' had to be applied by progressive thinkers who saw the Irish people 'as possessing the capacity to get ahead and to keep moving in line with the rest of the world in economic and social progress'. In other words, Fianna Fáil. According to Lemass, the change in policy might be 'subject to attack and criticism at the beginning', but it was 'certain that just as Fianna Fáil's original programme' had 'been accepted by all political elements', so too would the 'new programme become in time, accepted national policy'.[67]

In October 1955, the *Irish Press* published a special supplement on Lemass' proposals for state-led investment to kick-start the economy. The plan proposed to liquidate external Irish assets in order to fund the creation of 22,000 jobs per year over five years, a proposal that quickly disappeared when Fianna Fáil regained power in 1957. In reality the supplement was only a political kite flown to test the reaction of the party faithful, the electorate, the business community and other interest groups. Under the headline 'Fianna Fáil's Aim is Full Employment', the paper noted that 'the successful application of a sound development policy required a carefully prepared investment programme' involving the government and private enterprise joining together in a five-year spending programme to boost the economy.[68] The party had 'used the present period of release from immediate responsibility for government' to review its economic policy 'so that under Fianna Fáil leadership' the nation could 'experience another era of advancement'.[69] In an attempt to portray the policy change as a process of economic evolution, the paper noted that the proposals 'had their origins in the Fianna Fáil party's reassessment of the progress made during the past quarter of a century and its appreciation of the need for a vigorous new programme of economic development for the future'.[70] Indeed, the party had 'accepted the conclusion that the economic development programme which it initiated twenty-five years ago, notwithstanding its many and very substantial achievements and its subsequent acceptance by all political parties', had 'not proved to be sufficient to bring about all the economic and social progress' that the party desired and believed could be achieved.[71] The following day, the *Irish Press* expressed its wholehearted editorial support for Lemass' proposals and again portrayed the plans as economic evolution in which all could play a part. According to the paper, the party's proposals were ones 'which the community as a whole should carefully examine' because they suggested that the Irish nation had within 'its control the resources necessary to deal with the evil of emigration'. To do this, it had to develop 'further and on a more ambitious scale' its 'resources in land and industry'. It also had to 'be prepared to go out and seek markets', to explore its 'resources in material and human skills' and increase the 'level of productivity in field and factory'. Indeed, the paper noted that 'efficiency, enterprise and confidence' were 'vital to any practical solution of emigration'.[72]

Despite the party's idea of 'keeping Ireland for the Irish', it was obvious that the policy of protectionism had extended past its sell by date.[73] But while Fianna Fáil and the *Irish Press* were deliberately vague when discussing how to implement such fundamental economic change, the coalition government was more specific in its discussion of free trade and foreign capital. In 1956, the coalition government established a Capital Investment Advisory Committee, whose final report was extremely critical of protectionism and urged the courting of foreign investment. During the debate, Fianna Fáil reverted to its traditional position on protectionism coloured by nationalist discourse. And, despite their enthusiasm for Lemass' economic evolution, the Press titles were also used to propagate the party's criticism of free trade. According to the *Sunday Press*, 'the Fianna Fáil leaders questioned the policy, not in any narrow spirit' because foreign 'brains and modern techniques' could be of great service to industrial development. Instead, the party opposed the policy because the 'whole psychology behind the new move' was 'contrary to the Sinn Féin ideal on which the industrial revival in Ireland' had been based. That policy had best been described 'by Eamon de Valera as the old Sinn Féin ideal of developing our natural resources with our own capital, our own skills and our own labour'.[74] While the *Sunday Press* stated that although it was easy 'to call for a radical review of the policy of protectionism . . . it would obviously be very difficult politically to carry it out,'[75] Sean Lemass was quoted by the *Irish Press* as stating that 'in foreign owned concerns, the management personnel' were 'nearly always foreign and deny the chance of acquiring knowledge to Irish employees'. There was, proclaimed Lemass, 'a definite bar to the promotion of Irish personnel to the higher executive grades'.[76]

Disguising the switch as economic evolution would of course make it much more politically acceptable and it was this policy that Fianna Fáil and the *Irish Press* adopted. The following year saw Lemass and the *Irish Press* continue with their campaign to convince the party faithful and the electorate that economic evolution Fianna Fáil style was necessary. In January 1957, the *Irish Press* again published a major supplement in which Lemass was quoted as stating that Fianna Fáil had been 'engaged for some time on a comprehensive programme for the development of the country's resources'. The country had 'to face up in a realistic way, to the fact that the original Fianna Fáil plan' had not 'proved to be comprehensive enough to end unemployment and emigration' and so had to be 'extended'.[77] The following weekend, the *Sunday Press* carried an exclusive interview with Lemass, in which he potently stated that 'a permanent cure' to the country's economic difficulties entailed 'fundamental changes'.[78] This policy of disguising the change as an extension of current policy rather than promoting it as a radical new departure was described by one political commentator as 'a convenient cloak of seeming changelessness under which new policies, concerns and choices could be exchanged for old'.[79] Eventually the debate on how to stimulate the economy caused a split in the inter-party government and heralded its 'second inglorious exit from office', leaving in its wake 'confusion, disorder, impoverishment and unprecedented emigration'.[80] According to the *Irish Press*, by allowing 'the country to drift into an economic crisis' the coalition had lost 'the confidence of the people'.[81] Its 'greatest disservice' to the nation was its 'fostering of a spirit of disillusionment and cynicism'. The coalition members 'thought that they had found a formula for easy political success' and promises 'known widely to be false, deception and backstairs intrigues put them into power in 1954'.[82] During the subsequent election campaign, the paper observed that while the coalition parties had not yet fully learned the lesson of making false promises, 'the recklessness of the 1954 campaign' had not been repeated. Indeed, the Labour Party had 'even gone to the length of deleting from its official election programme any reference to the unemployed'.[83] On election day, it noted that the choice before the electorate was 'between a Fianna Fáil government with unity and purpose' and a coalition that had 'twice promised everything and fulfilled nothing'. It was a stark choice between 'a government of strength and conviction' and a government of 'disunion, weakness and self-induced disintegration'; a choice between 'a government of honesty and seriousness and a government of deception, incompetence and irresponsibility'.[84] The election result gave Fianna Fáil seventy-eight seats, a majority of ten seats over the other Dáil parties. It also marked the end of Clann na Poblachta which only retained one seat. The party leader, Sean MacBride, lost his seat and never regained it. Fianna Fáil was back in office and was to remain there for the next sixteen years.

But if 1957 was a good year for Fianna Fáil, it was an appalling one for the Press Group. Continuing the tradition of abrupt departures, the editor of the *Irish Press,* Jim McGuinness, resigned after a bizarre sequence of events. A former employee of the *Sunday Press* had been ordained as a priest and all of the Press Group's editorial staff had been invited to his first mass. McGuinness arrived at the church in plenty of time and secured for himself a prominent seat at the top of the church. Vivion de Valera arrived late, and taking exception to

McGuinness' good vantage point instructed him to move seats. At the reception afterwards both proceeded to have a blazing argument, during which McGuinness publicly aired his lowly opinion of the work conditions at Burgh Quay. His subsequent departure upset many 'seniors in Fianna Fáil' as he was well regarded in its higher echelons.[85] Nonetheless, McGuinness was replaced by another 'Fianna Fáil disciple' Francis Carty, who had fought under Sean Lemass in Wexford during the civil war and who had sub-edited the *Irish Press* during the Emergency.[86] The dismissal of reporter Dick Roche that same year also caused problems. Roche had worked on the industrial staff of the *Irish Press* before taking six months' leave of absence in May 1957 when he became ill with tuberculosis. He was later dismissed without notice when he was unable to return to work. The NUJ wrote to the general manager, Jack Dempsey, requesting that Roche be given three months' pay in lieu of notice, arguing that he had not received the statutory three months' notice of termination of employment and had not been told that his contract of service would be terminated automatically after six months' absence. Dempsey's rejection was forwarded to the union's head office in London, which advised that in the circumstances there was nothing more the branch could do. Roche subsequently got a job with the *Irish Independent*.[87]

Indeed, one of the major problems that the *Irish Press* had to deal with politically during this particular era was the rise of the trade union movement. Senior editorial executives 'had to watch every trade union story on the orders of the de Valeras. They studied them in microscopic detail and had to be careful of the various groups. They were scared of the political left, which was still minor enough at the time. The 1950s saw a great rush of unemployment, with marches all over the country but particularly in Dublin. Alongside this, there was still the IRA, the Sean South saga, and raids on the border.'[88] Such was the 'political sensitivity' at the time that Vivion de Valera decreed that 'no column of Brendan Behan's was to be published before it was vetted by him personally'. Behan was staunchly republican and Vivion regarded him as being 'strongly suspect'.[89] Vivion was particularly paranoid about the coverage given to the border campaign. Despite this, as editor-in-chief, he sought to interfere editorially only once:

> He often used to walk through the newsroom around lunchtime and ask 'what's doing today, what's the news?'. One day he came in and

> the main story was on one of the early border incidents and he just said to John O'Donovan [chief sub-editor] who had the page proof, 'is that the best lead you have?' John said 'yes, that's what the editor and I think is the best lead'. I said 'yeah, that's the story'. He said, 'are you sure?' and I said 'do you want us to change it?' He didn't say anything, he just walked off.[90]

It was, however, the resignation of *Evening Press* sub-editor Sean Cronin that shocked the Burgh Quay establishment most. Due to the American lilt in his voice, Cronin was assigned the unusual nickname of 'the sheriff', a law-keeper nickname that was to prove quite ironic in the light of later events. The paper had just gone to print one day, when Cronin, who 'had a great grasp of Irish history', approached editor Douglas Gageby for 'a quiet word'. Cronin told him that 'he had a personal problem; he wanted to go and to go now', so Gageby gave him his blessing.[91] While 'everyone in the newsroom knew that Cronin was strongly republican, no one realised that he was as involved as he seems to have been'.[92] A Garda raid on Burgh Quay failed to capture Cronin who was later arrested near the border and charged with membership of the IRA. Back at Burgh Quay 'there was an awful lot of surprise, shock and consternation when people realised what was going on'.[93] While the de Valeras were reported to be none too pleased with the episode, the opinions of 'those upstairs were never aired in public'.[94] But while differences were never aired in public, they were certainly aired in private.

In 1957, Sean Lemass clashed with Vivion de Valera over the *Irish Press*' use of the term 'six counties' when referring to Northern Ireland. In May of that year, the Fianna Fáil government announced that the term was to be gradually phased out of use on official government documentation. In explaining the change, it was emphasised that the adoption of the term 'Northern Ireland' had more to do with geographical convenience than political backtracking. According to Lemass, the term 'Northern Ireland' was a name for the geographical area comprising the six counties, rather than recognition of its political institutions.[95] Nonetheless, the decision was perceived as an acknowledgment of the north's constitutional position and regarded as an overture for cooperation in trade matters. The *Irish Press* ignored the change and shortly afterwards the paper printed an interview that Lemass had granted to the British *Guardian* newspaper and 'changed Northern Ireland Government to Stormont Government throughout the text'.[96] In reply, Lemass wrote to Vivion de Valera, criticising the paper's action and requesting that he not be misquoted in the future. According to Lemass, he had 'used the term government of Northern Ireland very deliberately' and had 'resorted to it with increasing frequency in Dáil statements'. The 'practice of substituting alternative terms like Stormont Government and Belfast Government' had, Lemass proclaimed, been the 'outcome of woolly thinking on the partition issue' and the 'continued reluctance to use this title in the conditions now prevailing' served 'no national purpose'.[97] Lemass' intervention was worthless as the *Irish Press* continued to address Northern Ireland as the 'six-counties' right up to the 1980s.

That same year brought another watershed in the form of T. K. Whitaker's *Programme for Economic Expansion*. Whitaker's document, which derived much of its findings from the report of the coalition government's Capital Investment Advisory Committee, provided the blueprint for Ireland's future economic development. Whitaker, who presented his report to the Fianna Fáil government in December 1957, concluded that rather than discourage foreign investment, the government should actively encourage it with generous tax concessions and grant incentives to any foreign industry willing to set up in Ireland. Increased state investment in and the modernisation of indigenous industry were also advocated, as were the cultivation and development of export markets. In essence, the report urged the government to prioritise economic development. Such a change in policy represented a shift from the constitutional and nationalist objectives as advocated by de Valera to the social and economic development objectives as advocated by his heir-apparent, Sean Lemass – an orientation shift from a cultural nationalist perspective to a renovated political nationalist perspective. Despite this, de Valera (by now aged 76 and almost blind) not only endorsed Whitaker's proposals but pronounced them as a continuation of long established party policy. According to de Valera, 'we set out those policies in 1926 at the formation of Fianna Fáil'.[98] Whitaker's plan was subsequently adopted as government policy and was published in November 1958. But before the plan was implemented, Lemass was to succeed de Valera as Taoiseach, helped in no small part by independent deputy Noel Browne who was 'instrumental in prompting him to leave office'.[99]

It was Browne who 'rumbled the shareholding issue' of the Press company and finally made public its carefully constructed financial structure.[100] In December 1958, Jack McQuillan, another independent deputy, came into possession of a number of Press Group shares and

1. Founding editor of the *Irish Press*, Frank Gallagher.

2. De Valera and Harry Boland in America, 1919. Boland played an integral role in the Irish Independence Bond Drive.

$100 This is the first bond certificate of the Republic of Ireland subscribed for and issued in the United States — Eamon de Valera. $100

REPUBLIC OF IRELAND

BOND CERTIFICATE

1 **ONE HUNDRED DOLLARS** 1

To Carmelite School. New York. Very Rev. Denis J. O'Connor. Pastor.

I Eamon De Valera, President of the Elected Government of the Republic of Ireland acting in the name of and by the authority of the elected representatives of the Irish Nation issue this Certificate in acknowledgment of your subscription of $100. to the First National Loan of the Republic of Ireland. This Certificate is not negotiable but it is exchangeable if presented at the Treasury of the Republic of Ireland one month after the international recognition of the said Republic for one $100. Gold Bond of the Republic of Ireland. Said Bond to bear interest at five per cent per annum from the first day of the seventh month after the freeing of the territory of the Republic of Ireland from Britain's military control and said Bond to be redeemable at par within one year thereafter.

Dated January 21st 1920

Seán ua Nunáin — REGISTRAR

Éamon de Valera — PRESIDENT

3. A Bond Certificate signed by Eamon de Valera. Many Irish-Americans subscribed to the bond drive.

4. An *Irish Times* cartoon succinctly captures the allegiances of the various national titles during the inter-party years.

5. An advertisement announcing publication of the *Evening Press*, 1954.

A National Hope Realised

THE FIRST ISSUE OF

The Irish Press

Ireland's New National Morning Newspaper

will be published on

FIFTH SEPTEMBER

ON Saturday morning next, September 5, the first issue of "The Irish Press" will be in the hands of the people of Ireland.

THIS new daily is the outcome of intensive effort and organisation. The object was to establish a first-class morning newspaper, and that has been done—a newspaper, national in its policy, distinctive in its make-up, and complete in all its services of news, pictures, and special features.

NOTHING has been spared to make this great enterprise a success. Staffs have been chosen for their ability and experience of the work required of them. Machinery, the latest of its kind, has been installed, so that better equipped Newspaper Offices do not exist in Ireland.

IN "The Irish Press" will be found just those things the average Irishman and woman want—home news, gathered by a large staff of reporters and hundreds of correspondents throughout the country; foreign news supplied by special correspondents and by two of the biggest Agencies in the world; a special Irish Language section; a daily Woman's section; regular Agricultural features; Literary notices, Motoring notes—all directed by Editors long accustomed to this work.

THE financial and commercial pages will be particularly full and authoritative. A special Sports Department will give "The Irish Press" the best reports and commentaries to be found in Ireland. A G.A.A. Editor, who is Ireland's leading expert, will handle the National Games. As for pictures, provision has been made to have each issue of "The Irish Press" attractively illustrated.

"TRUTH IN THE NEWS" has been adopted as the slogan of the new daily. It will not be a party organ or a political paper. It will be truly national in its contents, its vision, and its appeal.

INDEPENDENT in its comment, fearless in its assertion of national rights, scrupulously fair in its treatment of all sections "The Irish Press" will cater for the whole people.

Be Sure to Order Your Copy To-Day

Instruct your Newsagent to reserve for you a copy EVERY DAY. Why not place your Order NOW—while you think of it?

EVERY MORNING - ONE PENNY

6. An advertisement announcing publication of the *Irish Press*, 1931.

7. Legendary *Evening Press* sports journalist, Con Houlihan.

8. Irish Press Group chairman, Vincent Jennings.

9. Founding editor of the *Evening Press* and former editor of the *Irish Times*, Douglas Gageby.

10. De Valera lookalike (Arthur Riordan) launches *The Xpress* outside the Dáil.

11. Fianna Fáil leader Bertie Ahern reading a lockout edition of the *Evening Press*.

12. The Irish Press newsroom, 25 May 1995.

13. Irish Press Group workers march to the Dáil, May 1995.

14. Irish Press shareholder Nell McCafferty addressing the board at the IPN's wind-up meeting, September 1995.

15. Irish Press Newspapers' wind-up meeting in the RDS, September 1995.

16. Irish Press Group managing director, Eamon de Valera.

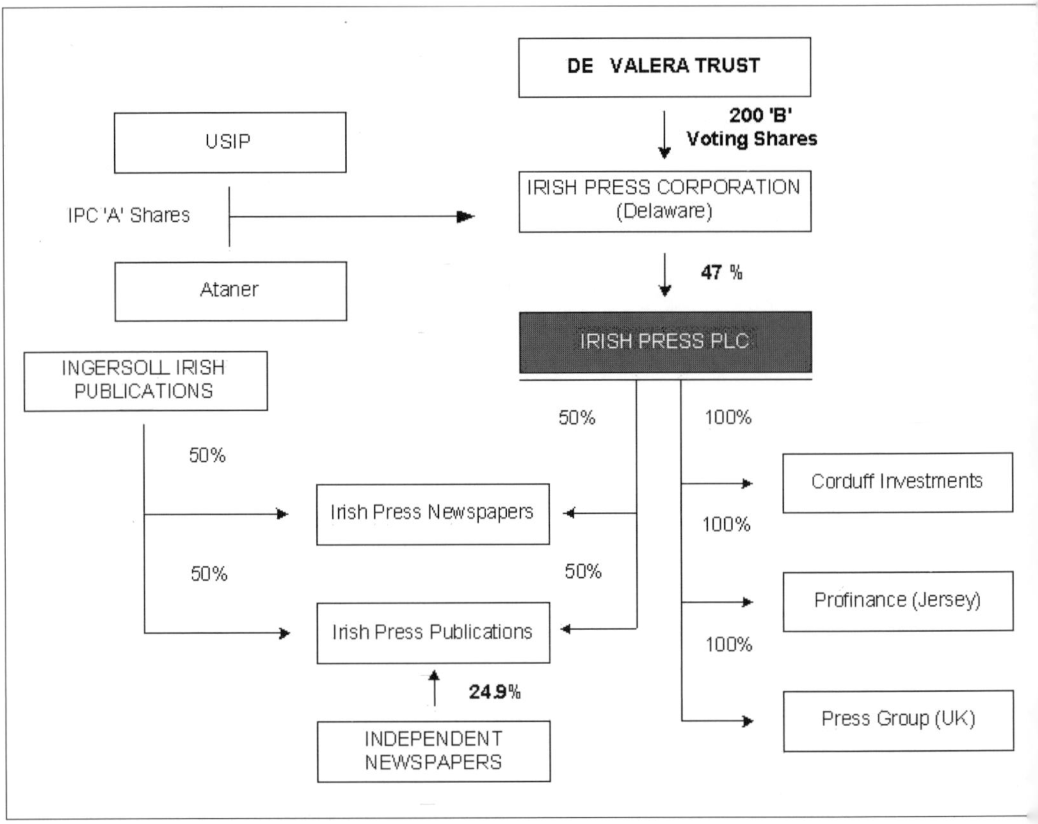

DE VALERA TRUST

200 'B' Voting Shares

USIP

IPC 'A' Shares

IRISH PRESS CORPORATION (Delaware)

Ataner

47 %

IRISH PRESS PLC

INGERSOLL IRISH PUBLICATIONS

50%

100%

50%

Corduff Investments

Irish Press Newspapers

100%

50%

50%

Profinance (Jersey)

Irish Press Publications

100%

24.9%

Press Group (UK)

INDEPENDENT NEWSPAPERS

17. The various holding companies and their relationship with Irish Press Plc.

presented Browne with a present of one share. Browne then exercised his right to examine the company records at its head office to determine exactly who owned what. In his autobiography, Browne recorded what he found. As he slowly 'turned the pages of the great volume of listed shareholders and transfers, it became clear that de Valera had systematically over a period of years become a majority shareholder of Irish Press Newspapers. Although he was controlling director of the newspapers, the share prices were not quoted publicly. The price paid by the de Valera family to shareholders was nominal. It was clear that de Valera was now a very wealthy newspaper tycoon.'[101] A lengthy struggle to make known the results of his investigation by means of a Dáil question then ensued. But no matter how Browne framed his question to the Taoiseach, he was refused permission to table it by the Ceann Comhairle, Paddy Hogan, a Labour Party deputy from Co. Clare who had 'no wish to antagonise de Valera supporters in the constituency he shared with him'. Accordingly, Hogan 'protected de Valera from embarrassing questions' for as long as he could. Finally, Browne was compelled to frame a motion for debate in the Dáil.[102] This was a much slower process and over a year later, on 12 December 1958, Browne succeeded in moving a private member's motion that stated that by continuing to hold the post of controlling director of the Press Group while acting as Taoiseach, de Valera held 'a position which could be reasonably regarded as interfering or being incompatible with the full and proper discharge by him of the duties of his office'. Browne also opined that de Valera had 'rendered a serious disservice to the principle of integrity in parliamentary government and derogated from the dignity and respect due to his rank and office as Taoiseach'.[103] Unusually de Valera left the chamber shortly after the debate began, leaving the case for the defence to be made by Sean MacEntee.

While conceding that it was common knowledge that de Valera, while Taoiseach, acted as controlling director of the Press Group, Browne argued that he should have adopted the usual practice of either resigning or asking for leave of absence without pay. Having not done so, Browne condemned de Valera for setting such a precedent, especially since it concerned a 'very influential industry'.[104] The post that de Valera had continued to hold while Taoiseach was a post of 'very wide responsibility, involving very important functions and considerable powers'.[105] According to Browne, the Taoiseach was 'morally bound to the shareholders and to his other directors to discharge these functions fully to the best of his ability'.[106] On the other hand, however, he was also morally bound to discharge his functions as Taoiseach. Holding both posts at the same time had, according to Browne, compromised de Valera's impartiality and left him open to the charge of whether he was working for the *Irish Press* or the Irish people.[107] As an example, Browne questioned de Valera's motivation for taxing imported newspapers and asked whether it was 'the newspaper-owner or the Taoiseach' that had decided that 'their admission to the country should be penalised or obstructed'. Was it, Browne enquired, 'from a national point of view' that de Valera did not like the imported papers or was it 'from a business point of view' that he did 'not like their competition'. According to Browne, de Valera had 'placed himself in a very false and serious position in allowing it to be suggested that he has either furthered the interests of the people and the Government at the expense of the shareholders of the Irish Press Limited, or has furthered its interests and prosperity and the expansion of the Irish Press Limited at the expense of the national well-being'. On one side there was 'a fairly prosperous, continually expanding and widely read chain of newspapers with an increasing circulation', but on the other side there was 'a position of almost national bankruptcy and social decadence of one kind or another, with emigration [and] unemployment'.[108]

Browne also reminded the house that on 5 June 1957, in reply to a question on ministers holding company directorships, de Valera had declared that 'no Minister should engage in any activities whatsoever that could reasonably be regarded as interfering or being incompatible with the full and proper discharge by him of the duties of his office, for example acting in a position such as a company directorship carrying remuneration'.[109] How, Browne asked, did the above fit with de Valera's 'Jekyll and Hyde existence as Taoiseach and controlling director of a chain of national newspapers?' According to Browne, there was no real substance in the words 'carrying remuneration' because if one were 'allowed to continue as controlling director of an evening newspaper, a Sunday newspaper and a daily national newspaper, as a politician one does not need any remuneration after that'. Instead, the politician was 'remunerated by having his speeches reported at great length'. That, according to Browne, was the essence of a politician's existence, 'his ability to make contact with the community as a whole'.[110] The position regarding remuneration was certainly at variance with the position adopted by de Valera in 1932, when in a public display of openness and transparency on the part of the new government, de Valera had announced that no member of the new cabinet would continue to hold directorships in any commercial concerns. In line with this decision and following discussions with de Valera, deputy Joseph Connolly resigned his *Irish Press* directorship at the same time that de Valera resigned as chairman. However, de Valera retained the much more powerful position of controlling director. During the course of his speech Browne also castigated the editorial ethos of the *Sunday Press* that 'carried gruesome scarlet colour cartoons illustrating the valorous deeds of republican violence during the Anglo-Irish and the civil wars'. According to Browne, de Valera could not 'disown personal responsibility for these warlike pictures: under his own carefully drafted articles of association, he was personally responsible for all editorial and administrative policy'.[111] Browne thus contended that it was wrong that the Taoiseach 'should be in a position where he is permitting a political policy in relation to his paper, that is, allowing these articles glorifying the gun on the one hand as newspaper director, and on the other hand as Taoiseach locking these young lads up who read his paper and think that a gunman is a very fine person'.[112]

When de Valera eventually returned to the Dáil chamber, he articulated a rather lame defence by claiming that there was never any secrecy surrounding his position of controlling director. The position was merely 'a fiduciary one'. Exploiting his self-made image of moral protector of the Irish people, de Valera claimed he had been 'given all the powers that seemed necessary' to enable him 'to safeguard the interests of those who subscribed the capital and the purposes for which the money was contributed'. It also enabled him to be 'in a position effectively to prevent the newspaper's policy from going in a direction contrary to that for which it was founded'. According to de Valera, never at any time had his duties 'conflicted in any way with the full and proper exercise' of his duties as Taoiseach. There was, he contended, 'such a thing as delegation'. He also claimed that it was never intended when he was made controlling director, that he should do all the things that he was given the power to do. He was, after all, 'one of a board' that looked after 'the ordinary work of supervising, controlling and directing the conduct of the business'.[113] It may be worth noting, however, that the powers that de Valera referred to were not so much given to him, as taken by him. Neither had he been pressurised to adopt the position of controlling director. He himself had drawn up the articles of association for the company and so had given to himself both the position and ultimate powers of controlling director. In his speech, de Valera claimed that the day-today running of the company was in the hands of the board and that while Taoiseach he had refrained from going to board meetings. He conceded that he would intervene if there was 'an important development . . . a new departure' that he considered contrary to the original aims of the paper.[114] According to de Valera, he had not made any money from the paper. Instead, profits had been 'used for expansion so as to achieve the original idea of those who founded the newspaper, which was not merely to have a morning newspaper but also an evening newspaper and a Sunday newspaper'.[115] Acknowledging that he had guided the editorial ethos of the papers, de Valera stated that from the start 'it was realised that divided control, anything like control by a group, could in certain events where differences would arise, lead to disaster for the enterprise as a whole'. Ever since, he had 'felt a certain degree of . . . moral trusteeship in the matter' and was 'quite satisfied' that there was 'nothing to suggest' that he had acted in a manner that was 'inconsistent with the dignity of the office of Taoiseach'.[116] In de Valera's defence, the Minister for Health, Sean MacEntee, claimed that the subscribers had 'trusted their savings . . . to Eamon de Valera as controlling director of the *Irish Press* . . . because they wished to see established an organ which would influence public opinion and keep the nation on the right path . . . an editorial point of view which prior to its establishment was not given any great publicity by the other organs of the press'.[117]

The vote on Browne's motion did not take place until 14 January 1959, when the debate resumed. Sean MacEntee opened this debate by claiming that the shareholders had subscribed money for de Valera's *Irish Press* 'to put the Republican position before the people, in order to keep the Republican flag flying, in order to put a Republican government in this Dáil and in order to give a Republican constitution to the people of Ireland'.[118] In his concluding remarks before the motion was put to a vote, Browne reminded the house that in reply to an earlier question put to de Valera regarding his financial interest in the *Irish Press*, he had replied 'I have no financial interest'. However, Browne then stated that his investigation into whether or not the Delaware Corporation that represented the American shareholders was still in existence had proved inconclusive. When he had telephoned the company secretary requesting the information, the secretary had sought leave to seek higher approval for the disclosure of such information. When Browne rang back he was refused any information, either confirming or denying that it was still in existence.[119] According to Browne, the reason that de Valera had refused the information was because he had 'a guilty conscience about the American Corporation and the American shareholders'.[120] He then proceeded to reveal that since 1929, de Valera had continually registered the shares owned by the American shareholders in his name. These shares had numbered around 55,000. Browne told the Dáil that since 1929, both de Valera and his son Vivion had been buying up shares in the company. Since then they had bought 91,983 shares bringing the de Valera holdings in the company up to between 140,000 and 150,000 shares.[121] By 1959, with the benefit of control over the American Corporation, the de Valeras were the effective majority shareholders in the Press company and controlled well over half the shares of a company then worth £918,000.[122] In a token gesture, de Valera had allocated a mere ten shares to the Fianna Fáil party, with either himself or his son appointed as trustee. Browne then contended that by not allowing the shares to be quoted on the stock exchange, de Valera had prevented the true commercial value of the shares being established and so had secured the shares at a 'grossly deflated undervaluation [that] deprived these poor shareholders of the right to a just price for their shares'.[123] According to Browne, the company was worth nearly £1 million and reeked of corruption and nepotism. De Valera had abused his dual role of Taoiseach and controlling director to create 'a very solid nest egg' and turn the company into a family concern by bringing his son Vivion and Vivion's brother-in-law onto the board.[124] Taking full advantage of parliamentary privilege, Fine Gael's Oliver J. Flanagan supported the motion in layman's terms by suggesting that the 'Minister for Justice should take action if Deputy Browne's statement that Mr de Valera is robbing the shareholders of the *Irish Press* . . . '.[125] As shouts of 'shut up' and 'sit down' rang out from the Fianna Fáil benches, the rest of Flanagan's comments never reached the annals of the official Dáil record. He was promptly expelled from the chamber, but before he left he crossed the floor and shook hands with Noel Browne and congratulated him on blowing the whistle on de Valera's control of the *Irish Press*. As de Valera left the chamber before the vote, the debate ended with cries of 'What will the *Irish Press* say tomorrow?'[126]

When the vote was finally taken on Browne's motion, the Fianna Fáil majority ensured its defeat. Earlier that day, it had been suggested to de Valera that with the presidency becoming vacant in the near future, it would be an ideal time for him to step down as Taoiseach.[127] The onerous task of suggesting resignation to de Valera fell to party stalwart and Press Group shareholder and director

Oscar Traynor, whose son Colm would also become a director of the company. The following morning's national newspapers gave page one prominence to de Valera's presidential ambition, while the reports of Browne's motion were relegated to the inside pages. Under the headline 'Censure Motion Defeated in Dáil', the *Irish Press* gave sparse coverage to the share holding controversy. Browne's claim that the American Corporation had ceased to exist was also denied by a very rapidly received letter from its board in New York. What the letter did not say, however, was that de Valera had complete control of the American Corporation. The paper also carried a letter of protest from de Valera that denied Browne's charges. According to the letter, Browne had made his allegations 'at a late hour' when there was 'no opportunity' for him to refute them. According to de Valera, while he owned only 'a few hundred personal shares', the 'block of ninety odd thousand shares to which Browne referred' was held by himself and his son Vivion 'on behalf of the persons who subscribed the money and to whom the dividend or other profits on these shares must be paid'. They were held 'to ensure that the purposes for which the money was subscribed' would not be departed from. It also stated that Browne's allegation that the de Valeras had engaged 'in a process of acquiring shares at reduced rates' or had 'built up a large holding of shares' was 'completely untrue'.[128] What the letter did not say was that while Eamon de Valera was absent from the Dáil chamber when Browne made his accusations, his son Vivion was present but declined the opportunity to refute Browne's allegations. Neither did the letter inform the public that de Valera had transferred control of the company and ownership of the crucial American Corporation voting shares to his sons Vivion and Terry the previous day. While the post of controlling director passed to Vivion, ownership of the voting shares of the American Corporation passed to Terry de Valera.[129] The latter did not express much interest in the affairs of the Press Group and essentially let Vivion run the company as he saw fit. Terry de Valera later become Taxing Master of the High Court. The announcement of a new boss made little difference to the journalists at Burgh Quay, where one journalist, Paddy Clare, remarked that 'it wasn't every young fellow that was given a newspaper company by his father to play with'.[130] While some Fianna Fáil members questioned the change in ownership, official objections did not materialise. However, some senior party figures were 'surprised and dismayed that he handed over control of the papers to his son Vivion rather than to the Fianna Fáil party' because 'thousands of members of the party put in much effort to collect a substantial part of the capital in small subscriptions'.[131] Nevertheless, it was not until the closing stages of his parliamentary career that anyone seriously challenged de Valera's right to control the Press Group, and that challenge had come from outside the party.

Although ownership of the Press newspapers had passed from Eamon de Valera's hands, they still provided him with reverential coverage for his presidential campaign, the date of which coincided with the referendum on changing the electoral system from proportional representation to the 'first past the post' system. The motivation for the change lay in the fear that the party could not survive without de Valera as leader. Since it was biggest party in the state, the straight vote would benefit Fianna Fáil more so than any other political party. Although the party stated that both ballots were being held on the same day because the opposition had delayed the referendum as long it could, this situation suited Fianna Fáil as both it and the *Irish Press* embarked on a campaign to convince the electorate to reward the 'father of the state' by granting him his last two wishes; electing him President and accepting the straight vote. While the *Irish Press* saturated its editions with past photographs and reviews of de Valera's political career in the run-up to polling day, the paper also promoted the merits of the straight vote at the expense of proportional representation. While the straight vote enabled people 'to choose between opposing policies and to return a government to office with sufficient strength to carry out the policy they have chosen', with proportional representation 'the life of each successive government' depended on the 'support of a combination of groups with conflicting aims'. According to the *Irish Press*, 'the minority parties created by proportional representation' had acquired 'a vested interest in the system' and so resisted any attempt to change it. The change was 'vital for the preservation of stable democratic government' and to avoid future decisions being 'swayed by the no-men . . . politically militant minorities with an axe to grind' or those who enjoyed 'obstruction for its own sake'.[132] Late on the day of polling, de Valera resigned as Taoiseach and leader of Fianna Fáil. The results of the ballots brought mixed results for Fianna Fáil and the *Irish Press* and were perhaps best summed up by the paper's headline; 'Mr de Valera is Elected – Majority for PR'.[133] It seemed that for de Valera, the power of the *Irish Press* had finally subsided. It would, however, be resurrected for his successor Sean Lemass, whose hour had finally come.

CHAPTER FIVE

A Changing Ireland – A Changing Media

I feel somewhat afraid . . . Never before was there in the hands of man an instrument so powerful to influence the thoughts and actions of the multitude.[1]

Eamon de Valera on the advent of RTÉ television

Sean Lemass succeeded de Valera as leader of Fianna Fáil on 22 June 1959 and became Taoiseach the following day. Transferring its allegiance to the new leader proved an easy task for the *Irish Press*. Noting the disastrous state of the economy and Lemass' plans for recovery, the paper proclaimed that 'the man and the hour' were 'surely matched'. According to the paper, 'few statesmen of any age' had been 'so well tried by experience'. His 'record of achievement' spoke for itself and 'the future of the country' was 'safe in the hands of Sean Lemass'.[2] As Taoiseach, Lemass began to implement Whitaker's *Programme for Economic Expansion* that was based on the belief that domestic capital lacked the ability to stimulate adequate economic growth and that growth would have to come from export orientated expansion. Despite Lemass' previous ambivalence towards foreign investment, by 1959 he was publicly proclaiming the need for foreign investment in the Irish economy. But since the party had so intimately associated protectionism with the struggle for Irish independence and freedom, the change to free trade required justification to both the electorate and the party faithful. This necessitated a considerable amount of ideological argumentation to justify a policy that encouraged foreign investment and reduced the nation's reliance on indigenous industry.[3] This policy was neither traditionalist nor nationalist; indeed it was anti-nationalist. Nonetheless, Lemass made an appeal for support to the electorate and the party faithful, an appeal that had recourse to traditional nationalist ideology to justify the new economic policy. The party and Lemass in particular, helped by the

Irish Press, associated the new policy with nationalism and patriotism and claimed that a successful new economic policy would result in the attainment of party goals such as the ending of partition and the restoration of the Irish language. It was, in effect, a return to the nation-building discourse so successfully utilised by de Valera and the *Irish Press* during the 1930s. It was thus an ideological appeal – an attempt to win support for the programme through the claim that its success would secure the nation's independence.

Lemass, helped by the *Irish Press*, propagated the argument that the post-revolutionary generation of the 1950s had a duty to 'consolidate the economic foundations' of their 'political independence' by concentrating their efforts on building up a viable economy.[4] No mention was made of the loss of economic independence that free trade involved. Lemass and the *Irish Press* merely presented free trade as a continuation of the struggle for Irish independence and freedom. Indeed, Lemass pointed to the economic crisis that the country had endured during the late 1940s and 1950 as a threat to the nation's survival and independence. It was, according to Lemass, a 'crucial period' in the attempt to 'build up an Irish state which would be capable of maintaining permanent independence'.[5] Economic planning was, according to Lemass, 'a constructive approach' to the 'task of nation building'.[6] Its aim was to raise 'up the people of Ireland from the depressed conditions to which external rule had reduced them'.[7] Again no mention was made of the fact that protectionism had failed to achieve this. Conversely, non-support was linked with betrayal of the nation's past struggle. According to Lemass, if the Irish people failed 'at this essential task' they would be 'false' to both their 'historic past and to the men and women who made it what it was'.[8] Thus the economic development programme was 'entitled on every grounds to first priority at this time'.[9]

The ideological campaign also made an appeal to patriotism. According to Lemass, economic development had to be 'as much the product of patriotism as of considerations of material or personal advantage'.[10] While the 'requirements of patriotism and the scope for national work' could vary with circumstance, the ultimate aim was 'always constant'.[11] That aim was to 'build in Ireland a worthy homeland for the Irish people in every sense' where they could 'develop their own way of life in accordance with their own traditions, their own cultural heritage, their own national characteristics'.[12] Those who answered Ireland's call 'testified to the courage and tenacity with which our people fought for their freedom'.[13] Thus Lemass' appeal for support, like de Valera's in the 1930s, looked back to the past to justify the vision that he had for Ireland. Lemass and the *Irish Press* also raised the possibility that a successful free trade policy would end partition once and for all. The failure of the Irish economy to develop, coupled with high unemployment and emigration had led to a legitimation crisis not only for protectionism but also for the viability of the south as an independent economic entity. Lemass argued that since unionists had used economic reasons for remaining within the UK, once the south had a buoyant economy there would be no reason for partition to continue. According to Lemass, there were 'people today in the north-east of the country' who believed that the people of the republic were 'paying an uneconomic price' for their freedom. Thus the people of the south had to demonstrate that they could 'bring about a higher level of achievement and greater progress with freedom than without it'. When this had been demonstrated, the southern people would have 'cleared away the one continuing argument' that was used to 'justify the partitioning of our country'.[14] According to Lemass, the southern people had to 'confound these northern defenders of partition who contend that joining us in freedom would be an economic disadvantage to the north-eastern counties by showing in the scale of our achievements that we, under equal conditions and in the exercise of our freedom can move faster and go further in economic progress that they can hope for, handicapped as they are'.[15] Lemass also argued that a successful free trade policy would be beneficial to the Irish language. He sought to encourage Irish language enthusiasts to support the new economic policy because it was part of the same philosophy of patriotism and nationalism that inspired the language movement. According to Lemass, patriotism was 'the produce of love of country and of traditions, culture and characteristics of our people and the Irish language is part of that heritage' and Ireland needed 'a strong patriotic urge to vitalise the economic programme'. To assert that there was 'no unifying link between our language policy and our economic policy' was 'a fundamental fallacy'. To 'neglect the forces that inspire patriotic endeavour' would put the country in 'economic peril'.[16] As well as reproducing Lemass' speeches for mass dissemination, the *Irish Press* backed his new policy editorially. Despite its previous denunciations of Fine Gael's plan for free trade, the paper noted that 'the policy of high industrial protection' had 'spent itself' and Ireland had to 'commence the process of shedding it'. Indeed, the policy had become 'something of a handicap' by inadvertently preserving 'inefficient and obsolete production methods' as well as 'restrictive labour practices'.[17]

But despite the ideological campaign waged by the *Irish Press*, there was considerable apprehension within Fianna Fáil in the run-up to the 1961 general election. As well as having to sell the new economic policy to the electorate, it was also the party's first election without de Valera as leader. Thus the party again relied on the *Irish Press* to promote both Lemass and his policy of economic evolution. It praised his guiding of the economy from the pre-war revival of industry and the foundation of semi-state bodies up to his present day 'daring spirit . . . patriotic ideals and service to the nation'. Lemass was, the paper noted, a man 'with his eyes fixed on the future' whose progress should not be 'thwarted by the paralysis of coalition'.[18] The election result was 'a foregone conclusion' because 'no real alternative to the present government existed'. According to the paper, 'the sole aim of the smaller parties' was 'to oust Fianna Fáil from office, or failing that, to rob the present government of an effective majority'.[19] When the party lost eight seats and failed to win an overall majority, the *Irish Press* observed that because Fianna Fáil was the largest party in the Dáil, it was 'evident that the main body of voters' still looked 'to Fianna Fáil for national leadership'. According to the paper, 'these and thousands of others of all shades of opinion' desired a continuance of the 'coherent progressive policy that Fianna Fáil provided'.[20] Lemass had a 'legitimate claim to form a Fianna Fáil government' and with the help of two independent deputies, Lemass formed a minority administration. To the *Irish Press*, this 'national . . . single party government', however unstable, was preferable to 'the uncertain whims and soft centred indecision of coalition rule'.[21] The paper also quickly shifted the responsibility of government stability from the minority government to the opposition parties. Government stability would only prevail if opposition parties were to behave 'with a proper sense of responsibility' and 'avoid any misguided and mischievous strategy designed to hamper and frustrate the proper government of the country . . . and the dynamic leadership of Sean Lemass'.[22]

That same year, Ireland applied for membership of the European Economic Community and in January 1962, Lemass made the formal presentation of Ireland's case to Brussels. The following month, the *Irish Press*' London editor Des Fisher interviewed Walter Hallstein, president of the EEC Commission, and enquired how Ireland's application for membership was faring. In response, Hallstein opened a drawer in his desk and showed Fisher an unopened folder that he said was Ireland's application. When asked why it had not yet been processed, Hallstein replied that since Britain was still Ireland's largest trading partner, the latter's membership depended on Britain becoming a member first. The *Irish Press* never published the high-profile interview. Vivion de Valera later informed Fisher that his article was spiked so as not to shock the Irish public.[23] Given the ideological campaign being waged by both Lemass and the *Irish Press*, the revelation would surely have shocked an electorate that was being encouraged to secure the country's economic freedom by embracing free trade. The suggestion by Hallstein that Ireland's economy was still subservient to Britain's would not have helped Lemass' campaign. Nearly a year later, Ireland's application to join ultimately failed when the French government vetoed Britain's application. Nonetheless, Lemass pursued his crusade to open up the Irish economy, with both he and the *Irish Press* continuing to link support for free trade with the achievements of past patriots. During a difficult budget debate in 1963, the paper bluntly opined that the country had to make a decision on the issue. It could 'plunge bravely forward into . . . the unknown and spend money in the process' or it could 'take things as they come', let the young people 'drift to England' and 'become a nice quiet backwater of Europe'. According to the paper, while the 'latter course would be easier', it would be 'a sore departure from the ideals of the men who died for Ireland' and 'an insult to the aspirations of the decent Irish man of today'.[24] Lemass' modernisation crusade culminated in the Anglo-Irish Free Trade Agreement of December 1965 that finally re-established free trade between Ireland and Britain.

As the tariff barriers that had been imposed for the purpose of economic protectionism were gradually lifted in the early 1960s, it became clear that while they had served their purpose in building up indigenous industry by preventing foreign capital spreading to Ireland, so too had they protected Irish culture from foreign cultural intrusions. As the barriers fell and Ireland looked outwards to Europe and America, the country opened up for the first time to the influences of foreign ideas, norms and values. As Ireland industrialised and modernised, the social structure that up to then had been predominately rural and relatively uneducated within a culturally isolated nation was changed utterly. The effects of foreign capital and foreign ideas, values and norms were reflected in various ways. The large inflow of foreign capital changed the economic emphasis from agriculture to industry and ensured the transformation of the labour force from a predominately agricultural one to one based on manufacturing and industrial skills. As the new industries arrived, a process of urbanisation began due to the employment available in towns and cities. Reciprocating this change was the phenomenon of rural decline; a factor that would hit the Press titles hardest in later decades, since rural areas were traditionally their main source of readership. As the demand for labour grew, emigration declined and there was greater participation of women in the workforce. The era also saw the development of a social welfare system and greater liberalisation in social attitudes and morals as the Second Vatican Council radically reformed the role and authority of the Catholic Church. The education system also underwent a major overhaul with free second level education being introduced in 1967. Sweeping curriculum reform in 1971 saw third level education selectively funded by the government and resulted in European languages replacing the Irish language in teaching priority. The subsequent economic boom saw living standards improve and also ensured the unprecedented growth of an affluent, professional, urbanised middle class in an increasingly urbanised Ireland. In essence, the era saw the rise of a consumer society in Ireland, wherein 'the Irish were enthusiastic in their embracing of the changes demanded by the economic transformation and were even more willing to enjoy the benefits of such a transformation, given concrete expression in increased personal incomes'. The late 1960s and early 1970s thus became 'a time of economic boom and a present-orientated, individualist, consumer mentality seemed to predominate'.[25] The emergence of a consumer mentality also led to two defining national cultural ideals being relegated in terms of relevance to the population – those of the revival of the Irish language and the goal of a united Ireland, both of which the *Irish Press* had been founded to promote and support.[26]

As Lemass pursued his policy of modernisation, the reforms inadvertently impacted on the nation's identity in both the material and normative sense. These in turn impacted on the structure of the Irish newspaper industry. When officially opening the new national television service, Radio Telefis Éireann, in 1961, Eamon de Valera expressed his reservations about the power of the new medium of communication. Never before, de Valera contended, had there been 'in the hands of man an instrument so powerful to influence the thoughts and actions of the multitude'.[27] In his speech, however, de Valera did not allude to the powerful media instrument that had helped put Fianna Fáil into office. For the previous three decades, the *Irish Press* had sought to legitimise Fianna Fáil in the 'thoughts and actions of the multitude'. In contrast to de Valera's fears, Lemass firmly believed that RTE was 'an instrument of public policy' and as such was 'responsible to the government' that had 'over-all responsibility for its conduct'. Lemass firmly rejected 'the view that Radio Telefís Éireann should be, either generally or in regard to its current affairs and news programmes, completely independent of government supervision'.[28] It was from this perspective that successive Fianna Fáil governments became embroiled in conflicts with RTÉ. Nonetheless, the rapidly changing social climate had serious consequences for the media in Ireland and, as de Valera predicted, the advent of television helped speed up the process. The serious competition posed by the new television service and the gradual emergence of an increasingly more educated, affluent and consumerist population presented newspaper proprietors with many dilemmas. In many ways, newspapers now had to compete with television and it was clear that the days of reverential political coverage were over: 'the advent of television led to a greater focus on the print media and exposed the propagandist press'.[29] Adjusting successfully to the new social climate was a fraught process. If a newspaper changed its tone and philosophy too quickly, it risked losing its traditional readers. Conversely, if it changed too slowly, it risked being left behind. When faced with political, economic, social or cultural change, organisations such as newspapers must undergo a process of role renegotiation or reinvention through 'relatively dramatic changes in mission or structure or both'.[30] As television replaced the newspaper as the medium for breaking news to the public, the various Irish national titles were forced to define a new role for themselves.

The *Irish Times* was first off the mark and reinvented its identity and company structure during the 1960s and 1970s. The Independent Group followed suit in the mid 1970s. Change also began to percolate through the corridors of the *Irish Press*. It was, however, a slow process. In 1961, a handbook on writing articles and reports for the paper instructing journalists how and when to use certain terminology was circulated. Journalists were instructed not to allow 'the six counties to be called Northern Ireland or Ulster, except in direct quotation'. Likewise members of the IRA were to be termed as 'a member of the IRA, or an IRA veteran, not a member of the old IRA'.[31] It was during the early 1960s that internal conflict over the content of the Press titles eventually surfaced and manifested itself in the power struggle between Vivion de Valera and the 'wily' editor of the *Sunday Press*, Matt Feehan. Both had been in the army, both were involved in Fianna Fáil and both held senior positions within the Press Group. Feehan 'was rather derisory of Vivion' of whom he thought 'he's not really his father's son'.[32] A clash of personalities was inevitable and manifested itself in arguments over the content of the *Sunday Press*. Vivion was determined to cut the paper's 'violently political'[33] nationalist tone and this resulted in 'rows that were heard all over'.[34] When tempers flared 'Feehan and Vivion had huge rows, a lot of them political. Feehan tended to be much more republican than de Valera would have liked to have shown. As to whether de Valera was republican or not, he certainly did not want the paper to be seen to be that republican.'[35] Eventually, in 1962, Feehan was 'almost summarily sacked, he was just told one day "you are not working here anymore"'.[36] Francis Carty, then editor of the *Irish Press* and regarded as a safe pair of hands by Vivion, was moved to the *Sunday Press*, while Joe Walsh who 'followed the party line and never rocked the boat' became editor of the *Irish Press*.[37] Nonetheless, Vivion's attempts to disinfect the Press titles met with opposition from an unlikely quarter – the Irish-American shareholders. The most vocal of these was the New York judge, James Comerford, who headed up the city's branch of the Ancient Order of Hibernians and who had once banned Brendan Behan from marching in the city's St Patrick's Day Parade. Behan had insisted on marching in the parade as an individual, an honour reserved for the parade's grand marshal. When Comerford insisted that Behan march as part of a group or float, the writer was infuriated. When asked by the *New York Daily News* to comment on the affair, Behan famously retorted that 'when St Patrick drove the snakes out of Ireland, some of them went to New York and became judges'.[38] Comerford, a Kilkenny born former member of the IRA, was a close personal friend of Vivion de Valera and was also the long time custodian of the American Corporation during the 1940s and 1950s. Comerford was extremely republican and 'used to put the republican arm on de Valera from the Irish-American perspective and clearly used to twist Vivion's arm quite a bit'. It was Comerford who 'tried at all times to represent the slightly more republican radical Irish-American influence'.[39] In an interview published in the *Sunday Press* during the 1970s, Comerford admitted that the Ancient Order of Hibernians was 'sending bags of money for guns' to the north. When the interview was published in the paper, Vivion was 'terribly embarrassed by the admission'.[40]

In another embarrassing encounter, a photographer who had worked for the Press Group since its foundation was suspended for three days for ascribing the wrong rank to a retired army officer in a caption for one of his photographs that was published in the *Evening Press*.

Tommy Lavery was suspended for wrongly describing the officer concerned as a Lieutenant General instead of a Major General. A few hours after the paper had been published, the art editor informed Lavery that 'there was awful trouble over a caption and that Major de Valera the managing director had been on the phone'.[41] Lavery was instructed to write a memo acknowledging the mistake to the managing editor, Bill Redmond. When he attempted to give the memo to Redmond, the latter refused to accept it and instead instructed Lavery to write a memo to the art editor who would then pass it on to him. He then retyped the memo only to be informed that he had been suspended for three days without pay. Lavery was 'most hurt and grieved and greatly surprised that the management could do such a thing to him'. In response, the group's chapel of the NUJ held an emergency meeting and demanded that Lavery be reinstated immediately without loss of pay and that no record be kept of the suspension. Management subsequently backed down when informed that the chapel knew that the army officer had not made a complaint to the paper because he was a personal friend of Lavery.[42] Such actions on the part of management did nothing to enhance industrial relations at Burgh Quay where 'blatant cases of dismissal, victimisation and suspension were wholly unjustified and often imposed for the most trivial of causes'. Nonetheless, there was 'a willingness on the part of the management to listen with reason to complaints and remedy them as far as is possible'.[43]

The arrival of television also impacted on the *Irish Press* and the consequences television exposure could have on a newspaper seen to be overtly supporting a political party were not lost on Vivion. With the advent of television, 'Vivion realised that the days of the slavish "my party right or wrong" type of coverage were over and through the appointment of Michael Mills, introduced a degree of impartiality that would have been unthinkable in the early days. Vivion tried to take the politics out, to disinfect the *Irish Press* and was very successful at the start but subtle coverage continued especially at election time.'[44] The move to dilute political coverage proved unpopular within Fianna Fáil and during the 1960s Vivion came under intense pressure from within Fianna Fáil to ensure that the *Irish Press* remained friendly to the party:

> All the de Valera's had a guilt complex about the paper, not over the coverage but the financial rip off. While Vivion maintained his Dáil seat, he was perpetually worried about the Fianna Fáil myth. He

> always expected a cabal of party members to reclaim the paper. People like Gerry Boland and Frank Aiken, big Fianna Fáil names who were involved in the foundation of the paper wanted it to remain strongly Fianna Fáil. Many were under the impression that the *Irish Press* was Fianna Fáil dominated, but in fact it was de Valera dominated. There were fierce rows and terrific pressure from the party, but the paper could not maintain the appearance of being aligned to Fianna Fáil.[45]

During the 1960s the 'biggest complainers were Fianna Fáil politicians who tended to think they owned the place. An awful lot of them, from ministers downwards would complain about particular paragraphs or that their speeches didn't get in.'[46] Despite such pressure, in 1963 Vivion appointed Michael Mills as political correspondent of the *Irish Press*. Significantly, Mills was 'the first political correspondent given a reasonably free hand'.[47] When offered the post, Mills told Vivion that he 'would try it for six months but would not write propaganda' – a condition that Vivion accepted. This new approach to political coverage did not endear itself to the party, but Vivion held out against the pressure. As *Hibernia* magazine noted, 'only a very strong man could be as much a part of Fianna Fáil and as independent of it'.[48] Indeed, Vivion was not very popular within the party and many other party members thought they would make a better job of running the *Irish Press*.[49] Since most Fianna Fáil politicians still regarded the paper as the party journal, Mills often incurred the wrath of the party, a threat that was countered by his frequent appearances on television:

> I had an advantage over previous political correspondents in that television had arrived and I appeared on several programmes and could often say on television what I might have difficulty saying in the *Irish Press*. There was opposition from sections of Fianna Fáil with many meetings passing resolutions trying to get the management to sack me. When the attacks came, Vivion resisted them and said he would stand by me. I used to get flack from TDs but I had regular access to television and radio which was a great help as I could reach a far greater audience there than by the *Irish Press*.[50]

Through the appointment of Mills, Vivion tried to transform the editorial ethos of the paper from its reverential coverage of the party to a 'Fianna Fáil friendly but not run by it' approach.[51] This new relationship between the party and the paper was encapsulated in the phrase 'fair to all, friendly to Fianna Fáil', although the latter 'was never allowed to get in the way of proper news-gathering, manifesting itself only in leading articles'.[52] Newswise, 'difficult stories had to be covered and political news that would cause discomfort to Fianna Fáil was reported, often first in the *Irish Press*'.[53] But in reality, such an approach reflected the slanting of stories rather than objective analysis. Ideologically, the paper attempted an orientation away from the blatant pro-Fianna Fáil coverage of old to a more subtle and disguised form of support. The new editorial ethos of 'fair to all, friendly to Fianna Fáil' was at best an oxymoron and at worst out of place in a modernising Ireland.

This new editorial ethos met its first major challenge in 1964, when for the first time a Fianna Fáil minister resigned over an issue of policy. In October of that year, Lemass' Minister for Agriculture, Paddy Smith, resigned. Smith, who epitomised the rural rather than the urban wing of Fianna Fáil, claimed that the government had capitulated to trade union 'tyranny' by intervening in a builders' strike. Conciliation talks had failed to resolve the strike and cabinet disagreement emerged over whether it should become directly involved. Smith resigned when the cabinet eventually agreed to meet the financial demands of the unions. His resignation caused chaos within Fianna Fáil and thus required a delicate approach by the *Irish Press*: 'in a flash, Vivion was over to see what was being done, to make sure the hand was right'.[54] The paper then threw all its energy into reporting the resignation and the reasons for it before any other paper could claim there was a split in the government. Under the headline 'Mr Smith Leaves Cabinet', the *Irish Press* reprinted his letter of resignation and Lemass' short letter of acceptance, documents the paper depended on its party connections to obtain. Smith's resignation letter was strongly worded and criticised the 'so called leaders of the trade union movement whom our Minister for Industry and Commerce has been chasing around for years'. The letter also described making agreements with unions as 'a fraud'.[55] In keeping with the new editorial ethos, the paper's editorial viewed Smith's resignation as 'a matter of principle', but also defended Lemass' policy of direct intervention in the strike. While the resignation was 'an exceptional occurrence and therefore the occasion of excitement and surprise', in reality it was 'but part of the democratic process'. The cabinet functioned through 'majority decisions and mutual consent' and if a minister felt he could not 'whole heartedly support the line taken by his cabinet colleagues' then resignation was an 'honourable course' of action. Defending Lemass' intervention, the paper noted that 'the government considered it would be worthwhile paying some premium over and above the average increase' because it felt 'that no effort should be spared to reconcile conflicting interests for the sake of the country's future'. After all, 'economic civil war would bring victory to nobody'.[56] The paper also published Smith's resignation statement that compared Lemass' policy of pampering industry with the party's aim of ruralism and putting people 'back on the land'. With Lemass' policy, it was impossible 'to relate the income of the people on the land to those in industry' if something extra was 'taken out of the national pool of wealth by industry at every turn' at the 'expense of the people' for whom Smith was responsible.[57] Although editorially the paper eventually sided with Lemass, the new approach whereby both sides of an argument were presented before editorial judgement was delivered contrasted sharply with the approach of previous decades whereby the paper merely propagated the official party interpretation of events and ridiculed all other interpretations.

Nonetheless, the paper continued to propagate the notion that only Fianna Fáil could deliver Ireland's economic salvation. A by-election in March 1965 saw Lemass warn that should the Fianna Fáil candidate be defeated, an election would be necessary to ensure that the government had the support of the electorate. As the by-election neared, the *Irish Press* warned that there could be 'no doubting the significance of the Taoiseach's statement'. A general election 'could result in another coalition government and that would mean the abandonment of the programme which had charted the nation's course to prosperity and its replacement by the hand-to-mouth politicking that characterised the two previous attempts at inter-party coalition'.[58] The paper subsequently described the defeat of the party candidate as 'unsatisfactory' and Lemass' subsequent decision to call an election as 'well justified'.[59] Following the lead of the party's election slogan of 'Let Lemass Lead On', the *Irish Press* blamed the inter-party governments for the economic crisis that had afflicted Ireland. The coalition's 'negotiations and disagreements at the top' had 'retarded social progress and came close to stultifying' the economy.[60] In contrast, 'the record of Fianna Fáil' was 'one of such progress, achievement and aspiration, as to justify an appeal to an intelligent people on that ground alone'.[61] In essence the choice was between 'a Fianna Fáil government with a working Dáil majority or a minority Fine Gael puppet government kept in power at the whim of the Labour Party'.[62] On voting day, the paper held that since it had 'pressed the reasons for supporting Fianna Fáil' it was now logical for it to urge all its readers 'to vote and to vote for Fianna Fáil'.[63] The party was subsequently returned with an overall majority and Lemass, supported as always by the *Irish Press*, resumed his modernisation crusade.

It was also during the 1960s that change at the *Irish Times* began in earnest. By this time the paper had started its own Sunday title, the short lived *Sunday Review*. Launched in November 1957, the paper suffered from a lack of advertising revenue because the *Sunday Press* and the *Sunday Independent* were the preferred choice of advertising agencies. Nonetheless, the paper introduced many innovations such as John Healy's 'Backbencher' column and Patsy Dyke's social diary on the various events held the previous Saturday night. When the paper eventually folded in November 1963, these columns transferred to the *Irish Times* and the *Sunday Press* respectively.[64] In 1960, the *Irish Times* acquired the *Evening Mail*, but in July 1962 it too ceased publication, mostly because of the phenomenal popularity of the *Evening Press*. In any event, it was the various talents of former *Evening Press* editor Douglas Gageby and former *Irish Press* journalist Donal Foley that combined to reinvent the identity of the *Irish Times*. In 1959 Gageby was approached by *Irish Times* director George Hetherington and offered the administrative position of managing editor. Gageby turned down this initial offer but added that were he also offered a position on the board of directors he would accept. In his own words, he 'did not want to be a hired editor'. Instead, he 'wanted a real say in running the paper'.[65] Three weeks later, Hetherington agreed. Deep inside, however, Gageby harboured a strong desire to edit and reinvent the *Irish Press*. If he had been offered that editorship he would never have left. It was not to be, however, and although the parting was amicable, Gageby was saddened to leave Burgh Quay because the place was his 'spiritual home' and the staff was 'very comradely'. When he gave his notice, both Jack Dempsey and Vivion de Valera quipped that they had taught him too much about newspapers.[66] In October l963, Gageby finally became editor of the *Irish Times*. In January 1964, Donal Foley joined him as news editor. Both immediately set to work on reinventing the paper that they gradually transformed to reflect the rapidly changing and more liberal Ireland. According to Foley, the paper played a central part in the opening up and development of Irish life:

> Ireland was changing. Truths learned at mother's knee and at school had begun, for many people, to take on a new meaning. Religion was

> no longer, to many, a subject for discussion in dark side chapels or confessional boxes, but a philosophy that should influence peoples' lives. It was a time for questioning: how, why, when? . . . It was a time for extending the frontiers and the advent of Radio Telefís Éireann was an important milestone in this development. People were looking for new answers . . . They were not satisfied with the old society in Ireland with its easy acceptance of poverty and injustice as part of the will of God. The role of the *Irish Times* was clear. It should be a forum for discussion, a mouthpiece for all minorities as well as the majority and a paper with a clear-cut radical viewpoint.[67]

Foley insisted that the paper give full support to Irish language. This was a major policy change for the paper as up to 1934, Irish words such as 'Dáil' were set in italics, a style usually reserved for foreign phrases. Foley also recruited several female reporters such as Eileen O'Brien with whom he began the 'Tuarascail' news feature in Irish, Meave Binchy, Mary Maher and Nell McCafferty, all of whom played a key role in the paper's success during the liberal 1960s. Previous to this, female journalists had generally been confined to writing about fashion and cookery, but Foley insisted that they write about politics and social affairs. Foley also began his legendary 'Man Bites Dog' column that offered an alternative and satirical interpretation of the week's political events. Gageby and Foley also added many new feature pages. The paper had the first expanded books page and was also the first to apply the concept of the specialist correspondent. The end result of their joint efforts was a phenomenal feat: 'at the beginning of Gageby's tenure the newspaper was the house journal of Irish middle-class and lower middle-class Protestantism. By the end of the 1960s, however, it had begun to appeal to the serious minded Catholic middle-class and moved to the pluralist position it holds today.'[68]

Change at the *Irish Press* was a lot slower. Despite Vivion de Valera's attempts to distance the paper from the Fianna Fáil, in 1966 it came under intense pressure from the party to retract a story. The story in question concerned the resignation of Sean Lemass and caught most party members unawares. The paper's political correspondent Michael Mills had been 'given a tip off by one of his political friends that he was about to retire' and the editor Joe Walsh accepted his 'word on the veracity of the story and ran it as a lead in the following day's paper'.[69] The article centred on Lemass' probable resignation claiming that 'sources close to the government were predicting that the Taoiseach would announce his retirement within the coming fortnight'.[70] The exclusive was news to most senior party figures and the story was vigorously denied. Pressure mounted on both Mills and Walsh to retract it. By the evening of the day that the story appeared, Walsh 'began to have doubts as other political correspondents attempted to knock the story on the basis of contacts with reliable government sources'. After two days of denial and pressure from Fianna Fáil and the rebuttal of the story by other newspapers, Walsh decided that the *Irish Press* would have to retract the story. Mills persisted, however and asked Walsh to 'hold off until the last minute in the belief that the story would be confirmed. Just before the deadline, a message arrived stating that a special meeting of the Fianna Fáil Parliamentary Party had been called for the following week.'[71] Lemass then announced his intention to retire as Taoiseach. Mills had been proved correct and later collaborated with Lemass to produce a major retrospective analysis of his life and career that was published by way of a series of interviews in the *Irish Press* in 1969.

The unexpected resignation meant that for the first time Fianna Fáil had to select a new leader. Unlike the transition from de Valera to Lemass, there was no preordained successor and Lemass' official announcement caused a flurry of activity in the party. Although Kevin Boland proposed Neil Blaney as a candidate, in reality both the leadership contest and the changes Ireland had undergone were encapsulated in the competition between George Colley, 'the clean-cut Irish speaking representative of old values', and Charles Haughey, 'the high-flying spokesman of business and financial interests'.[72] The choice between Haughey and Colley 'was a choice not just between two men, but also between different sets of values and different visions of what politics was all about'.[73] In effect, the contest divided the party into two factions separated not only by different visions but also by a personal bitterness that would haunt the party and the paper for decades afterwards. In the end, the contest became so bitter that Lemass persuaded Jack Lynch to stand as a compromise candidate. Just how much a compromise candidate Lynch really was, is open to question. In contrast to those actively seeking the party leadership, by firmly declining any interest in the position, Lynch further increased support for himself among those who did not want to see the party split. To avoid taking sides, the *Irish Press* declined to express an editorial opinion on the matter until the leadership race was a week old and it was clear that Lynch was going to win. Only then did the paper pronounce that it was clear that Lynch had 'emerged as

Mr Lemass' most likely successor'.[74] Neither did the paper report Sean MacEntee's harsh criticism of Lemass' decision to resign at the parliamentary party meeting convened to choose his successor. In his address to the meeting, MacEntree said he was 'appalled by the Taoiseach's decision' and stated that Lemass could 'not have chosen a worse time' to resign. By doing so, he was effectively relinquishing 'his responsibilities as head of the government and leader of Fianna Fáil'. It was, according to MacEntee, both 'astonishing and unjustifiable' that Lemass should seek 'to wash his hands of responsibility for the country's affairs'.[75] Despite the fact that several deputies objected to the way that Lemass had promoted the candidature of Jack Lynch, the latter became leader when both Blaney and Haughey withdrew and Colley was defeated in a vote.[76] To keep up the facade of party unity, the *Irish Press* noted that Lynch's success was 'a choice that reflected the very wide opinion of the party'. He was, the paper opined, 'a natural choice for the position of Taoiseach'.[77] Such natural selection was illusionary and in reality the paper had been caught unawares by the split that had marred Lemass' resignation. Editorially, the paper did not know which faction of the party to support: 'the old style republicans or the Mohair suit brigade'. While the party and other institutions were 'feeling the influence of free trade and questioning their relevance to a modernising Ireland, the paper did not take part in this process of self-evaluation and reinvention'.[78] It seemed that the best the paper could manage was its dilution of political coverage through the adoption of the 'fair to all, friendly to Fianna Fáil' editorial ethos.

Despite this, during the 1960s circulation figures for the Press titles grew to phenomenal heights with the titles regularly achieving the highest net sales of Irish newspapers. The year 1964 was a particularly good one for the Press Group as circulation increased by eleven per cent and advertising demand increased by thirteen per cent. With an ABC circulation of 148,336 readers in 1965, the *Evening Press* outsold the *Evening Herald*, while the *Sunday Press* also dominated the Sunday newspaper market with an ABC circulation of 419,948. Even the *Irish Press* had a high ABC circulation of 119,232.[79] Industrial peace was in short supply, however, and in June 1965 a printers' strike halted publication of the Press titles. Advertisers missed the *Evening Press* so much that a delegation from the City Centre Trade Group met with the Press Group's general manager Jack Dempsey and pleaded with him for the publication of the paper to be resumed because business had dropped by a massive thirty per cent. The delegation agreed to buy more advertising space and the extra revenue created by this literally paid what the striking printers were looking for.[80] The strike also suspended publication of the *Sunday Press* from the beginning of June to the middle of September 1965. When it resumed publication, the popularity of the paper was confirmed when, after such a prolonged absence from the marketplace, it suffered no loss of circulation. The paper had the most popular social column in the country at the time in the form of Patsy Dyke's back-page social diary. As sales of the Press titles increased, so too did the company's profits; they gradually rose from £42,834 in 1963 to £60,585 in 1968.[81] Although the precarious financial position of the company had seen it adopt a policy of holding any profits as reserve capital, during the 1960s both the *Sunday Press* and *Evening Press* were very profitable and some shareholders began to complain about the lack of return on their investment.

At the company's 1966 annual general meeting, Vivion de Valera was subjected to rigorous questioning over what was happening to the company's profits. Two shareholders, Nicholas Leonard (who later became a director of Independent Newspapers) and Alexis FitzGerald (a Fine Gael Senator), pressed for the payment of a dividend and organised 23,000 votes against the adoption of the accounts. At this time, Vivion de Valera and Sean Nunan were still trustees to the American Corporation and thus exercised its voting rights so that the motion was roundly defeated. Asked whether a stock exchange quotation for the shares was possible, Vivion rhetorically replied that it would be foolish for the company to apply for a quotation before it had paid a dividend.[82] After the company made a staggering profit of £500,000 in 1972, the board could no longer excuse the non-payment of a dividend, and the first one was paid to shareholders in 1973 as 'a strategic move to stop some people complaining'.[83] In another strategic move, rather than pay a dividend to the shareholders of the American Corporation, the board sold a unissued 16,400 shares to the Corporation, paid for by the dividends due and thus increased its shareholding in the Irish company even more.[84]

But despite the company's profitability, the lack of any industrial relations policy ensured that industrial unease prevailed at Burgh Quay. The appointment by Vivion de Valera of another former army officer and party supporter, Gerald FitzGerald, as personnel manager was greeted with scepticism among staff. Such individuals were 'just hauled in and became poles, token executives for the Major'.[85] There existed 'an uneasiness about the place that grew with every passing year. This regime of fear made people afraid of losing their jobs. Often people with twenty or more years experience left to go to the *Irish Independent*. These people were irreplaceable and left not because of money but because of the uneasiness.'[86] This situation was exemplified by the defections of Douglas Gageby and Donal Foley to the *Irish Times*, a loss that deprived the Press Group of two of the most influential Irish journalists of the latter half of the twentieth century. It seemed that if a journalist wanted to progress his or her career, then defecting to a rival publication was the only viable option. The Press Group 'was the nursery of Irish journalism . . . people came in for training and then left and executives used to boast about it'. In effect 'few opportunities existed for promotion to positions of real power because the de Valera family ran it'.[87] The origins of such an appalling industrial relations culture could be traced back to the paper's first leading article and especially the line 'we are not the organ of an individual or a group or a party'. This 'nudge and wink attitude blinkered people's view; it was believed that it was OK to say one thing and to do another'.[88] Indeed, Vivion de Valera, who could sometimes be 'a very deceptive man', did much to foster this culture. Staff always knew when an election was on the way by the type of car being driven by him. Most of the time he travelled to and from the office in his Mercedes. When electioneering, however, he would leave the Mercedes at home and requisition an *Irish Press* staff car, a Volkswagen Beetle, to acquire the common touch that meeting the public required. His frequent walkabouts in the newsroom also instilled a sense of paranoia in the staff who 'could be collared at any particular time'. Most of the time, 'staff often read praise as meaning something else'.[89]

Vivion did much to discourage rather then foster an atmosphere of modernisation. In 1966, the editor of the *Evening Press*, Conor O'Brien, attempted to bridge the gulf that separated management and editorial executives by reorganising the company's management structures. O'Brien proposed that at least one of the group's editors should sit on the company's board of directors. In this way, editorial executives would always have a direct link to management, while the latter would also be kept more informed about what was happening on the shop floor. O'Brien was also in favour of a representative organisation for editorial executives – department heads such as news editors, sports editors and chief-sub editors – to ensure independence from both the board of directors and the NUJ. Both suggestions were rejected by Vivion, who did not appreciate such initiatives being presented to him without prior consultation. Spotting his potential, Independent Newspapers offered O'Brien the editorship of the *Sunday Independent* and so the Press Group lost another innovator. Senior executives at the company were dismayed 'and de Valera lost the loyalty of many of them'.[90] O'Brien was replaced as *Evening Press* editor by Sean Ward, whose father Terry had been London editor of the *Irish Press* during the war years. Ward later recruited the celebrated sports columnist Con Houlihan to write for the paper.

It seemed resistance to change was endemic. Even though 'the staff detested the black dirty tempo heavy print of the Press titles, any suggestions for a new design or change of layout were quickly shot down, simply because the papers were on the pig's back'.[91] There was, it seemed, a 'total de Valera veto on everything' and every Tuesday all three editors of the group's titles held a weekly meeting with editor-in-chief Vivion de Valera at the company's business offices in O'Connell Street.[92] Indeed, the only change that did occur was change that suited the de Valera family. In 1967 Vincent Jennings, a sub-editor of the group's evening title, replaced Francis Carty as editor of the *Sunday Press*. During that year, Lemass' Committee on the Constitution issued its report and Carty took the rare step of writing a leader that agreed with the need to amend de Valera's 1937 constitution. Two days later, Vivion sent a clipping of the leader back to Carty with a five-letter word scrawled across it. Carty took the hint and retired shortly afterwards.[93] Over the next twenty years, the paper's circulation fell significantly, due mainly to the growth of television and the arrival of the *Sunday World* in 1973. With television having practically taken over the function of breaking news, the *Sunday World* placed its emphasis on sports, gossip, features and entertainment and hit upon a winning combination to the detriment of the *Sunday Press*. For advertisers in particular, it represented a downmarket, mass circulation newspaper with equal rural and urban appeal and colour advertising facilities that slowly but surely ate into the advertising base of the *Sunday Press*.

One of the first issues that Jennings had to deal with as editor was that of the 'closed shop'. During the late 1960s, the issue of non-journalists contributing columns to the paper became a contentious one. One such individual was Gay Byrne, then 'the biggest thing in Ireland'.[94] After one such external column criticised the paper's journalists, the NUJ chapel demanded that no column be written by outsiders. When management rejected this, a dispute erupted and on instructions from their trade union, *Sunday Press* staff refused to handle outside copy. Eventually, every staff member of the paper, which at that time numbered just seventeen, was called individually into Jennings' office and sacked. At this time editorial executives could still produce and print the newspaper because they were not members of the NUJ. It was only when management realised that the print unions were about to become involved in the dispute that it relented. The resulting compromise saw all the staff rehired and agreement reached on the use of outside copy.[95]

As the decade drew to a close, Vivion de Valera continued his policy of diluting the Fianna Fáil influence at Burgh Quay. In January 1968, he removed Joe Walsh from the editorial seat of the *Irish Press* for a number of reasons; circulation was falling, he wanted a 'more independent approach'[96] and he wanted the paper to have 'a more youthful image'.[97] In keeping with what by now seemed like tradition, Walsh arrived for work one morning to be informed that he was no longer editor and had been transferred to the company's business offices in O'Connell Street. Ironically, Walsh's replacement as editor was Tim Pat Coogan, the son of a former Fine Gael TD for Kilkenny. Coogan faced a daunting task, as up to then the *Irish Press* had literally ignored the changes such as 'the paperback revolution, the easing of censorship, the Vatican Council, and new currents in popular journalism' that had occurred in Irish society.[98] The paper had done 'nothing to face up to this new challenge because there was a lack courage in facing up to the arrival of modernity over the decade'. While Vivion de Valera 'often asked for innovative ideas, he was always worried about cost control. Changes should have been implemented earlier because while the party reformed, the paper did not.'[99] Oblivious to the need to change its appeal from a declining rural, working-class readership, to a growing urban, professional middle class, the *Irish Press* failed to move with the times:

> As the fifties slid into the sixties, Ireland began to notice the outside world and to want some of the new freedoms and the new sophistications that were flowing in from America and Europe. The bedrock of the *Irish Press*' beliefs was being challenged. At first the Irish dailies responded nervously, but before long the pot was bubbling with new ideas and developments. The sixties saw the *Irish Independent* and the *Irish Times* striding into the modern world. The *Irish Press,* however, seemed hobbled by its past. Somehow the hardy frugality that was right in the thirties looked very outmoded thirty years later. The paper needed to reinvent itself, to get rid of its downbeat, cloth-cap image. Only a long-term strategy involving considerable investment in

> content, size and printing could achieve this. Sadly, the *Irish Press* never got that investment. By then Burgh Quay was also publishing the *Sunday Press* and the *Evening Press*, papers that made more money and always got more marketing than the flagship.[100]

Nonetheless, Coogan did his best to drag the paper into the modern era. In the mould of founding editor Frank Gallagher, Coogan again sought to make the *Irish Press* a paper that celebrated Irishness, albeit a more modern version. In April 1968, a new feature page appeared in the paper. Entitled 'New Irish Writing', it attempted to revive the tradition of short story writing that had declined after the publication of short story periodicals became no longer viable. Every Saturday the paper devoted one page to a new Irish short story and the feature, edited by David Marcus, soon won wide critical acclaim. The appointment by Coogan of female journalists Anne Harris and Mary Kenny also gave a modern, liberal touch to the paper. Their articles on prostitution in Dublin and the ban on contraception caused storms of protests and woke the public up to the fact that Irish society was indeed beginning to change. With the arrival of Kenny and her dyed blonde hair and wardrobe of hot-pants and mini-skirts, the already hot temperature at Burgh Quay increased considerably. Pipe smoking was no longer confined to male journalists, although bra burning somehow remained a female preserve. Kenny was, nonetheless, 'a very serious career minded girl' and soon moved on to become features editor at the London *Evening Standard*.[101]

Politically, Coogan was viewed as being neutral and he allowed journalists 'do their own thing . . . he ensured that what they wrote was published when other people might worry about what the party might think'.[102] Among those who contributed to editorials during Coogan's tenure were eminent broadcaster Brian Farrell and Fine Gael Senator Maurice Manning. During the 1960s, the paper also had a good relationship with those training for the legal profession at the King's Inn. Among the trainee barristers who worked for the *Irish Press* were Hugh O'Flaherty, later a supreme court judge, Niall Andrews, later a Fianna Fáil European MP and his brother David Andrews, later a Fianna Fáil government minister. According to the latter, who worked as a sub-editor at the *Irish Press* between 1959–62, while there may have been pressure on management, there was no pressure on journalists to be friendly to Fianna Fáil. However, as Andrews pointed out, while the original reporters for the *Irish Press* had been of the Fianna Fáil persuasion, by the late 1960s this had changed, resulting in an altered relationship between the party and the paper. According to Andrews, 'during the late 1960s and 1970s, the *Irish Press* did not reflect the views of the party and there was dissent within the Fianna Fáil ranks at the publication, which was looked on as a party mouthpiece'. While the paper had been 'originally set up to compete with the *Irish Independent* and the *Irish Times* and to give Fianna Fáil a voice, somehow it lost contact'. The new journalists employed at Burgh Quay from the 1960s onwards 'were not in the mould of Fianna Fáil and were imported from other political parties, and this was reflected in their writings'.[103] It was not management but rather the journalists already employed there who were responsible for the recruitment of additional reporters. This 'old boys' network meant that the paper was 'fed almost totally from the provincials and what you were dealing with were experienced and generally unbiased reporters and not Fianna Fáil hacks'.[104]

Despite this gradual estrangement from the party, during 1968 the *Irish Press* and the *Sunday Press* were the only national newspapers to support Fianna Fáil's second attempt to replace proportional representation with the straight vote. This change would effectively eliminate smaller parties to the benefit of bigger parties, a fact exploited by an opposition that highlighted the spectre of Fianna Fáil 'dictatorships'. In response, the party, helped by the *Irish Press*, dismissed such fears and instead hyped up the instability of coalition government that proportional representation inevitably produced. According to the paper, while the case in favour of the straight vote was 'logically made and so presented in print', the upholders of proportional representation merely 'impugned Fianna Fáil's motives by raising the bogey of dictatorship'. While the benefits of the straight vote had been clearly articulated, much of what had 'been urged against it' was 'irrelevant' because the protagonists of the straight vote had made no suggestion 'as to how the problems of minority coalitions' could be 'avoided or solved'.[105] But despite the support of the Press titles, the proposal was defeated even more heavily than the previous referendum. In the 1959 referendum, fifty-three per cent of the electorate had rejected the straight vote. In 1968, this rose to sixty per cent.[106] The election campaign of the following year saw the *Irish Press* note that although the electorate preferred 'proportional representation more than any other electoral system', in using it the electorate also had a duty to ensure that the country got a 'stable government'. Fianna Fáil could 'govern well and govern fairly from a position of strength' and so the paper expressed the view that the party's 'mandate should be renewed for that purpose'.[107]

This was the first election campaign to take place under the editorship of Tim Pat Coogan. The reverential praise of Fianna Fáil and the demonisation of other parties that up to then had been the basis for *Irish Press* election editorials literally disappeared. Instead, the paper concentrated its energy on promoting the concept of Jack Lynch as a true statesman more worthy of support than any other party leader. This was primarily done through the columns of the paper's political correspondent, Michael Mills, who accompanied Lynch on his tour of constituencies. While Mills would not tolerate party propaganda, he was a friend of Lynch and his reports had the effect of depicting Lynch as a true statesman. According to Mills' reports of the tour, Lynch was a 'different man' when he got away from 'government functions'. His manner became easier and he was 'more at home with the people'. They came up to 'shake his hand on the streets' and mothers brought 'up their children to be introduced'.[108] Lynch also developed 'a nice technique in dealing with hecklers'. He did not merely 'give a short answer' but treated 'their questions seriously'. According to Mills' reports, if a Garda moved in on a heckler, Lynch would intervene and insist on answering any question the heckler cared to ask.[109] A former GAA star, Lynch's rapport with the electorate saw Fianna Fáil win its biggest electoral victory since 1957. For the paper, it looked as if the 'fair to all, friendly to Fianna Fáil' philosophy had been a success. By concentrating its energies on exalting the virtues of Lynch rather than demonising the opposition, the paper had garnered support for the party that now looked united under Lynch's leadership.

Such unity, however real or imagined, was extremely short lived as the north exploded amid sectarian strife and 'imposed great strains' on the party.[110] The heavy-handed response of the northern authorities to demands for civil rights from the nationalist community created an atmosphere of impending crisis. That crisis manifested itself in August 1969 during the unionist marching season and the north rapidly descended into a state of near civil war. How to respond to the situation provided the Irish government with a massive dilemma and created a split within the cabinet. The cabinet division was essentially that that had developed during the Lemass succession race. At an emergency cabinet meeting, Lynch found himself under intense pressure from Neil Blaney, Charles Haughey and Kevin Boland to consider several options as a response to the deteriorating northern situation. While an incursion by the Irish army to relieve the beleaguered nationalist community and create an international incident was considered, the cabinet eventually agreed that army field hospitals be sent to the border to receive refugees, a move that excited Irish public opinion.[111] A text for Lynch's address to the nation was also agreed. This included the infamous statement that the Irish government could 'no longer stand by and see innocent people injured and perhaps worse'.[112] The cabinet also agreed that a special fund administered by the Minister for Finance, Charles Haughey, be made available to northern representatives. The subsequent revelation that some of this money had been paid to a German arms dealer for an aborted arms delivery to Dublin airport resulted in Lynch's decision to request the resignation of not only Haughey but also for those of the Minister for Justice Michael Ó Móráin and the Minister for Agriculture Neil Blaney. While Ó Móráin immediately agreed to resign, both Blaney and Haughey refused. The spin put on Ó Móráin's resignation was that it was purely on health grounds and, despite the rumours of the impending arms crisis, he was wished a speedy return to 'good health' by the *Irish Press*.[113] Two days later Lynch sacked both Blaney and Haughey from the cabinet. However, Lynch took this action only after the leader of Fine Gael, Liam Cosgrave, threatened to make public information he had received from the Gardaí implicating government ministers in the purchase of arms.[114] The fallout continued with the subsequent resignations of the Minister for Local Government, Kevin Boland, and his deputy minister, Paudge Brennan. The *Irish Press* described the revelations of attempted gun running as 'more serious than anything we have known in our politics since the ending of the Civil War'.[115] Initially, however, the paper adopted an empathetic tone towards Blaney and Haughey, noting that they 'acted as they did not out of hopes for personal aggrandisement but to bring strength to the beleaguered Catholics of the north, terrorised by the events of last year's bloody August. In so doing they put political careers of merit and long standing at hazard and they have paid the price.'[116] But sensing the in-party strife that lay ahead, the paper soon reverted to its traditional policy of supporting the leader of the day.

According to Tim Pat Coogan, the arms crisis resulted in severe pressure being put on him by both sides of the party split to articulate their views in the paper. In particular, the journalism of Michael Mills was again criticised by sections of the party: 'there was a fallout within Fianna Fáil and I got a lot of flack about the coverage by Michael Mills. Pressure was put on me as editor to sort him out, but I left his copy untouched. This approach was unpopular but I think the average Fianna Fáil member respected that.'[117] According to Mills himself, the paper was caught between a rock and a hard place during the arms crisis, as the two factions competed for their side of the story to be given more prominence and perhaps editorial backing. While Vivion de Valera came under strong pressure from the nationalist wing of party to destabilise Lynch's position, he resisted the pressure. According to Mills:

> no matter what you said you were wrong, but Lynch's position had to be sorted out. He believed that the northern problem could be solved only by peaceful means. Jack Lynch was the first party leader to challenge the party on this and he succeeded. Vivion de Valera was a Jack Lynch supporter. He may have been critical but he never tried to undermine him. Vivion had a difficult role, he was caught between both party and paper.[118]

But while the legitimacy of using force to attain political objectives was the central issue of the crisis that caused the unprecedented party infighting and dissension, Lynch, with the help of the *Irish Press*, skilfully reorientated the issue around to that of party unity and loyalty to the leadership and thereby outmanoeuvred the vociferous militant element of the party. Indeed, the paper's editorial column became a bulwark of support for Lynch's policy of turning the issue on its head. According to the paper, Lynch had 'shown himself to be resolute and decisive in discharging his responsibility to safeguard the interest of the people'. It also praised the party that had 'reciprocated his action by a display of loyalty and sound sense' by its 'endorsement of Mr Lynch's action in dismissing the two ministers concerned'. The party's reaction was a 'reassuring and steadying one'.[119] Indeed, despite having previously compared the crisis as 'more serious than anything we have known in our politics since the ending of the Civil War',[120] the paper later noted that 'before the crisis broke, people here were rightly concerned with the other major concerns of the day to day living'.[121] The paper harshly denounced northern nationalist politicians who dared question Lynch's actions and expressed the curious view for a nationalist newspaper that the state did 'not need northerners either coming in or being brought down to take sides in its internal affairs'.[122] It also continuously dismissed the need for an election. It seemed no credible alternative to Fianna Fáil existed. The opposition consisted of 'a Labour Party to the left of the British Labour Party and a Fine Gael party something to the right of the Tories'. Ignoring the huge dissention within Fianna Fáil, the paper opined that 'such a coalition could not hold at a time of national crisis'.[123]

The subsequent arrest and charging of Blaney and Haughey[124] with conspiracy to import arms brought a mixed response. While editorially the paper had nothing to say on the development, Kevin Boland accused Lynch of 'an unparalleled act of treachery and felon setting' and called for both Lynch to resign as leader and for an emergency ard fheis to discuss the crisis. The *Irish Press* responded by describing Boland's call as 'a broadside . . . pitched to strike a emotive response' and noted that 'to call an ard fheis allegedly to put Fianna Fáil's house in order would serve to burn down the house in the heat of emotion of debate'.[125] The paper also defended Lynch's decision to send files and instructions to the Attorney General by accusing Boland of wanting 'to set aside judicial procedures' in favour of the 'judgements of individuals'.[126] Thirty-one years later, the 'judicial procedures' used in the case became a controversial issue when it emerged that a key statement from the Head of Irish Intelligence, Colonel Michael Hefferon, had been heavily edited to remove any reference to the Minister for Defence Jim Gibbons, being aware of the attempted importation. Such knowledge, if established, would have made the attempted importation legal and rendered the prosecution's case null and void. O'Morain's replacement as Minister for Justice, Des O'Malley claimed state privilege over Hefferon's original statement on the grounds of 'public policy and interest' and the statement lay in government files until released to the National Archives under the thirty-year rule governing all government documents.[127] In the 1980s, O'Malley and Haughey would fight head to head for supremacy within Fianna Fáil. Boland's subsequent expulsion from the parliamentary party was described by the paper as a 'regrettable necessity . . . in the interests of public order'.[128] Boland, along with his father Gerry Boland, a founding father of both the party and the paper, resigned from the Fianna Fáil organisation three weeks later. Despite Lynch's popularity with the electorate, for many party members the sackings, resignations and Lynch's policy of non-intervention represented a 'sense of retreat, of betraying Fianna Fáil's moral community' – that of the besieged northern nationalist community.[129] The *Irish Press* was only too painfully aware of this fact and, because of the very specific explanation given, Boland's resignation caused panic within Fianna Fáil and the *Irish Press*:

> I remember on the night of Boland's resignation, Vivion de Valera, editor-in-chief of the *Irish Press* came into the office. He was obviously consumed with anxiety to read my leader. He considered that, given Boland's stated reasons for his departure, it was the most important leader I had ever written. It was the most fraught certainly, for the balancing act between the reality and the fear of retreat was particularly

difficult to maintain at that time and in that atmosphere. But reality won out.[130]

The editorial described Boland's resignation as 'inevitable . . . he had set himself on a collision course with the leader not alone of his party, but also of the country'. The paper also denied that the resignation would cause disunity with the rank and file members of the party because 'every responsible person in Fianna Fáil and in the country generally' was well 'aware of the need for calm and responsible behaviour at this time'. According to the paper, now that the 'nettle of Mr Boland's defiance' had been 'grasped', the party could 'go forward on a firm low-keyed united approach towards the pressing problems which beset us'.[131] The paper made no comment when party deputy Sean Sherwin resigned in sympathy with Boland, nor when the arms charges against Neil Blaney were dropped. When Boland founded his own political party, Aontacht Éireann, the paper dismissed it as 'yet another divisive group in the ranks of those who are opposed to unionism'. According to the paper, those opposed to partition should unite and not be 'undermined by the protracted and recriminatory debate on the nature of republicanism as outlined yesterday in Mr Boland's speech'.[132] As the crisis progressed, management at the *Sunday Press* decided that because of the 'political sensitivity of the case, the Arms Trial would not be covered on a weekly basis'.[133] At the conclusion of the case, the *Irish Press* again sprang to Lynch's defence when Haughey was cleared of the arms charges and at a press conference asserted that 'those responsible for the debacle' had 'no alternative now but to take the honourable course open to them'.[134] According to the paper, the 'rush to the microphone and the press conference to attack the Taoiseach' could 'only have the effect of weakening the party'.[135] Lynch's winning of a vote of confidence in the government was described as 'a personal triumph for the Taoiseach and a further manifestation of the sheer professionalism of the Fianna Fáil party'.[136] Such uncritical, partisan defence of the leader of the day, combined with Vivion de Valera's interference with editorials, heralded a return to the reverential political coverage of old. It would be another nine years before the paper revoked its support for Lynch in spectacular fashion.

CHAPTER SIX

Troublesome Times – The 1970s

Irish Press Plc was ruled by the proxy vote of the Irish Press Corporation, which was used by the de Valera family at shareholders' meetings. The de Valera family had ultimate control but the shareholders still showed up year after year, many with only a handful of shares.[1]

Michael O'Toole on the share structure of the Irish Press

After the turbulence of the arms crisis, within the Fianna Fáil party 'there was retrenchment and the protection of the state tended to be the first priority and caution the watchword'.[2] This caution exploded into the public domain in October 1971, when the Minister for Post and Telegraphs, Gerry Collins, invoked Section 31 of the Broadcasting Authority Act for the first time. Collins acted after the RTÉ current affairs programme *Seven Days* broadcasted recorded interviews with members of the IRA. His directive ordered RTÉ to 'refrain from broadcasting any matter that could be calculated to promote the aims or activities of any organisation' that engaged in or promoted 'the attaining of any political objective by violent means'. It also compelled RTÉ 'to refrain from broadcasting any particular matter' at the Minister's discretion.[3] Despite the implications for the freedom of the press, the *Irish Press* defended the censorship. According to the paper, while Irish people should 'not be dependent for information on what is going on in the north from the BBC', it was 'understandable that the government, faced with recent RTÉ programmes concerning the great events which now convulse our nation . . . should feel touchy on the subject of violence'.[4]

The first test to the censorship came in November 1972, when RTÉ's news features editor Kevin O'Kelly read quotes from an interview with the IRA chief-of-staff Sean MacStiofain during the current affairs radio programme *This Week*. The quotes were raised in the context of interviewing a panel of northern politicians that included a unionist on the subject of the troubles. Although the original interview was not broadcast and MacStiofain did not appear on the programme or take part in the discussion, Gerry Collins immediately wrote to the RTÉ Authority asking what action it intended to take. Although technically the ministerial directive had not been breached, the *Irish Press* defended the reactionary response of the Fianna Fáil administration. While conceding that to broadcast only unionist opinion would lead to an imbalance, the paper turned the issue on its head by stating that the row really centred on 'the question by whom and how is RTÉ to be controlled'. According to the *Irish Press*, the government had 'the right and duty to do so and in theory should be able to direct that this or that should be done or not done'.[5] When Collins subsequently sacked the RTÉ Authority and replaced it with seven nominees of his choice, the paper commented that while it was 'incontestable' that the government had 'the right to control RTÉ', it was 'highly debatable' whether this was 'the right way to go about it'. In its mild criticism of the action, it noted that the new Authority would be viewed as trying to 'muzzle RTÉ so as to prevent any comment or reportage the government might not like'. It was 'a childlike adult fantasy to expect that evil will go away simply because we pretend we do not know it exists'.[6]

Shortly afterwards, the government introduced its Offences Against the State Amendment Bill that granted extra power to the Gardaí and could, according to the *Irish Press*, be used to compel journalists to reveal their sources if required to do by a court. In an editorial, the paper expressed the view that if a newspaper published an article that incorporated a statement made by an unnamed person that either expressly stated or implied that they were or had been a member of an illegal organisation, then the newspaper could 'find itself implicated in the proceedings'. According to the editorial, the 'authorities could call the reporter who was responsible for the report to identify the speaker, with the accused as the person who made the statement, and he might, if he refused to answer, find himself in jail'.[7] But despite the obvious implications for journalistic integrity, confidentiality and safety of sources, the paper described the bill as 'a mandate to defend Dáil Éireann and its institutions from the threats that face them'. It also described Fine Gael's opposition to the bill as 'political gamesmanship'[8] and noted that 'the furore over the bill from the so called liberal forces' had only served to create 'an emotional atmosphere'.[9] The paper would later express the very opposite sentiments in the anti-censorship crusade that it launched when the subsequent coalition government sought to broaden the definition of incitement to include newspapers. Although both the Labour Party and Fine Gael opposed the bill, the latter relented after two bombs exploded in Dublin city centre on the day of the vote. Fianna Fáil TDs Paudge Brennan and Des Foley voted against the government and were subsequently expelled from Fianna Fáil. These expulsions, like that of Neil Blaney (who had been expelled the previous July), warranted no editorial comment from the paper.

But despite all the controversy that dogged the Fianna Fáil administration, the subsequent general election of 1973 was a rather dull affair. When the party was criticised for its disunity on the northern problem, the *Irish Press* again defended the status quo, noting that 'no government in ancient or modern times was subjected to greater stresses than Mr Lynch's'.[10] It felt compelled to point out that 'Mr Lynch did not hesitate to purge his cabinet of some of his most senior ministers when he became convinced that they were pursuing a policy towards the northern crisis divergent from the one he had laid down'.[11] Again it chastised the proposed 'bargain basement coalition'[12] of Fine Gael and the Labour Party by pointing out that two months earlier, both parties had opposed each other on the vote on the Offences Against the State Bill. According to the paper, while 'the murderous blasts that occurred in Dublin that night blew a little sanity into the minds of the mutinous hotheads of Mr Cosgrave's party', the same could not be said for the Labour Party. Indeed, the parties who now presented themselves 'as an alternative to the Fianna Fáil government were unable to coalesce on this issue of vital importance, although the state was in peril and they knew it'. If this were the case, the paper opined, 'what chance would they have of making a successful, cohesive administration?'. Only a hunger for power could have brought about 'such an ill-omened alliance'.[13] The paper also felt compelled to criticise Kevin Boland's party, Aontacht Éireann: it was 'an Adam's rib of a party doomed to turn politically gangrenous'.[14] Despite such sentiments, the paper was gracious when Fianna Fáil was defeated at the polls. It complimented the 'discipline of coalition supporters'[15] in transferring preferences and noted that 'when Fine Gael and Labour finally decided to form a coalition and to draw up a positive programme after the Taoiseach had called an election, the new ideas met with a response'.[16] The paper also acknowledged that the internal 'difficulties and dissensions which racked Fianna Fáil during 1970 certainly must have had a bearing on the election's outcome'. In an effort to keep spirits up, the paper noted that the party had 'lost before and came back to win'. Optimistically, the paper predicted that it could do so again.[17]

Notwithstanding the internal party strife of the early 1970s, the *Irish Press* retained its republican philosophy throughout the decade and, in an era of aroused nationalism in the south, it enjoyed a reputation as being the most nationalist of all the national papers, highlighting the root causes of the conflict rather than supporting the IRA. It was only later, when an economic depression gripped the south, revisionism set in and 'Coogan stuck un-popularly to his guns' that the paper was labelled as pro-IRA.[18] In one particularly unfair criticism, *Magill* magazine claimed that 'in the early days of his [Coogan's] editorship the attitude of the first leader to the Provisional IRA was an indication of whether he had been around the night before or not'.[19] Despite the tragic occurrences in the north, there were some humorous moments. In early 1972, the group's northern editor Vincent Browne was shown a sub-machine gun that the IRA claimed was one of many that had been manufactured by loyalists at a Belfast engineering works. Browne phoned the British army press office for a comment and was asked whether he could get his hands on one of the guns. Browne's article in the *Sunday Press* attracted a lot of attention from other journalists and he informed them that he might soon have temporary possession of a gun. Browne subsequently collected the gun from a bar on the Falls Road and arrived at the Europa Hotel to find the city's press corps and a posse of RUC special branch officers waiting for him. Browne was arrested, held overnight and charged with possession of a machine gun. He was later convicted and received the lenient fine of £20. Browne left the Press Group shortly afterwards.[20] Nonetheless, the multitude of political beliefs then present at Burgh Quay saw many differences of opinion emerge on the northern coverage. According to one journalist, 'the strong nationalist tone of the paper during the 1970s was seen by many as support for the Provisional IRA and may have damaged circulation and alienated readers'.[21] According to another, however, the *Irish Press* 'enjoyed something of a short golden age in the late 1970s and early 1980s':[22]

> Superbly reliable news coverage and a sparkling feature section drove circulation slightly over the 100,000 mark. At this point the paper could conceivably have developed a radical constituency similar to that enjoyed by the *Guardian* in England. Unfortunately circulation fell back for various reasons including intensifying competition and a series of stoppages. There was also a view that the *Irish Press* was soft on the IRA – whether this stood up under analysis hardly matters since we're talking about perceptions.[23]

In spite of, or perhaps because of, such perceptions, Vivion de Valera advocated a more balanced approach to news coverage. When Michael Keane was appointed northern editor in 1972, Vivion took him aside and informed him that coverage was to be 'absolutely down the middle'. Keane was to be 'balanced and fair and was not to yield to pressure from any side'. If he felt any pressure he was to report back to Vivion. The latter also warned him that if he discovered that Keane had 'yielded to pressure', he would be in trouble.[24] The paper subsequently cultivated a reputation for fairness among all sections of the northern population.

One of the paper's most vocal critics was John Healy, an ex-Press Group journalist who wrote the weekly 'Backbencher' column for the *Irish Times*. By this time, Fianna Fáil was back in opposition and Lynch's position as leader of the party again looked vulnerable. In his column, Healy continually claimed that the *Irish Press* was both anti-Lynch and pro-IRA. The publication of an article in the *Irish Press* entitled 'Fianna Fáil; The future in Opposition', in which the anonymous writer made some mild criticism of Lynch's leadership, was highlighted by Healy to justify his beliefs. The article suggested that the party had become complacent in opposition and called on Lynch to reassess his 'party's position on national and international affairs'. According to the article, Fianna Fáil needed to be 'revitalised' and have 'a new dynamism injected'. In fact, a coherent 'party policy' was needed, and Lynch faced a 'major challenge . . . to rebuild the party as a credible alternative government'.[25] Thus Healy contended that the *Irish Press* was trying to hound Jack Lynch from his position as leader of Fianna Fáil because his stance on the north was not republican enough:

> The party's official organ is running a lovely anti-Lynch line . . . and savaging Lynch's dove policy. It is true you'll find Lynch's picture in the paper now and again. You'll even find his speeches. But don't look for Jack's words of placatory wisdom in the editorial section . . . When Big Daddy was in Jack's shoes, leading the Soldiers of Destiny . . . every syllable he uttered would be reproduced and endorsed word for word and called timely and eulogised as the true voice of the Irish people . . . It behoved all of us to consider the implications of what Mr. de Valera said . . . But times change and leaders change and if you think that Jack Lynch is the embodiment of Fianna Fáil Republicanism, you don't know the Burgh Quay scene or Big Daddy's Fianna Fáil Party . . . Burgh Quay, by making hawkish noises ensures that true blue Republicanism survives in Fianna Fáil thus keeping faith

> with the past. Don't mind what Jack is saying, Jack has to make the appropriate noises – but we know the score and we have the measure. Thus the doves will follow Jack at the ballot box, and the hawks will follow the lead which Vivion through his paper, the official journal, is giving the faithful.[26]

According to Healy, there were two distinct ideologies within the Fianna Fáil party. While Lynch and his official Fianna Fáil represented the wholly constitutional party, Vivion de Valera and the *Irish Press* represented the slightly constitutional party of old. Within the party there existed 'a feeling among some that Fianna Fáil had drifted from its roots and no longer reflected the republican vision that had inspired its founders. The removal of Lynch and his replacement by Haughey was regarded by them as a way of changing the underlying philosophy of government and reverting to the original Fianna Fáil ethos of vibrant nationalism.'[27] But while it was public knowledge that there were two factions within Fianna Fáil, nobody really knew which side, if any, the *Irish Press* supported. Nonetheless, this attempt by Healy to demonstrate that the paper was anti-Lynch had an ulterior motive. Healy was a lifelong friend of Charles Haughey, who was still biding his time for the leadership of Fianna Fáil.[28] By exaggerating the lack of support for Lynch within Fianna Fáil and the *Irish Press*, it was Healy himself who was trying to undermine Lynch's position. For its part, the Lynch faction had no complaints to make about the *Irish Press*. Indeed, the political coverage was probably more favourable to Lynch given his friendship with Michael Mills. According to one Lynch supporter, the party did not notice an anti-Lynch agenda in the paper. While it was 'perhaps a stronger advocate of awareness of Northern Ireland . . . the *Irish Press* was not anti-Lynch, it was neutral'.[29] Healy's campaign was relentless, however, and in 1974 Healy again proclaimed that Vivion de Valera and the *Irish Press* were trying to hound Lynch from office by undermining his northern policy:

> His paper's tacit concern for the Provos has often been attributed to Tim Pat Coogan, the current editor, but old Burgh Quay hacks think that in political matters it is de Valera's policy that is printed . . . He has been careful to keep his roles separate, and sentiments of understanding of the Provos which appear in his paper have not been repeated in Dáil Éireann. . . . Sean Lemass began the de-stalinisation process, he gave de-facto recognition to Stormont . . . we heard nothing from Major Vivion de Valera and his paper echoed the chorus of approval for the stroke of Sean Lemass going to Stormont . . . In all

> the years when Jack Lynch worked towards Sunningdale, publisher Vivion de Valera signalled his reservations, but deputy Vivion de Valera kept his civil tongue in his loyal party head.[30]

This was also a misrepresentation of Vivion's Dáil speeches, as the sentiments expressed were the same as those articulated in the *Irish Press*, namely highlighting the root causes of the northern conflict. While Vivion often referred to the troubles as 'the product of an unnatural situation in the north', he also often reiterated that he held 'no brief' for the IRA.[31] Lynch's leadership troubles were given a brief respite when the party's founder, Eamon de Valera, died on 29 August 1975. The following day's edition of the *Irish Press* led with a full front-page portrait of its founder. As well as devoting four pages of news coverage to his death, the paper also published a ten-page memorial supplement on de Valera's long career in Irish politics. Its half-page editorial lamented that 'the passing of Mr de Valera' marked 'the end of a heroic era in Irish history'. Referring to his role in founding the paper, it noted that 'the *Irish Press* was born out of Mr de Valera's resolve to see Ireland become a really independent nation and of his concern for social justice and economic development in Ireland'.[32] The paper, like the rest of the national media, also gave extensive coverage to de Valera's state funeral, during which the country came to a standstill. In a curious move, however, the coalition government kept the public offices of all its departments open on the day of the burial – a move that was criticised by the *Irish Press* as being disrespectful to one of the state's founders. The campaign against Lynch's leadership recommenced soon afterwards. Healy was a passionate follower of Haughey and 'believed that whatever went against Haughey was bad for the country'. In 1976, when the first challenge arose, 'Healy supported Haughey while the *Irish Press* took a neutral line'.[33] In its coverage of the party's 1976 ard fheis, it was anything but anti-Lynch. According to the paper, the 'ard fheis was a notable triumph for the leader Mr Lynch'. His presidential address was 'the highlight of the gathering' for which he received 'an enthusiastic reception'. It was clear that he had 'rallied the party' and was 'soundly in control and firmly set to continue in the leadership'.[34] Indeed, when Haughey asked Vivion to propose him as leader in 1979, the latter refused and finally put paid to the rumours that he was a Haughey advocate.[35]

As the coalition's term of office continued, all of the nation's papers commented on the emergency legislation that it introduced in response to the escalating conflict in Northern Ireland and the assassination by the IRA in Dublin of the British ambassador to Ireland, Christopher Ewart-Biggs, in July 1976. The Emergency Powers Bill and the Criminal Law Bill were both introduced in 1976 and included the declaration of a state of emergency within the republic and a provision for the detention of suspects for seven days without charge. Section 3 of the Criminal Law Bill dealt directly with incitement and was the most ambiguous and the most contentious section of the bill:

> Any person who, expressly or by implication, directly or through another person or persons, or by advertisement, propaganda or any other means, incites or invites another person (or other persons generally) to join an unlawful organisation or to take part in, support or assist its activities shall be guilty of an offence and shall be liable on conviction on indictment to imprisonment for a term not exceeding ten years.[36]

The government's attempt to cover all possible sources of incitement, without defining exactly what constituted incitement, meant that the wording of the section was extremely ambiguous and could be interpreted to suit the state on a case by case basis. It was in this way that the section had implications for the way the media reported court proceedings of those charged with political crimes. For example, if a member of an illegal organisation availed of his or her right to give a speech from the dock, reporters could fall foul of the law by merely reporting the general thrust of the speech. The same dilemma applied to a newspaper printing readers' letters that were partisan or sympathetic to the views of illegal organisations. By extension, the same applied to a newspaper's editorial column. In essence, the proposer of the section, the Labour Party's spokesperson on the north, Conor Cruise O'Brien, 'tried to introduce a Section 31 type restriction on papers; the letters to the editor column in any newspaper is a podium for free expression, but now the editor was to be held responsible for the views expressed'.[37] While the NUJ demanded that the section be dropped, the *Irish Press* – the newspaper that came closest 'to expressing the undercurrent of sympathy that still remains for the IRA goal of a united Ireland' – also condemned the section.[38] In one interview, Tim Pat Coogan stated that of all the nation's editors he felt most vulnerable and that he was certain that the *Irish Press* would be 'intimidated'. As editor, he would 'either hold back an exposé of mistreatment of IRA men in our jails' or understand that he 'would have to join them'.[39] The above situation was remarkably similar to Frank Gallagher's attempts to highlight the beating of IRA prisoners in 1932 and the government's reaction of trying to silence it by a military tribunal. Given that O'Brien proposed the legislation shortly before the *Irish Times* exposed the existence of a 'Heavy Gang' of interrogators within the Garda Síochána and the ill-treatment of prisoners in custody, the similarities are striking.

The controversy really erupted when Bernard Nossitor of the *Washington Post* interviewed Conor Cruise O'Brien. In the course of the interview, O'Brien opined that there was 'a cultural problem' in the south with regard to both the IRA and the north.[40] Nossitor thus got 'the distinct impression' that Section 3 was 'regarded by the minister as one attempt to change the cultural setting'. According to Nossitor, O'Brien then 'began pulling out letters that he regarded as typical products of a wrong-headed culture'. When asked whether he would 'prosecute the letter writers, he said he wouldn't do that, but he indicated that he was interested in the medium that gave them print'.[41] O'Brien then 'read from two letters to the *Irish Press* which had been sent in by indignant readers complaining that the fund set up in honour of the murdered Ambassador . . . was a desecration of the memory of 1916'. According to Nossitor's interview, O'Brien's view was that this material was part of 'a whole framework of teaching, of ballads of popular awe that enabled the IRA to survive, even to flourish and most of all to recruit young and impressionable people'.[42] After O'Brien had produced the *Irish Press* letters file to Nossiter, the latter went directly to the Press Group offices and told Tim Pat Coogan about the file. The paper's political correspondent, Michael Mills, was immediately dispatched to interview the attorney general Declan Costello about the legislation. Costello confirmed that 'if the *Irish Press* continued to print such letters then he would charge the editor'.[43] According to Mills, within the coalition 'there was a feeling that the *Irish Press* was subversive to the state; that it was justifying and provoking IRA killings'.[44] The fact that Vivion de Valera was on holiday allowed Tim Pat Coogan to, in his own words, 'run the *Irish Press* like a real paper' and the revelation that O'Brien had kept files on the paper led to several bitter exchanges between both.[45]

In one particularly strong editorial, the paper warned readers that the legislation paved 'the way for full-scale political censorship' and noted that 'the Letters to the Editor which appear on weekdays in the *Irish Press* appear only a few centimetres away from this editorial column – a very short step indeed could cause Dr O'Brien and those who think like him to cross under the umbrella of their infamous Act and further suppress opinion'.[46] The editorial also compared O'Brien to the former American president Richard Nixon who had used 'the red scare technique and the compilation of hate lists similar to Dr O'Brien's dossier'. According to the editorial, by using 'the IRA scare, the Irish version of Mr Nixon's tactics', anyone who objected to Section 3 could be 'attacked in just the same way as the proponents of the continuation of the Vietnam War called its critics soft on communism'. In Ireland this could 'be adapted in view of the appalling crimes of the IRA to supporting the IRA'. By doing this, O'Brien had set out 'to undermine the freedom of the press in this country, inhibiting public discussion and the free flow of information to the electorate'.[47] In a subsequent Dáil debate, O'Brien admitted that he believed that newspapers were the favourite medium of 'recruitment propaganda' of the IRA, but claimed that the *Irish Press* had misrepresented his position as he kept the file only in his capacity as a legislator. He had 'started this terrible collection of newspaper clippings' in this capacity because it seemed 'that some of the matter being carried in the correspondence columns of the *Irish Press* . . . between the time of the murder of the British ambassador and the recall of the Dáil, was relevant to the legislation now before the House'.[48] O'Brien also read one letter from the file which he personally found objectionable into the Dáil record. The letter in question objected to the setting up of a memorial fund for the assassinated British ambassador. In response, Neil Blaney expressed his sorrow that the objectionable sentiments came from the paper's letters page and not its editorial column. Despite this, Blaney observed that he should at least be thankful that the *Irish Press* would 'occasionally publish such a letter' either as 'an attempt to hold on to some of their circulation' or as a 'genuine effort on the part of their editorial and management staff to display both sides of the coin'.[49]

In any event, O'Brien sought to reassure the nation's media institutions by stating that it would not be him but rather the Director of Public Prosecutions who would enforce the contentious section. He also stated that once the section was law, it would pose no threat to newspapers as they would be too afraid to publish anything that might be interpreted as breaching the section. According to O'Brien, an editor contemplating the publication of a letter similar to the one he had quoted from 'would be likely to consult his legal advisors' with the net result of a 'significant diminution in the publication of pro-IRA propaganda'. In a convoluted use of logic, O'Brien stated that 'those who publish such material' as he had quoted would not 'be in any danger under the new law' because they would 'rightly take good care not to break the law'. They were, O'Brien observed, 'not the stuff out of which martyrs are made although they have published material which may have made martyrs out of other people'.[50]

This statement that newspapers would be extra careful about what they printed once the section became law was nothing more than a thinly disguised threat, as the section was so ambiguous that no newspaper would know how the law would be interpreted until it unwittingly fell foul of it. However, outspoken Fine Gael deputy Oliver J. Flanagan, whose thinking on the subject was very much in line with O'Brien's, defended Section 3. According to Flanagan, the press had 'grave responsibilities' to the state and was useful for 'molding public opinion, expressing views, in publishing truth' and swaying public opinion.[51] It was, however, very possible for 'an irresponsible person' to become an editor and, as a consequence, irresponsible editorials had been published. According to Flanagan, the publication of some articles that he had read constituted 'gross misuse of journalistic privilege' and thus he supported Section 3 in the hope that it would end such a practice.[52] The following day, the *Irish Press* took both O'Brien and Flanagan to task for their justification of Section 3. According to the paper, 'all Dr O'Brien could do, even in the privileged confines of the Dáil, was root out one isolated letter and quote from it', whereas the paper's correspondence columns had given 'a fair hearing to both points of view in the controversy'. It also criticised Flanagan's 'notably foolish speech'. According to the paper, when Flanagan had spoken of irresponsible editorials that had been published in the past, what 'he meant was editorials which had attacked him over some of the extra-ordinary things he has said in the past'. It also opined that while both O'Brien and Flanagan knew exactly 'how the proposed measures could be used as a stick to beat the press under a general guise of a drive on the IRA', they also had an ulterior motive – to 'exact retribution for past criticisms of themselves and to stifle other such criticisms being made in the future'. O'Brien had produced his file of readers' letters 'as evidence of the sort of thing he found distasteful in Irish life and indicated that far from wanting the debate enlarged, he wanted it curtailed'.[53] To prove its point, the *Irish Press* reprinted all readers' letters that it had published commenting on the killing of the British ambassador. While some letters condemned the killing, others, while not condoning the killing, pointed out that as long as there was a British presence in

Ireland, conflict was inevitable. Altogether, the letters page adopted an objective approach in printing both sides of the debate.

In the subsequent Dáil debate deputy Barry Desmond of the Labour Party called on those who were 'howling blue murder about the appalling imposition' that Section 3 would have on the freedom of the press to do 'some internal analysis on the pressures that shareholders, directors, and advertisers exert on the policies and articles of such newspapers'.[54] He then reminded the house that the *Irish Press* was 'owned and controlled by a Member of this House' and noted that the 'irony should not be lost in the context of the debate'. To those who spoke about freedom of the press, Desmond posed the question of how free were 'some of the workings of that paper over the years' but resisted the 'temptation to comment on the editorial policy of individual newspapers, particularly that of the *Irish Press*'. While the paper had the 'best political correspondent in the country', he could only wish that he could 'say the same about the editor'.[55] But despite such sentiments, Desmond conceded that the section was 'more a statement of principle than a piece of legislation', a 'blank cheque' and 'a licence to go ahead and prosecute very widely'.[56] Eventually, due to mounting public opposition to the section, the government caved in and accepted a Fianna Fáil amendment that ensured that the words that could be interpreted as pertaining to the media (from 'who' down to 'incites') were deleted. The amendment was welcomed by the *Irish Press* and, in an article entitled 'Triumph for the Press', the paper termed it as 'one of the most notable victories for the freedom of the press since the foundation of the state'.[57] The paper's editorial noted that it was 'extremely gratifying for the *Irish Press* . . . that the government should so greatly water down the infamous section of the Criminal Law Bill which had given rise to such widespread fears of press censorship'.[58] Accusing Conor Cruise O'Brien of trying to impress northern unionist politicians, the paper pointed out that both the *Belfast Telegraph* and the *Belfast News* had editorially condemned Section 3 and that the northern unionist community would respect southerners more after 'being allowed to see us freely discussing ourselves, warts and all'.[59] To Coogan, the fact that O'Brien lost his Dáil seat in the following year's general election was 'significant'. Likewise, he found it 'ironic' that the Fianna Fáil party that had been responsible for the draconian Section 31, 'suddenly stood up for free speech'.[60] By the time Vivion de Valera came back from his honeymoon, the controversy was over, but Coogan had shown 'how strong the paper could be'.[61] But the harsh criticism directed at the coalition government for its censorship measures was very much at odds with the support the paper had given to the previous Fianna Fáil administration that had invoked Section 31 and introduced the Offences Against the State Amendment Bill. While censorship for public service television and radio and abolishing confidentiality for sources were acceptable to the *Irish Press* under a Fianna Fáil government, press censorship to prevent incitement under a Fine Gael/Labour government was totally unacceptable. Notwithstanding the fact that Conor Cruise O'Brien had produced *Irish Press* readers' letters as a basis for the move, the principle of censorship was the same. The fact that the paper had defended censorship under a Fianna Fáil administration and campaigned against censorship when the party was in opposition seemed lost on both the party and the paper. Despite the adoption of the 'fair to all, friendly to Fianna Fáil' editorial philosophy, it seemed as if the paper's policy was still influenced to some degree by official party thinking. This was clearly demonstrated during the 1976 presidential crisis.

When the emergency legislation was finally passed by the Dáil, President Cearbhall O'Dálaigh, having consulted with the Council of State, signed the Criminal Law Bill but referred the Emergency Powers Bill to the Supreme Court to test its constitutionality. When the court ruled in favour of the legislation, O'Dálaigh duly signed the bill into law but shortly afterwards the country was plunged into a constitutional crisis. Described by one colleague as 'a very legalistic man . . . very strong in integrity . . . if he felt a certain way, he'd push for his rights under the law of the constitution to say it, right up to conflict point',[62] Cearbhall O'Dálaigh had been a staunch Fianna Fáil activist with a distinguished career as Irish language editor of the *Irish Press*, as Attorney General between 1946–48 and as Chief Justice between 1961–72. O'Dálaigh became president in December 1974, following the sudden death of Erskine Childers, but sensationally resigned less than a year and a half later. His resignation was precipitated by comments made by the coalition's Minister for Defence, Fine Gael's Patrick Donegan, to which the president took grave exception. The comments arose from O'Dálaigh's decision to refer the aforementioned Emergency Powers Bill to the Supreme Court. During a speech at an army barracks, Donegan called the president 'a thundering disgrace' and stated that 'the army must stand behind the state'.[63] The significance of a government minister criticising the head of the defence forces in an army barracks and implying that the president, unlike the army, was not loyal to the state was not lost on the only journalist present, Don Lavery of the *Westmeath Examiner*, who passed the story on to the national papers. Given that government ministers hold office by virtue of the seal bestowed upon them by the president, a constitutional showdown was inevitable. O'Dálaigh considered the constitutional relationship between his office and that of the Minister for Defence as 'irreparably breached'.

In a strong attack on the coalition, the *Irish Press* noted that 'as often happens with a decaying government', it was 'lurching from crisis to crisis' with the latest one being 'highly discreditable to any cabinet'. According to the paper, any minister 'so utterly oblivious to the constitution . . . and so discourteous to the person who gave him the seal of that office' deserved to be 'dismissed out of hand'.[64] Although Donegan offered to resign, Taoiseach Liam Cosgrave rejected it. Fianna Fáil subsequently tabled a Dáil motion calling on Donegan to resign and when this was defeated, O'Dálaigh resigned 'to protect the dignity and independence of the Presidency as an institution'.[65] Again taking a swipe at the government's emergency legislation, the *Irish Press* stated that since the people's rights had previously been attacked 'by a reactionary, censorious, window dressing government, determined to use the law and order issue in place of an economic plan', it was no surprise that the president, as custodian of the constitution, was attacked in such a 'rude fashion' wherein Donegan had called 'into question the President's right to exercise his function'.[66] In response, the paper's nemesis, Conor Cruise O'Brien, condemned the paper's 'self-righteous howl for blood'. According to O'Brien, the 'cry of the Fianna Fáil pack' was the 'natural product of ravenous political hunger'.[67] The task of finding a successor to O'Dálaigh posed a problem for the coalition; by standing over a gross insult to the president, it received the blame for the constitutional crisis. As a result, both Fine Gael and the Labour Party declined to field candidates and agreed with Fianna Fáil that if a compromise candidate were selected from that party, then he or she would be returned unopposed. Vivion de Valera was proposed but proved unacceptable to the coalition. Jack Lynch was also put under pressure from within the party to run, but insisted on staying on as party leader.[68] In the end, the coalition and Fianna Fáil agreed on Patrick Hillery. Thus began the 'Draft O'Dálaigh' campaign. Organised by members of Dublin City and County Community Councillors, the campaign was basically a nationwide crusade to convince O'Dálaigh that he had 'a national duty' to renominate himself as a candidate for the presidency to ensure that 'the integrity of the Presidential Office be kept intact and clear of party politics'.[69] The campaign took the form of a series of adverts during November 1976 that criticised Fianna Fáil's agreement with the coalition government on a compromise candidate, thus dispensing with the need for an election. According to the advert, Fianna Fáil's statement that it awaited the announcement of the coalition's candidates so the public would 'have an opportunity of electing their President' reeked of 'political chicanery' because 'it was generally known that the coalition would not nominate anybody provided Dr Hillery was nominated by Fianna Fáil'. According the advert, O'Dálaigh was the only person that could 'prevent the Presidential Office from being degraded by the political parties for their own ends'.[70] Readers were thus encouraged to fill in a form within the advert, urging O'Dálaigh to renominate himself. The advert was accepted by and appeared in both the *Irish Independent* and the *Irish Times*. However, although the *Evening Press* had accepted classified adverts from the same group for other public campaigns, such as the Dublin Bay Oil Refinery Campaign, this particular advert was refused by the Press Group (it made it to the stone of the *Sunday Press* before being withdrawn) simply because it highlighted Fianna Fáil's collusion with the coalition government in appointing a successor to O'Dálaigh without consulting the electorate.

While the paper had all the appearance of a formidable medium, internally the rot was slowly beginning to manifest itself, particularly in the realm of industrial relations. The task of dealing with the various trade unions fell to personnel manager Colm Traynor who was 'always up front in negotiations . . . he was never a de Valera hack and would tell you straight that there was very little he could do at times'.[71] A sudden printers' strike during the 1973 general election had resulted in the *Irish Times* finally breaking the 'one out, all out' agreement that the Dublin Newspapers Management Committee had adopted to weaken the bargaining power of various trade unions (particularly the print unions). Stripped of the protection of other managements, the Press Group now had to deal with trade unions on its own. In July 1974, after six months of negotiations, management and the NUJ agreed a comprehensive three-year productivity deal. While staff received enhanced wages, the company secured agreement for 'greater flexibility in working hours, range of duties and effective use of manpower'.[72] Significantly, the agreement also stipulated that middle management could join the NUJ and be bound by its rules.

One such rule was that of attendance at mandatory meetings of the chapel. On previous occasions when journalists had been summoned to a mandatory meeting, editorial executives had produced the papers. Under the new agreement this could no longer happen. Negotiations for the agreement's renewal began some months before its expiry and a new twelve-month deal was agreed. But despite this progress, change in the upper echelons of the company was non-existent. By 1975, the average age of the company's directors was sixty-nine. At sixty-four years of age, Vivion de Valera was the youngest director on the board that still included Sean Nunan (seventy-eight), P. B. Pierce (eighty), C. S. Furlong (sixty-seven) and former general manager Jack Dempsey.[73] Dempsey had held the position of general manager for thirty-five years before he retired in 1977 but he continued as company chairman until 1981. Indeed, it was the duo of Dempsey and Vivion de Valera that essentially controlled the Press Group. While Vivion controlled the editorial side, Dempsey concentrated on the business and organisational aspects. While such an aged board probably kept the traditional republican ethos of the *Irish Press* alive, in the long term it had detrimental effects on the company. While such a traditional style of management may have suited the populist era of the 1930s, it was wholly inappropriate to the competitive newspaper market of the 1970s. Whatever about its performance in the past, it was hardly a collection of men that was likely to successfully deal with the problems of modern newspaper production methods. As the 1970s wore on, Vivion became ill with cancer but still retained control of the company, despite pleas that he train in a successor. He resisted such pressure with the assertion that he was determined to keep 'close in'.[74] But as *Hibernia* magazine pointedly noted, 'if he [Vivion] dropped dead in the morning, the present structure would be ill-prepared to carry on'.[75] Thus unlike its competitors, a recomposition of the board to bring modern ideas to the company never occurred. The lack of mechanical modernisation also concerned both management and staff. According to one editor, 'although the company was successful in the 1960s, it did not modernise its plant machinery. There was union intransigence – they did not want to know about the new technology. But if de Valera had hammered out an agreement, while costing a lot at the time, in the long term it may have ensured the company's survival'.[76] However, according to one former union negotiator, 'as far back as 1974, house agreement documents were advising management to move into technology. For management to subsequently claim that the unions were hostile just doesn't wash.' While the print unions wanted 'redundancy deals, extra money and all sorts of things . . . any right management would have found ways of negotiating on these points'. Money was in short supply, however, and 'staff never knew much about the profits or where they were going. They certainly weren't ploughed into plant machinery that the company was crying out for.'[77] Vivion also rejected many innovative ideas that were suggested by staff. When journalists advocated the development of a specific agricultural section or supplement, 'general manager Jack Dempsey would listen but the Major would not'. The *Irish Independent* and *Irish Times* again took the lead with the introduction of agricultural and property supplements. Indeed, Vivion was 'particularly anxious regarding the development of property supplements because he thought it could lead to corruption among the staff'.[78] While allegations of excessive coverage of certain building developments by journalists at another newspaper only strengthened this belief, the paper's rivals flourished because of the extra advertising revenue. Indeed, in later years, the *Irish Press* found it almost impossible to attract property advertising, simply because both the *Irish Independent* and the *Irish Times* had the market sown up.

The mid-1970s also saw an economic downturn hit the Irish newspaper industry hard. The cost of wages and newsprint soared and during the first five months of 1975 the volume of advertising in the Dublin dailies dropped by an average of twenty-six per cent. Management at the *Irish Times* responded rapidly and acclimatised to the new economic environment by establishing the Irish Times Trust that replaced the board of directors with a board of governors. The trust committed itself to publishing 'an independent newspaper primarily concerned with serious issues . . . free from any form of personal or of party political, commercial, religious or other section control'. News was to be 'as accurate and as comprehensive' as possible while 'comment and opinion' were to be 'informed and responsible' and 'identifiable from fact'.[79] Despite some criticism about the financial arrangements surrounding the establishment of the trust, 'it was generally accepted that the move to trust status gave the newspaper greater independence and secured it against takeover possibly from outside the state'.[80] Fundamental change also occurred at Independent Newspapers, where T. V. Murphy had to find the resources to modernise and preserve the titles, a dilemma that saw him sell them to one of Ireland's most successful businessmen, Tony O'Reilly. The latter brought 'a business ethic to Independent Newspapers; this included modern management techniques, accepted industry standards, specialised departments to handle financial, circulation, advertising and editorial matters as well as introducing the use of consultants and market research'.[81]

The process of modernisation began with the reinvention of the *Evening Herald* in the late 1970s. At the time the *Evening Press*, with a circulation of 170,000, was the preferred choice of advertisers and the new owner knew 'something drastic had to be done with the *Herald*'.[82] Intensive market research suggested a more aggressive competitive approach to newsgathering and the addition of new features. While 'the old image of the *Herald* was that of an inner city working class paper', the new management 'moved it out of that rut by including a section on junior soccer'. This had the effect of creating 'a new audience as well as retaining the old readers and the subsequent market research showed the reception of the paper to be good'.[83] The paper was relaunched as a tabloid aimed at a younger, urban-based readership in 1982 and this change saw sales drop by over seven and a half per cent as the paper lost some of its older traditional readership. Despite this, the paper still managed to close the gap on the *Evening Press* by attracting a larger share of the under thirty-five-year-old readership and thus a larger share of advertising. Where once there had been a difference of 45,000 copies a day between the two papers, by 1983 this had dropped to 26,000 – the difference mainly being that the *Evening Press* had a larger rural readership, whereas the *Evening Herald* was aimed primarily at the Dublin market.[84] The reinvention was funded by O'Reilly's other business interests; capital was redeployed to remould the paper, compensate for its drop in circulation and market the new product until it established a niche for itself in the marketplace.

The next title tackled was the *Irish Independent*. Again the first step the company took was to commission extensive market research into how the paper was perceived by the public. Lansdowne market research found that the public viewed the paper as 'dull, sensational, parochial, rural, unreliable, lacking in appeal to females and that no-one identified with it'.[85] Nonetheless, the market research paid dividends, as the talents of editor Vincent Doyle and marketing director Joe Hayes combined to change the paper. What the market research showed them 'was that the Farming Independent supplement was regarded as basic agricultural news whereas a service such as advice on what machinery to buy etc. was in big demand. The change was tremendously successful.'[86] While this ensured the retention of the provincial readership, the introduction of a news analysis section, a property section and a modern business section all played crucial parts in attracting the much sought-after urban upmarket readership. The results of subsequent market research showed just how much the paper had changed; it was now 'seen to display the common touch with authority, had a core audience right across the social spectrum, had an improved layout of content and was perceived to be trying harder'.[87] The paper had in effect evolved from a family controlled paper with a recognised party allegiance and fixed moral view to just another commercial enterprise dominated by financial considerations.

The reinvention of the group's third title, the *Sunday Independent*, did not begin until 1984 under the editorship of Aengus Fanning, who steered the paper away from traditional Sunday journalism to its present-day magazine style format. According to Fanning, he preferred to edit 'a Sunday newspaper described as show business as distinct from the self-importance and pomposity of the Fourth Estate'. With its 'entertainment, information, analysis, opinion, provocative pieces and gossip', the paper became 'a magazine wrapped up in a newspaper'.[88] The rethink saw the paper successfully reorientate itself from its traditional and ageing readership to a younger, urban and more affluent readership. By encapsulating the social and economic changes that were making Ireland increasingly urbanised and consumerist, the paper soon became the preferred choice of advertisers. Initially the reinvention was a spectacular success, with the paper attracting A and B category readers in thousands. It also increased its share of the C and D readership market, something that normally proves impossible for a newspaper to do without losing A and B readers. Although the paper was extremely successful as regards circulation, there was a price to pay in content. With the paper continually trumpeting the opinions of its columnists, opinion fatigue soon set in and readership figures began to drop, reflecting the fall in popularity of what market research called the paper's 'pub and disco journalism'.[89] By the mid-1990s, market research found that readers viewed the paper as 'trivial, cheap, predictable, sensationalist and lacking credibility'.[90] Given the paper's venomous anti-republican ethos, sales in Northern Ireland and the republic's border counties were found to be particularly weak, with readers advocating 'a more balanced coverage'.[91] Numerous events in the late 1990s finally forced the paper to take stock of what it had become. The notorious Gordon Thomas interview with Bishop Eamon Casey in April 1993 and the murder of the paper's crime correspondent Veronica Guerin in June 1996 saw many criticise the paper's policy of a story at any price.[92] The gradual assimilation of Sinn Féin into mainstream politics made the paper's virulent anti-provo ethos outdated while its venomous attacks on personalities such as John Hume made the paper look out of touch with an Ireland that was searching for peace. The marathon libel action against the paper taken by Proinsais de Rossa in 1997 and the embarrassing revelation that high-profile social columnist Terry Keane had not written what was printed under her by-line for several years also undermined the credibility of the paper. Despite all this, the paper's standing reached an all-time low in October 2000 with its bizarre front-page article on the Paralympics.[93] The public revulsion to the Mary Ellen Synon opinion column resulted in some shops refusing to stock the paper and health boards threatening to withdraw advertising worth £8 million per annum from the paper. At a company where profit is of paramount importance, the controversy again focused minds on the paper's identity.

At the Press Group no such radical change occurred. Instead, in an attempt to weather the storm of the economic crisis, management increased the cover prices of the Press titles. Management also sanctioned cut-backs in overtime and expenses, much to the chagrin of the company's already hard pressed workforce. Shortly before the expiry of the 1977 productivity deal, negotiations began in April 1978 for a replacement deal. In the negotiations, the NUJ sought a twelve per cent increase in pay (as opposed to a national pay agreement rate of eight per cent) and a reduction from thirty-five working hours to thirty-two. According to one union negotiator, while 'the reduction in hours was universal throughout the EU', inflating pay demands were par for the course in negotiations. The twelve per cent pay increase 'would have been reduced in the course of negotiations through a nod and a wink here and there'.[94] Management seemed unprepared for haggling and after two weeks of negotiations, offered a mere two per cent pay increase and the requested reduction in hours. It was from here that the company descended into industrial chaos, with each side blaming the other. For its part, the NUJ chapel was 'more than willing to meet and discuss all aspects of the new house agreement but was faced by the general tardiness on the part of *Irish Press* management'.[95] While the latter had agreed to meet a minimum of three times a week, it cancelled the opening meeting because they had not prepared their proposals. Negotiations finally opened the following week but the undertaking to meet three times a week was only honoured for the first fortnight. The chapel was then informed that the acting general manager, Michael Walsh, had a long-standing engagement dating back to the beginning of the year to visit America on company business. As a result, the negotiations were summarily adjourned with the promise of a full week of talks on his return. The negligence of management was exemplified when the existing house agreement lapsed at the end of June: 'at no stage was there any request from management to arrange any interim continuation of the agreement pending the conclusion of the talks'.[96]

The company also faced difficulty in dealing with the printing unions:

> The printers were frequently on go-slows which ensured that the *Evening Press* was constantly late in the marketplace. This kind of industrial action made proofreading virtually impossible and the papers were filled with misprints. The motto seemed to be 'It'll do'. Stoppages of one kind or another were frequent. Some sections of the technical staff had a 'sick roster' which ensured that a specific number of overtime shifts would be made available through bogus illnesses.[97]

Such actions were, of course, disastrous for the Press Group. With the *Evening Press* arriving late on the market, it gave a distinct advantage to its rival the *Evening Herald*, thus reducing the Press Group's revenue and competitiveness even more. Furthermore, during the 1970s, the *Irish Times* and Independent Newspapers carried out extensive market research, examining readership profiles and targeting the young, urban and affluent generation of readers as the older, rural generation of readers steadily declined. The Press Group made no attempt to tap into or relate to this new market and instead relied all too heavily on its existing ageing and rural readership. At Burgh Quay, the only modernisation to take place during the 1970s was the rebuilding of the company's premises. Rebuilding began in 1971, with an outlay of £300,000 saved up by Vivion de Valera. Costs soared and rather than borrow money to continue the work, it was stopped until the company raised more cash from its own resources. As one journalist politely put it, the company had 'a most prudent management in money matters'.[98] This novel approach to renovation ensured that the process of rebuilding took nearly eight years to complete, making life at Burgh Quay even more uncomfortable for those working there.

But despite the festering internal problems at the Press Group and the perceived uneasiness between Jack Lynch and the *Irish Press*, both Fianna Fáil and the paper rallied together for the 1977 general election campaign. Reflecting the global economic changes that the end of the post-war boom heralded, Fianna Fáil's manifesto concentrated on economic matters, such as how to combat rising unemployment and inflation. A new Department of Economic Planning and the abolition of car tax were just two of the many proposals put forward by the party to entice voters. In contrast, the coalition badly misjudged the public mood and concentrated all its energies on security issues. During the campaign, the *Irish Press* was highly defensive of Fianna Fáil. This was prompted by several hysterical anti-Fianna Fáil outbursts by the paper's adversary, Conor Cruise O'Brien. With the party's manifesto receiving huge public attention, the coalition desperately tried to swing the debate around to security issues. In this respect the 1977 election resembled the 1932 election when the Cumann na nGaedheal government used the threat of communism to scare the electorate off voting for Fianna Fáil During the 1977 election, the coalition government used the security scare to the same end by trying to use the arms crisis to discredit Fianna Fáil's commitment to constitutional politics. Similarly, just as in 1932, the *Irish Press* sprang to Fianna Fáil's defence and castigated the coalition's scare-mongering. According to the paper, the coalition's efforts 'to make a Fianna Fáil victory appear a harbinger of onslaughts by gunmen on the north with official connivance' was merely 'a cynical exercise in dirty politics, played at the expense of the feelings and the real interest of the north of Ireland people'.[99] The paper also condemned O'Brien's 'attempts to use the events of the arms trial era as a stick to beat Fianna Fáil with, rather than adopting the more responsible approach of debating the contents of the Fianna Fáil manifesto as opposed to those of the coalition's'. His misuse of the northern situation demonstrated his 'pretty shoddy method of demonstrating his real lack of concern for the people of Northern Ireland'. He had not 'elevated it out of any concern for the north or its people, but only to try to do down Fianna Fáil through the person of Mr Haughey'.[100] It was widely acknowledged within the coalition that O'Brien's outbursts were doing it more harm than good and so when it decided to challenge Lynch on the northern problem, it replaced O'Brien with Garret FitzGerald, a move that did not go unheeded by the *Irish Press*. The paper noted that the 'coalition did not allow their more customary hitman, Dr Conor Cruise O'Brien, to attack Mr Lynch . . . Dr Garret FitzGerald was chosen to do the job instead'. According to the paper, Fitzgerald's 'carefully chosen fluencies unveiled the fact that a note of desperation' underlay 'the unfeeling use of the northern issue by the coalition'.[101]

The paper also pointed out 'the note of hypocrisy in the coalition's protestations about threats to democracy arising out of the attitudes to the north on the Fianna Fáil side'. Considering the coalition's preoccupation with security legislation and emergency powers, there was 'ample evidence of threats to democracy arising out of attitudes to the south on the coalition's side'. According to the paper, 'talking about the fears for constitutionalism under Fianna Fáil' conveniently overlooked the fact 'that it was a coalition cabinet's blatant disrespect for constitutional procedure which led to the first resignation of an Irish President in the history of the state, less than a year ago'.[102] It also reminded its readers that it was the *Irish Press* that had 'spearheaded a campaign that finally forced a change in legislation that would, if passed, have posed the greatest threat to the freedom of the press in any European country outside the Iron Curtain'. According to the paper, it was 'this debate and the events that followed which first exposed the myth of the coalition's invincibility and placed them where they now stand, on the slippery slope to electoral defeat, grasping ignominiously and meanly at straws blown from the northern whirlwind'.[103] On polling day, the *Irish Press*' acrimonious relationship with the coalition saw it 'unequivocally recommend that Fianna Fáil be returned to power',[104] and when the party won the biggest overall majority in the history of the state, the paper observed that the defeat contained 'a sharp rejection of the coalition, its personalities' and the 'condescending, academic irrelevancies of the "don't want to know" outgoing administration'.[105] Indeed, so big was the majority that, in words that the paper would be forced to eat two years later, it observed that 'the by-election, so long regarded as barometers of mid-term public opinion' would now 'almost be an irrelevance'.[106]

Despite the friendship between the party leader Jack Lynch and the paper's political correspondent Michael Mills, the latter never let it interfere with his job. This was certainly shown to be the case during the political upheaval of 1979 that ended Lynch's political career. In August of that year, the IRA assassinated a member of the British Royal family, Lord Mountbatten, in Co. Sligo and later that same day blew up a British army bus from the southern side of the border. In response, the British government demanded border security concessions from Lynch's government. The *Irish Press*, in the guise of Michael Mills, was the first paper to reveal that both governments had agreed a ten-kilometre over-flight zone along the border.[107]

> We had a very good relationship until the story about the cross-border flyovers. Of course it upset the relationship, but I was a journalist with a good story and I could not sit on it. I knew new security arrangements had been made and there was only one place that it could be – the air. When I put my idea to certain people they were visibly upset by my knowledge. I ran the story but it was denied by the government.[108]

The unconfirmed revelations caused consternation within Fianna Fáil but Lynch refused to reveal the details of any new arrangements. Thomas McEllistrim, a north Kerry deputy, immediately put down a motion for the forthcoming parliamentary party meeting seeking clarification on the matter from the Taoiseach. At the meeting, McEllistrim asked Lynch whether Mills' report was true and stated that if it were, Fianna Fáil would lose thousands of votes in the next election.[109] When McEllistrim had finished speaking, over thirty-five deputies raised their hands to contribute to the motion, but after hearing only a handful, Lynch ended the debate by stating that 'as of now, the British have not permission to over-fly the border'.[110] Despite the ambiguity of Lynch's answer, and despite the fact that other deputies wished to question Lynch further, McEllistrim decided 'not to question the Taoiseach's veracity' even though the issue 'left a lot of tension within the parliamentary party'.[111]

After the meeting, the *Irish Press* reported that Lynch had given an assurance that 'Irish sovereignty would not be affected in any way by any security arrangements made with the British government'. The strongest anger at the meeting was reserved for 'the press setting up these hares around the place . . . There was apparently strong criticism at the meeting of the reports first carried in the *Irish Press*'.[112] It was obvious, however, that in light of what the *Irish Press* had discovered, its support for Lynch was fading. A fortnight later, with Lynch under pressure to deliver two by-election victories in his native Cork and despite the unwritten rule of governments rarely winning by-elections, the paper noted that 'if Fianna Fáil lost both seats there would certainly be a re-evaluation of certain policies'.[113] When the government lost both contests, it noted that the defeats were a 'personal setback' for Lynch and that 'questions about the leadership' would 'certainly resurface'.[114] The following day, Lynch let a fatal truth slip from his lips when answering questions at a news conference in Washington. In one of those strange quirks of history, Sean Cronin, who had fled Burgh Quay in the late 1950s but who was by then the Washington correspondent of the *Irish Times*, asked Lynch about the new security arrangements. In an uncharacteristic slip of the tongue, Lynch finally admitted that security concessions had been granted to the British in the aftermath of the Mountbatten killing. That night Mills sent over his story stating that Lynch had confirmed his original story:

> It was at the Washington news conference that Jack slipped up. In reply to a question from Sean Cronin of the *Irish Times*, he replied that there was no change. He should have stopped there but then he said 'except in one slight respect'. This confirmed my story. The story appeared in the *Irish Press* and Bill Loughnane made an attack on Lynch. Lynch tried to have him expelled but failed. Of course our relationship suffered. He blamed me, but my duty was to the paper not to Jack.[115]

Mills' report stated that Lynch had 'confirmed that a new arrangement had been made by the British and Irish governments in regard to flying across the border for limited distances by military aircraft'. According to the report, Lynch had been asked 'by journalists at the National Press Club why the details had not been disclosed earlier, to which he replied that reports of the so called air corridor were without foundation. It was an assumption made by certain people he stated, that had no basis in fact. He then corrected himself and said "it had very little basis"'.[116] In the paper's first ever editorial directed against a Fianna Fáil Taoiseach, the *Irish Press* commented that 'if the Dáil, the Fianna Fáil parliamentary party and the Irish people could not be told at home about these arrangements, it seems curious that they should be made aware of them via Washington'.[117] In strong language, the paper criticised Lynch's cooperation with the British government, and more or less stated that for his leadership, the writing was on the wall:

> Here we have a proposal which has aroused and is going to arouse, very great passion not least among Fianna Fáil supporters about a real

> or imagined loss of sovereignty . . . And why are we doing it? To improve British security when Britain cannot even improve her own on the territory over which she claims sway against the wishes of the majority of the Irish people . . . Even in isolation, the Taoiseach's announcement would cause controversy but coming in the wake of the Cork by-election results, it seems certain that the much used cliché of a winter of discontent has suddenly received a new and very powerful validity.[118]

The paper's revelation caused turmoil in Fianna Fáil. While the country awaited Lynch's return from Washington, deputy Bill Loughnane publicly accused Lynch of misleading the parliamentary party in his response to McEllistrim's motion. Lynch immediately instructed the Tanaiste George Colley to have Loughnane expelled from the parliamentary party. But many senior backbenchers, including Vivion de Valera, resisted the move. Such was the consternation within the party that the issue didn't even get as far as a vote. The *Irish Press* also criticised the secrecy surrounding the new security measures and accused the Minister for Defence of 'stonewalling on details'.[119] As the pressure on Lynch mounted, however, the paper relented and commented that while 'there was bound to be criticism of the party leader . . . it should not be of a sort that makes a bad situation worse'. It noted that in Lynch's absence 'voices were raised against the Taoiseach within Fianna Fáil in a manner which would have been unacceptable had they been on the opposition side', whereas the leader of Fine Gael had 'showed himself mindful of the respect owing to the Prime Minister [*sic*] abroad on his country's business'.[120] Although the paper appealed to the party to drop 'the internal, disedifying party wrangling' and unite 'unequivocally behind resolute leadership', the damage had been done.[121] A petition demanding Lynch's immediate resignation had already begun to circulate and, when word of this leaked out, Lynch indicated that he intended to resign. When Lynch announced his resignation, the *Irish Press* commented that it was received with 'general regret', but noted that 'the dispute on the over-flights issue . . . had caused dissenting voices to be raised against him'. While it was inevitable that this 'created a note of challenge and uncertainty within the party and within the country', the paper praised Lynch's decision to resign to 'give his successor a chance to pull the party and the government together'.[122]

In the subsequent two-day tussle for the leadership, George Colley and Charles Haughey again did battle, with Lynch and most of the cabinet supporting Colley. Reporting the intense lobbying in a matter-of-fact way, the paper did not publish an editorial on the succession race, save for one that merely listed issues and priorities for the 'new man'. It did, however, publish five pages of reports on the division within the party and the last minute change of camps by some deputies. By this time, the Fianna Fáil 1977 manifesto had run into serious difficulties. The spending spree coupled with the international energy crisis saw public debt spiral upwards at an alarming rate. Capitalising on the disquiet within the party over this and the sovereignty surrender issue, Charles Haughey made a strong bid for the leadership. In a secret ballot, Haughey beat Colley by forty-four votes to thirty-eight and was thus elected party leader and Taoiseach. In an ironic sign of things to come, the ballot papers were burned in a metal bin, the smoke from which set off the fire alarm in Leinster House. According to the *Irish Press*, Haughey's succession 'generated a sort of glow of appreciation in the community, a realisation that someone of flair, drive and initiative' had taken over the helm at the nation's top post.[123] Opposition politicians were less than impressed with the party's choice and, upon his election as Taoiseach, many made stinging speeches attacking Haughey. These included Fine Gael's Garret FitzGerald. In what then looked like a bitter speech, Fitzgerald stated that he also spoke 'for many within Fianna Fáil who may not be free to say what they believe or to express their deep fears for the future of the country under the proposed leadership'.[124] He described Haughey as having 'an overweening ambition' not to serve but rather 'to dominate, even to control the state'. The new leader, he declared, came with a 'flawed pedigree'.[125] The *Irish Press* immediately sprang to Haughey's defence and condemned the 'petulance, vituperation and political distaste' displayed towards Haughey, whom it described as 'a pretty formidable opponent'.[126] In the years ahead, however, this formidable opponent was to have a most acrimonious relationship with the paper, as the all too frequent leadership heaves against him tore the party apart and again left the paper exposed to pro and anti-leadership faction fighting.

As the 1970s drew to a close, the paper itself had to deal with its own internal bickering over its northern coverage. During the winter of 1980, there occurred an incident described by one journalist as 'a palace revolution'.[127] At the time, seven republican prisoners were on hunger strike in the north's Maze Prison for recognition as political prisoners. In November, the former leader of the SDLP, Gerry Fitt, made a speech in the House of Commons in which he urged the

British government not to grant political status to the hunger strikers, arguing that it would escalate rather than diminish violence by enhancing recruitment to the IRA. The *Irish Press* responded to Fitt's speech with a hard-hitting editorial accusing him of 'succumbing to the old disease of the Irish at Westminister, the tone of the house, that siren call of English manners and English interests that has seduced so many Irish representatives away from their allegiances and those of the people who returned them in the first place'.[128] The editorial also condemned Fine Gael leader Garret FitzGerald for 'attempting to play politics with the hunger-striking H-Block men in the Dáil yesterday by pursuing his curiously personal vendetta against the Taoiseach with a would-be clever, coat-trailing invitation to the Taoiseach to join him in an exhortation to the hunger-strikers to call off their strike'. According to the editorial, 'their pronouncements over the last couple of days can only have served to ensure the British government to persevere with their hard-faced attitude and to press on to disaster'.[129] The editorial caused furore among *Irish Press* journalists, already divided over the paper's northern coverage. Many regarded this editorial as the last straw and felt the opening paragraph exceeded the boundaries of fair comment. Thirty-one journalists then took the unprecedented step of publicly disassociating themselves from the editorial by signing a telegram stating this to Fitt. According to one journalist involved, 'those who signed the telegram were the more independent souls' at the paper. The paper did not take any disciplinary action and there was no recrimination because 'the NUJ was very powerful at the time'.[130] Nonetheless, during the 1970s and 1980s, along with the *Sunday Press*, the *Irish Press* was the only national mainstream media voice to continually highlight the root causes of the northern conflict. In the south, it was easier to concentrate media coverage on the effects rather than on the root causes of the conflict. Successive government policy in the guise of censorship sought to block coverage of the northern problem from broadcast and print media. Such a policy reflected the hope that the problem would go unheeded by southern voters: 'for two decades censorship largely ensured that unpalatable truths were not aired. Republicans and entire nationalist communities were demonised. They were atavistic, reactionary, locked into an inexplicable nationalism that spawned mindless violence.'[131] The *Irish Press*, however, never engaged in such demonisation. While it condemned the violence, it sought to educate the southern population as to the root causes of the conflict and promoted compromise from both sides as a solution. In the mists of atrocity after atrocity, this philosophy gradually became associated with support for the IRA. In the light of the peace process and the radical revisions other national media such as the *Irish Times* and the Independent titles have had to make regarding republicanism, it is arguable that the paper's approach was correct in the long term. During the 1980s, however, it was the leadership of the Fianna Fáil party that dominated the paper's agenda.

CHAPTER SEVEN

One Leader, One Voice – The Haughey Years

> The paper was not subservient to Fianna Fáil. It stood for the party ideals but not individuals. The paper was friendly but was not a lackey – a friend will sometimes tell you when you're wrong. I never let Fianna Fáil determine editorial policy. Although there was pressure and Haughey had me over to Kinsealy several times to win me over, my loyalty was to Vivion.[1]
>
> *Tim Pat Coogan on Fianna Fáil and the* Irish Press

As Ireland entered the 1980s, there began an era of political upheaval and economic depression. An ever-growing government deficit, the eruption of the H-Block hunger strike in the north and three general elections between June 1981 and November 1982, combined with the continuous leadership heaves against Charles Haughey, led to a period of profound political and economic instability. In January 1980, Haughey went on national television to address the country on the critical state of the economy and in a now infamous turn of phrase warned that the country was living beyond its means. The Press Group, it seemed, was also living beyond its means. In 1980, Vivion de Valera's son Eamon joined the board of the Press Group as an executive director, beginning his career amid the economic crisis that caused a severe downturn in the newspaper industry. The following year, 1981, the Press Group celebrated its fiftieth anniversary but made a loss of over £1.5 million. Increased competition from British newspapers and the growing popularity of television as an advertising medium caused a huge reduction in revenue. In 1979 national newspapers had held fifty-two per cent of all advertising revenue but by 1983 this had dropped to just over thirty-three per cent. During the same period, RTÉ's share of advertising rose from thirty-three to forty-three per cent. To offset such losses, the cover price of all the national daily titles increased. Between July 1981 and July 1984, the price of the *Irish Press* increased from sixteen pence to thirty pence, while the *Irish Times* rose from twenty-five to forty-five pence. Likewise, the price of the *Irish Independent* doubled from twenty pence to forty pence.[2] Inevitably, the price increases had an adverse impact on sales. As the recession began to bite, the Press Group noted 'a severe reduction in the volume of advertising . . . as increased cover prices resulted in very significant consumer resistance and reduced sales in the second part of the year'.[3] In addition, the introduction of a Saturday night vigil mass in 1983 saw the transfer of approximately twenty per cent of church congregations from Sunday morning mass to Saturday night mass which resulted in a decline in the sales of Sunday papers. Sales of the *Sunday Press* dropped from 369,156 in 1981 to 281,992 in 1984 while sales of the *Sunday Independent* fell from 267,109 to 227,003 during the same period.[4] The decline in the popularity of the Press titles was mirrored in the fall in support for Fianna Fáil.

The first of three general elections within seventeen months occurred in June 1981. This was Haughey's first election campaign as party leader and so the *Irish Press* attempted to mend the bitter rift within the party that had been caused by the leadership battle. When Haughey and Lynch appeared together at an election rally, the paper observed that 'Mr Haughey's appreciation of Mr Lynch's service to political life seemed to mark the end of the long standing hostility between them'.[5] According to the *Irish Press*, Haughey started 'with an edge over his rivals' because of his 'track record' as an innovative minister. In contrast the opposition parties were in disarray, had 'the disadvantage of having no agreed coalition platform worked out . . . and the even greater disadvantage of clearly stated policy differences.'[6] While Fine Gael's policy document was 'vaguely reminiscent of the sort of posturing which Mrs Thatcher engaged in prior to her election',[7] the Labour Party manifesto, by wanting to 'take the economy off to the left . . . put the tin lid on their chances in forming a coalition with Fine Gael'.[8] The 'mutual antipathetic policies'[9] merely reflected the 'size of the gulf in ideology, attitudes and policies currently dividing the two opposition parties'.[10] The choice was plain. Voters could either return a Fianna Fáil administration to tackle the country's problems or they could return 'two ideologically opposed parties with conflicting policies' that had to 'attempt to bridge the unbridgeable' before forming a government that would 'operate on a programme of patched up policies that have never been put before the electorate'.[11] The electorate opted for the latter, with Fianna Fáil losing a total of six seats including two vital border seats to H-Block candidates. As coalition negotiations began between Fine Gael and the Labour Party, the *Irish Press* noted that Fianna Fáil 'with its strong working class support would make a more natural ally for Labour than the deputies of Fine Gael, whether from the law and order school or the new breed of middle class liberals'.[12] Despite this, Fine Gael and Labour, through the support of independent deputy Jim Kemmy and the abstentions of independent deputy Noel Browne and Joe Sherlock of the Workers' Party, formed the first of their two coalitions during the 1980s.

Despite the economic crisis, the new Taoiseach, Garret FitzGerald, launched a 'constitutional crusade' to make the south a 'genuine republic'.[13] According to FitzGerald, the southern laws, constitution, practices and attitudes reflected a majority ethos and were unacceptable to northern Protestants. To Fianna Fáil, the crusade was 'manna from heaven' and allowed Haughey to portray FitzGerald as 'having launched an attack on the very integrity of the Irish state'.[14] According to the *Irish Press*, FitzGerald's crusade was an 'ill-temperate attack on what he called the sectarian nature of the laws, attitudes and practices under which the citizens of the republic live'.[15] The 'so called crusade' was 'a politically unworthy manoeuvre designed to distract attention from the country's economic plight'.[16] Three months later, this economic plight caused the collapse of the coalition when the Minister for Finance John Bruton attempted to impose VAT on children's clothing and footwear. Independent deputy Jim Kemmy, on whom the coalition depended upon for support, voted against the measure and the government fell. During the subsequent election campaign, the *Irish Press* accused the coalition of producing a 'harsh budget' that contained 'obvious psychological flaws'. Thus the 'verdict of the electorate on Fine Gael and more particularly the Labour component of the coalition' would be 'harsh'.[17] According to the paper, Labour had performed abysmally in coalition by letting itself being 'completely subsumed into Fine Gael on the right while allowing the independents to outflank them on the socialist left'.[18]

Although the paper noted that Haughey had 'to contend with a very personalised style of attack from Dr FitzGerald',[19] it also expressed the view that Haughey had 'always concerned himself with the media and with image making, setting up a high profile with all the attendant dangers of this backfiring'.[20] This was in reference to the resurfacing of discontent with Haughey's style of leadership while in opposition. During the election campaign the paper called on the party to unite behind Haughey who was 'beyond doubt one of the ablest and most effective politicians this country has ever seen'. It also criticised his critics whose 'personal grudges and ambitions are not alone damaging their party but also their stated ambition to form a stable government'.[21] Two days before polling, Vivion de Valera died and the paper devoted much of its space to his obituary at the expense of election coverage. On polling day, however, the paper rallied round and admitted that it 'advocated voting for Fianna Fáil' because it offered a 'one party coherent approach to the nation's problems'.[22] Being returned as the biggest party but without a majority saw the paper declare that although Fianna Fáil did not have 'a clear mandate', its mandate was 'clearer than that of Fine Gael and Labour'.[23] While it could not 'give an absolute guarantee of stable government', it was 'certainly in a better position to attempt it'.[24] The balance of power again rested with independent deputies and the Workers' Party. But before attempting the formation of a government, the issue of Haughey's position as leader of Fianna Fáil had to be settled. In order to quell rumours about his unpopularity, Haughey put down a motion for his own re-election as leader for the parliamentary party meeting of 25 February 1982.

A member of the anti-Haughey camp, Des O'Malley, also put his name forward and in an unprecedented move, former leader Jack Lynch issued a statement supporting O'Malley.[25] Haughey was forced to meet the challenge head on, albeit with some help from the *Irish Press*. According to the paper, O'Malley's challenge had the 'most serious implications, not alone for the future of Fianna Fáil or the fate of the next government, but the fundamental issue of the stability of the state'.[26] The challengers showed 'no apparent regard for the serious economic situation' of the country, nor for the 'parlous state of Northern Ireland'. Motivated by 'personal animosity, memories of the manner in which Mr Lynch was removed from office or chagrin at not getting more seats in the election', they were prepared to 'support Mr O'Malley's challenge to Mr Haughey, which could have the effect not only of preventing the party taking office but of permanently weakening it'.[27] According to the paper, the attempt to unseat Haughey was 'not just an effort to change horses in mid-stream but a lemming like urge to drive over the cliffs to destruction'.[28] Such sentiments, combined with the Haughey camp's strong canvass of O'Malley's supporters, ensured that the challenge collapsed. Finding little support, the latter withdrew his leadership challenge.

With the issue of his leadership settled, Haughey was free to court the independent deputies to secure their support. The three Workers' Party deputies pledged their support and in return for his support, Tony Gregory, an inner-city independent deputy, secured a £50 million deal from Haughey for his constituency. Despite Haughey's earlier contention that the country was living beyond its means, the *Irish Press* saw fit to criticise Gregory more than Haughey for the infamous deal. Although the paper noted that Haughey 'might have shown himself to be more aware of the need to share out any funds . . . in a more equitable fashion', the bulk of the criticism was reserved for Gregory. According to the paper, 'as a socialist, Mr Gregory should have been aware that the exorbitant amounts he was making for his own area would not be in the best interests of the poor and the deprived in other areas'. All socialists had 'a duty to consider the national interest as well as that of their own constituents'.[29] Although Fianna Fáil formed a minority administration, the issue of Haughey's position as leader would not go away. In October, deputy Charlie McCreevey was critical of the leadership and tabled a motion of no confidence in Haughey as party leader and Taoiseach for the parliamentary party meeting of 6 October 1982. McCreevey issued a statement declaring that he no longer considered Haughey the best man for either position. According to McCreevey, Haughey's reign was marred by 'political strokes, deals and convulsion policies' as well as 'reckless and daft economic proposals for electoral gain'.[30] The first that Haughey heard of this new challenge was when the *Irish Press* rang him for a comment. He optimistically told the paper that the motion would not get much support. For its part, the paper was critical of McCreevey for causing dissent as it noted that his action had 'plunged the party and the government into turmoil' at a time when the country needed 'stability and confidence in leadership above all else'.[31] Neither the resignations of Des O'Malley and Martin O'Donoghue from cabinet on the day before the meeting, nor the fact that Haughey broke from party rules by insisting on an open vote warranted editorial comment from the paper. After a marathon twelve hour meeting, Haughey survived by fifty-eight votes to twenty-two, prompting the *Irish Press* to declare that since Haughey 'emerged the clear winner . . . there at least for the foreseeable future the matter should be left to rest'.[32] According to the paper, the 'best course now for the country and for the party' was for Fianna Fáil to unite and concentrate 'on the issues facing the country not on personalities'.[33]

A month later, however, Haughey's government fell after losing a vote of no confidence. The party's policy of cutting back on spending, especially in health, cost it the support of the Workers' Party. Again the *Irish Press* called on the party to unite behind Haughey, noting that if its members could not be seen to support each other, they could not expect the public to support them.[34] Despite its call for unity, the paper was assailed by the pro-Haughey camp for not doing enough to secure his position. In an *Irish Press* interview during the campaign, when asked if she believed that there was a media conspiracy against her husband, Maureen Haughey replied that the media was 'blatantly unfair'; even the *Irish Press* had 'gone like the others' and was 'no longer dev's paper'.[35] This despite the fact that the paper had already criticised the 'gang of 22 skulking in the background'.[36] Despite carrying half-page adverts for Fine Gael, the paper accused Garret FitzGerald of 'personal animosity' towards Haughey and of being 'one of the architects' of the smear campaign against him.[37] According to the paper, what the country needed was 'an undiluted party capable of forming a government and staying in power long enough to do the job'. Thus, 'reflection on this point before entering the polling booths should give Fianna Fáil both the edge and the election'.[38] When Fianna Fáil was replaced by a Fine Gael/Labour coalition, the paper identified the 'so called Haughey Factor and the presence of a substantial body of Fianna Fáil parliamentarians vociferously opposed to his leadership' as playing a major part in the defeat.[39]

In January 1983, the coalition government revealed that the previous Haughey administration had authorised the Garda Síochána to bug the telephones of two journalists to stop information regarding cabinet meetings and the heaves against Haughey being leaked to the media. Although the Garda Commissioner, Patrick McLaughlin, and his deputy, Joe Ainsworth, resigned, Haughey denied any knowledge of the affair. While the *Irish Press* could not be seen to condone the bugging of phones, neither could it be too harsh on the party for fear of losing the loyalty of its Fianna Fáil readership. Despite the implications for the freedom of the press, the paper claimed that much of the 'flood of rumour about phone tapping' was 'encouraged by a coalition happy to see attention diverted from the internal strains already showing in economic policy'.[40] Nonetheless, the paper was critical of the 'stupidity and incredible distrust revealed by the bugging controversy'.[41] Noting that 'the bugging of the phones of two journalists and of certain politicians . . . was closely connected with the recent challenges to the then Taoiseach Mr Haughey', it called on the 'political masters . . . who twisted the system and betrayed their trust' to 'be made face the music even though now removed from the centre of power'.[42] The *Sunday Press*' new political correspondent, Geraldine Kennedy, also revealed that Haughey had personally attempted to identify her Fianna Fáil sources in a conversation with Hugh McLaughlin, the proprietor of her former newspaper, the *Sunday Tribune*.[43] The revelations were followed by intense speculation within Leinster House that Haughey was seriously contemplating his resignation.

On the day of a parliamentary party meeting, under the page one headline 'Haughey on Brink of Resignation', Michael Mills contended that 'the resignation of Mr Charles J Haughey as leader of the party was imminent'.[44] But it was the paper's infamous two page political obituary that carried a detailed account of Haughey's political career that caused most damage between it and the party. Most of the obituary material had already been prepared in line with the standard newspaper practice of compiling biographies of national figures ready for immediate publication should the need arise. Other material was added as the rumours of Haughey's impending resignation intensified. The obituary, by its context and its content, was assumed by both Haughey supporters and critics as evidence that the paper thought Haughey should resign the leadership. There is no definite account of how the political obituary got into the paper. Michael Mills and Stephen O'Byrnes (who later joined the Progressive Democrats) were the *Irish Press* reporters on duty in Leinster House the previous night. While the first edition of the paper was being printed, an unusual editorial conference took place to decide whether or not the obituary should be included. All the indications pointed to Haughey's resignation, and since the last news received at Burgh Quay was that the government would announce his resignation by four o'clock in the morning, it was decided to include the obituary in the city edition. Whoever made the final decision to include the obituary has always been shrouded by mystery. While deputy editor John Garvey had the night off, chief sub-editor Jack Jones always insisted that the decision to include the obituary was taken at a higher level than him.[45] According to editor Tim Pat Coogan, the obituary 'was put aside with a note attached telling the printers to include it in a supplement if Haughey was ousted, but it was put in by mistake. It was a cock-up rather than a conspiracy'.[46] Although Haughey blamed the paper's political correspondent, according to Mills himself, he had nothing to do with it:

> It was extraordinary. I left Leinster House at twelve midnight and the last words I gave to the news editor on duty was that no matter what he heard from his sources Haughey had not resigned. I knew Haughey was not of the resigning character. In the morning I heard about the political obituary on the eight o'clock news. I was astonished. I told my wife that Haughey would stay and there was no way the *Irish Press* would make him resign. Of course everyone passed the buck but it was nothing to do with me.[47]

There were 'no ulterior motives to the political obituary – all that Coogan wanted was a scoop ahead of the *Irish Independent*'.[48] The paper certainly got the scoop it wanted. No other paper reported the political death because Haughey did not resign. Most party figures were surprised at the stance taken by the *Irish Press* and the obituary caused some ill-feeling between the party and the paper:

> It was not very perceptive but it is fair to say it could have been anticipated. It caused some ill-feeling within the party and the party took a very poor view of it. The *Irish Press* was not performing to the tune of the soldiers of destiny. The anti-Haughey stance was read in this light – as a bias against the party and the party leader. Of course Haughey was upset – who wouldn't be? But from the day Haughey became leader of Fianna Fáil to the day he left as Taoiseach, the party was riven by dissent with much side taking and factions. The party never settled but the *Irish Press* did not have any effect or influence on the splits.[49]

At the parliamentary party meeting that morning, there was intense criticism of the media, and in particular, the *Irish Press* for its premature announcement of Haughey's resignation. When the pressure on Haughey to resign was attributed by some supporters to a media conspiracy, the paper's editorial retorted that such allegations were 'simply not true . . . the phone-tapping, the bugging and all the rest of it were not the media's doing'. In an effort to mend fences, however, it also complimented Haughey for showing 'incredible political tenacity . . . under the most extreme pressures'.[50] Describing events at the meeting, Michael Mills reported that 'deputies who formerly supported him [Haughey] called publicly yesterday for his resignation'. Mills also reported that Haughey had told some deputies that 'he now accepted that the fight to retain his leadership had been lost and that he accepted the inevitable – that he should resign'.[51] That same day, the *Evening Press* printed an article on Haughey's financial affairs. Written by financial journalist Des Crowley, and based on what he referred to as 'well informed speculation', the article noted that it had been 'rumoured in discreet financial circles for years that Mr Haughey owed one million pounds to a major bank and that the bank had held its hand because of his elevated position'.[52] The revelation increased the pressure on Haughey and prompted Allied Irish Banks to dismiss the report as 'outlandishly inaccurate'. As later events would prove, it was the bank rather than the newspaper that was 'outlandishly inaccurate'.[53]

When Haughey eventually refused to resign, Mills' front page story reported that Haughey was facing 'a massive revolt' after forty-one of the party's seventy-five deputies had signed a petition demanding an immediate meeting 'to bring the leadership crisis to an end once and for all'.[54] The paper's editorial column remained neutral and merely persisted in its call for the party to 'solve the leadership issue once and for all'.[55] But while the *Irish Press* tried as much as possible to remain editorially aloft from the leadership crisis, the *Sunday Press* gave extensive coverage to the anti-Haughey camp, including a hard-hitting interview with Charlie McCreevey on the day before the meeting to decide Haughey's fate. According to McCreevey, under Haughey's leadership Fianna Fáil had been reduced to a 'self-centred, advance-seeking cabal of opportunists', while Haughey himself was a 'disgrace to the democratic tradition of Fianna Fáil and the Irish nation'.[56] While the publication of such criticism of a party leader by a Press title would have been unthinkable in the past, the publication of the McCreevey interview demonstrated that times, at least for the *Sunday Press*, had changed. While the *Sunday Press* was never perceived as being as partisan towards Fianna Fáil, all the Press titles faced a dilemma during the Haughey years – 'which part of the party were the papers to support?'[57] Nonetheless, the *Sunday Press* was regarded as being more editorially independent. When the paper's last editor, Michael Keane, was appointed in 1986, he was never formally instructed on political angles:

> Fianna Fáil was never mentioned and neither was political policy, although it remained in the hands of Eamon de Valera [son of Vivion de Valera] – he would make the final decision. We were friendly to Fianna Fáil but not run by it. I felt free to criticise Fianna Fáil in or out of government once the criticism was fair and balanced. At election times though, it would be taken as read that the papers would be friendly to Fianna Fáil – what you were dealing with was by and large a Fianna Fáil constituency.[58]

On the morning of the meeting to decide Haughey's fate, Mills' page one column held that 'Haughey's hopes of holding on to the leadership of Fianna Fáil . . . appeared to be very slim'. Since the revelation of the phone tapping, Haughey's support had 'gradually diminished'.[59] Editorially, the paper urged the party to unite rather then divide. What was at stake was the 'political future of Fianna Fáil' – a party that appeared 'crippled by bitterness and internal feuding'. The substantive issue was 'not how the party got to its present disarray' but what could 'be done to heal the wounds and get back the cohesion and unity of purpose that made Fianna Fáil the natural party of government in this state'. Instead of the 'splits, attempted coups, strokes and scandals', the country needed 'a credible and critical opposition' to offer something more hopeful than the 'coalition's cutbacks'. Thus the paper expressed the hope that the outcome of the vote would herald the 'first step back along the road to . . . the old Fianna Fáil' that was 'synonymous with unity not division'.[60] When Haughey won by forty votes to thirty-three, the paper observed that there was not 'a fighter to equal him in Irish politics nor anyone with the obvious capability of taking the leadership away from him in the ranks of Fianna Fáil'. While it acknowledged that the vote was close and showed 'a marked division of opinion' it was 'the will of the party that he should continue in office'. Now, the paper proclaimed, was the 'time to bury the hatchet and get on with the job of reuniting the party'.[61]

It was during this period of political turmoil within Fianna Fáil that both Vivion de Valera and Jack Dempsey died. Shortly before he died in February 1982, Vivion turned down an offer from Allied Irish Banks for a very substantial loan to invest in new technology. This would have allowed the company to make generous redundancy payments, speed up the transition to new technology and avoid any industrial unrest. However, the bank made it a condition of the potential loan that it appoint one director to the board of the Press Group to oversee the modernisation effort – a condition that proved too bitter a pill for Vivion to swallow. In any event, Vivion's death left a power vacuum at the Press Group, a vacuum quickly filled by his son Eamon who became the first controlling director of the company not to be a Fianna Fáil deputy. According to one researcher, his 'disciplinary background [science] and work with a subsidiary of Cement Roadstone had proved insufficient business or managerial experience for his new role. It can be viewed as an example of duty and responsibility being thrust on a male family member to continue the tradition.'[62] Eamon also took control of the company at a time of extreme economic instability. But despite the uncertainty over the financial status of the company, Vivion de Valera had 'left one real bridge for the future'. This took the form of Donal Flinn, a former managing partner with the auditors of the Press Group, Coopers and Lybrand, who had been coopted onto the board as chairman, and Sean McHale, a business consultant who had been appointed as a director.[63]

Both arrived at Burgh Quay in May 1983 and both were pragmatic and hard-nosed businessmen who knew how to run a business.[64] The following month, the Press Group NUJ chapel held a mandatory meeting to discuss the company's pleaded inability to pay the twelve per cent wage increase granted to the other national newspapers. Such mandatory meetings were never called 'except for the most serious of reasons' and although the tactic was 'occasionally overplayed it became practice for a skeleton staff to keep production going'.[65] All editorial and executive staff attended the meeting and work did not recommence until 4.45pm. This seriously disrupted the publication of the *Evening Press* and so it did not carry late news or sports results that day. Management observed that 'the custom of holding these meetings with the view to causing the minimum of disruption to publications had not been observed'. Such actions it argued, 'would have a most damaging effect' and jeopardise 'the long term success and economic viability of the company'.[66] In response, management docked the wages of forty-two editorial staff members who it deemed as not having completed their full shifts and issued protective notice to its staff. Two weeks later, publication of the *Irish Press* was suspended for a month over the issue. The company's 1983 annual report welcomed the Flinn and McHale appointments in the knowledge that they brought with them 'a wealth of experience' that would be invaluable to the company.[67] The appointment of such an experienced businessman as chairman with his emphasis on modernisation gave rise to some premature speculation that marketplace realities had finally penetrated Burgh Quay. It was a widely held view in the business community that the new directors would 'take the Press Group by its roots, shake off many of its traditional legacies and make it grow'.[68] Indeed, in his first statement as chairman, Flinn ruffled a few feathers as he spoke of how the company had been left behind while other newspaper groups had scrambled towards modernisation. According to Flinn, there had been 'for a considerable time a lack of realism in attitudes to the relationship between employment, efficiency, productivity and profitability'.[69] In February 1984, the board threatened to close the company unless agreement on a business survival plan was reached by May of that year. The board said that 'unless there was an early acceptance of new technology, the abandonment of retarding work practices [and] an acceptance of necessary redundancy', it would be impossible for the company to continue trading.[70] At a meeting between management and the company's group of unions at the Gresham Hotel in April 1984, the various survival options were discussed. While the dropping of the *Irish Press* title and the rationalisation of the other two titles were considered, three hundred redundancies were also sought. According to management, 'if the Press was to have a future it was not as a national newspaper group'.[71] It (the management) had 'invented neither the recession nor the technology' but was governed by both. Staff therefore had to show commitment to the new technology; time was precious and there was no time for 'ritualistic negotiations or sectional interest'.[72] While the unions initially resisted the redundancies, a compromise of two hundred and fifty redundancies was eventually agreed upon.

As chairman, Flinn's first priority was the reshaping of the company's internal financial structure to pay for the introduction of direct input computerised technology. This plan would have wrested control of the company from the de Valera family but it eventually came to nothing. That same year, the international news agency Reuters floated on the stock exchange and brought a financial windfall to shareholders. Various Irish newspaper groups, including the Press Group, held shares in the Press Association which in turn owned a forty-one per cent stake in Reuters. The Press Group, thus received a dividend of approximately £4 million. The company then used over half this money to pay for the new technology, thus negating the need for a restructuring of the antiquated company structure. With the dividend from Reuters and a share holding restructure, the company could have made a clean break from its past, but it chose not to. It was clear that the de Valeras intended to remain in control of the Press Group. In late 1984, a Coopers and Lybrand report on the structure of the company recommended that executive control of the company be handed over to a business team. The matter of how to convince the de Valeras to let an experienced business team run the company occupied the minds of Flinn and McHale for several months but it was clear that a showdown was inevitable. The Coopers and Lybrand report 'recommended radical changes. This led to furious board meetings and the crunch meeting occurred in May 1985.'[73] At that meeting, the two main items on the agenda were the appointment of Elio Malocco (husband of Eamon's first cousin, Jane de Valera) as a director and the contentious Coopers and Lybrand report. Previous to this, however, Eamon had bought a block of one hundred, or half, of the voting 'B' shares in the American Corporation from his uncle (and Malocco's father-in-law), Terry de Valera, for £225,000.[74] Malocco thus became a director and took over the company's legal affairs. He would later be imprisoned on charges connected to monies unaccounted for in the company's libel fund.

The decision to appoint Malocco incensed Flinn. As chairman of the board he was not consulted on the appointment – he was simply told that Malooco was joining as a director. Flinn found this totally unacceptable and resigned. Eamon de Valera, who already held the positions of controlling director and editor-in-chief, then assumed the position of chairman.[75] In the company's 1985 annual report, it was politely noted that Flinn had resigned 'following differences with the controlling director on company policy'.[76] At the company's annual general meeting in July 1986, Flinn argued that had it not been for the Reuters money, the company would have been liquidated long ago. Almost foretelling the future, Flinn declared that for the company to survive, it would have to immediately implement direct input and achieve a significant reduction in the workforce. In response, de Valera replied that direct input was 'not the be-all and end-all, but one step in rebuilding the industry'. Nonetheless, Flinn stated that while 'drastic action' was urgently required, he did not believe the board 'was capable of such action'.[77] He claimed that if the Press Group were a normal company, the shareholders would replace the board. As Flinn noted, however, the company was anything but normal and was controlled by 'a minuscule shareholding based in Delaware'. This entity, Flinn proclaimed, held 'the voting power' and 'should be disassembled'.[78] Flinn also asked the board why the Group's solicitors J. S. O'Connor and Co. had been 'removed from office'. In response, de Valera merely replied that a new firm, Malocco and Kileen, had been awarded the company's legal contract.[79] Shortly afterwards, the other 'bridge for the future', Sean McHale, resigned over disagreements 'concerning the board's business strategy in relation to the company's problems'.[80]

While the board flirted with business reality and fought over control of the company, morale among staff plummeted as they sought to produce the papers:

> None of these 'fly by nights' had much of a relationship with the floor. We used to look at these people coming in and wonder at them. I'm sure some of them tried to change things on the board, but I'm equally sure none of them ever got anywhere. The attitude on the floor was

'get the sheet on the street and to hell with them'. The sheet was the critical thing and it always hit the street despite them.[81]

Deprived of the business acumen of Flinn and McHale, the subsequent negotiations on the implementation of the 'Rationality and Technology Programme' were fraught with difficulty. As the negotiations continued, a deadline of the end of April 1985 was set for the changeover to the new technology. Staff were trained on a rota basis, but as the deadline approached it became apparent that it would not be met. The deadline was extended but a print union ballot was deferred several times, preventing the company from meeting more changeover deadlines. Eventually, the company halted production on 20 May 1985 and laid off all eight hundred and fifty staff 'to protect the long term viability' of the company.[82] The previous day's *Sunday Press* bade goodbye to its readers and expressed its hope that the 'unique voices' of the three Press titles would not be 'long silent'.[83] The board subsequently declared that publication could only resume 'using the new system'.[84] As the lockout continued, the blame was firmly placed at the feet of the print unions by de Valera who bluntly stated that they could 'choose between a willing acceptance of the new techniques, with a relatively small reduction in jobs on favourable redundancy terms, or . . . reject the changes with a consequent loss of all jobs on nothing more than statutory redundancy terms'.[85] The six-week closure eventually ended after a compromise was reached on the basis that for at least four years only printers and not journalists could operate the new direct input technology. According to one editor, this represented management's willingness to agree 'crazy deals with the unions . . . The deal meant that all workers, regardless of their skills were equal, and this meant that people were let do jobs that they were not qualified to do.'[86] Indeed, de Valera later admitted that this interim concession stage slowed down production of the papers as all material was doubled handled.[87]

Both the *Sunday Press* and the *Evening Press* reappeared on the market at the start of July, the latter explaining its absence as 'the result of the difficulties and traumas that go hand in hand with the introduction of new technology', but the *Irish Press* did not reappear for a further six weeks.[88] This gap was 'the greatest blow suffered by the *Irish Press* . . . the company made the title look like the least important of its papers'.[89] For a considerable time after the strike, all three titles were marred by production delays that resulted in a loss of crucial revenue. The *Irish Press* in particular 'was always late and was basically going down the tubes. Taxis were used to distribute the paper in Galway, as it often arrived too late to be distributed by the vans waiting for the Dublin papers.'[90] Having been missing from the market for three months, the *Irish Press* never truly recovered and its readership base began to rapidly erode. The Press Group made a loss of over £3 million in 1985, most of it attributed to lost circulation and advertising revenue during the strike. As with most industrial disputes, both sides blamed each other. Management held that 'the unions did not want to know about the new technology and wanted a guarantee that no jobs would be lost',[91] but the unions held that 'the company was ahead of its competitors in getting acceptance for computer based systems but it failed to capitalise on the advantage. Poor advance planning, including inadequate staff training resulted in production delays. . . . Despite a compliant and flexible workforce who were paid considerably less than their counterparts in competing newspapers, circulation continued to decline.'[92] In 1985 the Press Group bought Southside Publications Ltd, a company that published seven free local newspapers in the Dublin area. Although the original papers were profitable because they concentrated on local advertising, when the Press Group took over, resources were ploughed into the journalistic side of the papers. Within two years the company was forced to close.

The infighting within the Press Group was mirrored by the internal dissent within the ranks of the Fianna Fáil parliamentary party. The publication of the coalition's *New Ireland Forum Report* of 1984 again saw the *Sunday Press* criticise and expose Haughey's weakness as leader. The forum report sought to unite Irish political parties on northern policy so that a common position could be forwarded to the British government. It suggested several solutions including a federal, confederal or joint authority state. When British Prime Minister Margaret Thatcher infamously rejected all three proposals as being 'out, out, out', the *Irish Press* castigated her 'flint-edged . . . set piece iron-maiden performance'. It also bemoaned Taoiseach Garret FitzGerald's 'positively cringing' response to Thatcher's outright rejection of the suggestions from his 'laboriously cobbled together and expensively mounted and sustained New Ireland Forum'.[93] Before any party discussion could be held on the report, Haughey declared that it called for a 'unitary state' which was the 'official policy of the party'. The fact that Haughey made such a statement before any party discussion prompted Des O'Malley to publicly call for northern policy to be formulated by the party as a whole rather than just the leader as was tradition. Exposing Haughey's perennial weakness as leader, the *Sunday Press* claimed that his outburst was prompted by his dependence on the nationalist element within Fianna Fáil to survive as leader. According to the paper:

> Haughey genuinely feared that he had not got enough to placate the more republican elements of his own party. He admitted often in the Forum that he felt 'trapped' and argued constantly that he couldn't sell this point or that point. Mr Haughey's fear was that Ray MacSharry, Rory O'Hanlon or Jim Tunney – the people most often mentioned, would find the report not green enough. And if Mr Haughey upset the green element in Fianna Fáil, he could lose his power base for the leadership.[94]

In the following weeks, the paper reported almost verbatim on the public exchanges between Haughey and O'Malley. In a page one interview, O'Malley condemned the 'air of paranoia around the leadership' where putting forward a different idea was 'seen as a preliminary to a coup'. The paper also published the infamous 'Uno Duce, Uno Voce' (One Leader, One Voice) off-the-cuff remark by Haughey's press secretary, P. J. Mara, to which Haughey took great exception.[95] But while the Press titles may not have had an influence on the infighting within the party, the power struggle was damaging to the papers, particularly the *Irish Press*, as its appeal to the party faithful became strained.

> The Haughey splits and leadership heaves did not help the *Irish Press*. The paper always had a policy of supporting the leader of the day, even though it had reservations about the way Haughey did things. The pro-Haughey faction said that the *Irish Press* did not do enough for him, while the anti-Haughey faction said it did too much.[96]

Shortly afterwards, Fianna Fáil and the *Irish Press* clashed again over the paper's political correspondent, Michael Mills, who had been invited by the coalition government to become Ireland's first ombudsman. The fact that the coalition chose Mills for such a position only demonstrated his widely acknowledged sense of impartiality. Mills' acceptance of the position caused consternation within Fianna Fáil and 'some elements of Fianna Fáil, especially the Haughey wing, regarded Mills as a "Quisling" for accepting the position. They hounded him for this and tried to have him removed when in power, but Mills won.'[97]

Haughey's opposition to the Anglo-Irish Agreement signed in November 1985 also caused a split in the party and was the final straw for many within the anti-Haughey camp. Mary Harney was promptly expelled when she voted with the coalition for the agreement, and the foundation of the Progressive Democrats in December 1985 by both she and Des O'Malley saw the *Irish Press* predict a dismal future for the party. While conceding that the expulsion of Mr O'Malley had been 'a major loss of talent to Fianna Fáil' and that he would 'undoubtedly attract a large number of people to his banner', it noted that the Irish political landscape was 'littered with the skeletons of new parties promising a new approach'.[98] It also dismissed its policies as 'neither radically left wing nor radically right wing' and criticised its genesis from a clash of personalities rather than one of policies. What was most dubious about O'Malley's actions was the fact that he had 'not questioned the strategy or politics of Fianna Fáil in any significant detail'. Instead, his main emphasis had been 'on the style of leadership of Mr Haughey, the way in which Mr Haughey dominates party thinking and the way the party has according to Mr O'Malley opted for political opportunism on occasions. The basis for the new party, to judge from this analysis seems more of personality than principle'.[99] Thus the best the party could hope for was 'to hold the balance of power in a tight electoral contest'. Shortly afterwards, two more anti-Haughey figures, Bobby Molloy and Pearse Wyse, defected from Fianna Fáil to the new party.

But while the *Irish Press* criticised the Progressive Democrats for a lack of radical policies, it also deplored Fianna Fáil's policy of abstaining from the divorce referendum campaign of 1986. Sitting comfortably on the opposition benches, the party sat back and watched the Fine Gael/Labour coalition try to convince a depression-ridden Ireland that divorce was a social necessity. While officially Fianna Fáil left it to the discretion of individual deputies to decide whether or not to support the constitutional amendment, in effect most campaigned against it. The party was subsequently criticised by both the government and the *Irish Press* for sitting on the fence on such a fundamental issue. But according to one party strategist, 'on the so called liberal agenda, Fianna Fáil's instinct was to proceed cautiously trying to build the maximum consensus for change, rather than engage in constitutional crusading that rode roughshod over traditional values and sensibilities. This more cautious but also more productive approach earned a lot of hostility from the media.'[100] However, according to editor Tim Pat Coogan, the party's position was 'an equivocal and totally hypocritical stance'. The paper itself advocated the acceptance of the amendment and because of this came in for 'lots of flak from the party'.[101] Although the paper's stance was republican in the truest sense of the word, it differed from the beliefs of the majority of its rural readership. According to the *Irish Press*, the acceptance of divorce would make Ireland a place of 'tolerance and generosity ready to accommodate the differing views and traditions of people of all religions and none'.[102] At the company's annual general meeting that year, some criticism was expressed at the stance taken by the paper. During the meeting, one shareholder enquired whether the company 'had adopted a policy of smut' and claimed that the 'the objectives of the papers and their ethical policy was so wrong that sales had suffered'. In response, de Valera replied that the coverage had been 'fair and unbiased'.[103] Despite the high hopes of the *Irish Press*, the amendment was defeated at the polls – with a majority of rural voters rejecting the proposal. Again drifting from the beliefs of its older rural readership, the paper bemoaned the fact that divorce had been rejected. While it wondered whether 'the failure of Fianna Fáil to show the courage of its republican convictions was the key factor that the coalition claims it to have been', it concluded that the rejection of divorce would make it 'more difficult to argue the case for Irish unity or for any Dublin government to pose as champion of the minority'.[104]

The four-year coalition between Fine Gael and the Labour Party ended in January 1987 when the latter walked out of cabinet over the spending cuts proposed by Taoiseach Garret FitzGerald. Since it was unlikely that Fine Gael and Labour would again join forces in coalition, the only alternative was one composed of Fine Gael and the Progressive Democrats, a prospect that neither Fianna Fáil nor the *Irish Press* relished. It would, according to the paper, be a government defined solely by spending cuts. Both parties were 'bitterly competing' over who had 'the sharpest axe' and both were committed to policies of 'cutting public spending and social services' and 'selling off the state industries'. Such policies only meant 'fewer jobs and more misery'.[105] Neither party seemed fit for government. While the policies of the PDs were 'tailored to the demands of the young and upwardly mobile', Fine Gael cared only 'about balancing the books and pleasing the economists' and no longer seemed 'to care about people'. Such a coalition would only please 'right wing economists'.[106] Thus, the paper concluded on election day, the only party that could 'offer coherent government policy' was Fianna Fáil; 'after the last four years of calamity' the paper noted, it was 'time to stop the messing and start progress again'.[107] Haughey's failure to win an overall majority for the fourth time saw the *Irish Press* again discount the 'Haughey Factor' for the party's poor performance at the polls by bizarrely noting that it was 'no use blaming whatever factors affected the results'. Instead, it held that the scale of problems 'raked up by the outgoing administration' was so 'horrendous' that all Fianna Fáil could do was 'get in there and govern'. None of Haughey's legendary 'deals, strokes or nifty footwork' would 'impress either the electorate or make for an improved Dáil majority'. The paper reminded the electorate that 'Sean Lemass led one of the best governments in the history of this state from a minority position'. Now, the paper noted, his son-in-law had the option of doing the same.[108] The administration survived for two years but only by securing consensus on legislation and budgets with Fine Gael. For instance, during the 1988 legislative year, Fine Gael voted with the government on forty-two occasions and only twelve times against it.[109]

As the 1980s wore on, the exodus of staff from the Press Group for better pay and conditions at other national papers reached an all-time high. By 1990 the pay gap between the Press Group and other Dublin papers was a massive fifteen per cent.[110] In 1988 there was a continuous stream of 'executives leaving and taking lower money in other jobs just to get a little security'.[111] The departures of high profile journalists such as social columnists Angela Phelan and Terry Keane to the Independent Group, and the defection of film critic Michael Dwyer to the *Irish Times*, continued the exodus of talent that had been traditional since the company's foundation. The *Sunday Press*' political correspondent Geraldine Kennedy also left, leaving the paper without a political correspondent during the 1987 general election in which Kennedy was ironically returned as a Progressive Democrat deputy. The Press Group was 'always hampered by the superior resources of Independent Newspapers' and was 'continually losing talented people'. At Independent Newspapers 'there was job security but it was always a struggle with the Press Group. The titles were always susceptible to losing people and when you lose your best journalists you lose the very reason why people bought the papers in the first place.'[112] The company was also critically short of cash and this hindered attempts to improve the readership profile of the *Sunday Press*, once the great money-spinner of the Press Group. In essence, 'the company was in trouble and there was little money to market the paper, although a number of initiatives were planned'. While the company 'wanted to bring the paper upmarket', the change did not go down well with readers.[113] The main problem was that 'there was a perception that the *Sunday Press* was a rural paper. When it was founded, it was aimed at a rural readership because the *Sunday Independent* was an urban paper. The *Sunday Press* always suffered from that fact as advertisers wanted a large Dublin audience with big buying power.'[114]

The Press titles were by now losing readers on a massive scale as their ageing rural readership base gradually declined. Between 1981 and 1986, sales of the *Irish Press* fell from 104,768 to 78,641 while sales of the *Sunday Press* fell from 403,833 in 1980 to 256,146 in 1986. The *Evening Press* also suffered, with sales dropping from 145,031 in 1983 to 125,347 in 1986. By that year, the group had accumulated losses of over £8 million for the first five years of the decade. The stalemate over direct input technology was still raging and even though the technology had been installed, it was not being fully utilised. By the time management finally got the system installed and accepted, it had become outdated and expensive to maintain. According to one editor, 'the wrong technology was chosen and the Harris system was finally installed one month before the Harris Corporation pulled out of Europe, forcing the Press Group to fly engineers in from America'.[115]

In 1986, Vincent Jennings was appointed managing director and as the *Phoenix* magazine commented, the reasons for his appointment to such a pre-eminent position were 'best known to Eamon de Valera himself'.[116] That same year an executive committee was set up to examine the future of the *Irish Press*. It proposed many editorial changes, including a tabloid format for the paper. As editor, Tim Pat Coogan was effectively given the option of accepting these changes or vacating the editorial chair. The strained relationship between Coogan and the board was reflected in the absence of Coogan from several crucial meetings on the tabloid change. Although Coogan resisted moves to bring the paper downmarket and argued that the change would essentially destroy the Irish ethos of the paper, Jennings had the support of de Valera and the board which hired two London based newspaper consultants – Larry Lamb and Vic Giles – to redesign the paper. It was their idea to make the paper a tabloid with a broadsheet content. Coogan however, made one last stand:

> The tabloid market was saturated and the *Irish Press* could never have worked as a tabloid. The decision to go tabloid was like the hauling down of the flag – an admission that the paper could not make the grade. The idea was touted and then abandoned until Jennings was appointed when the idea of a tabloid was raised again. I made one last

> stand and put together a document to save the paper. It called for investment, better production facilities, more pages and better quality. The document was backed by the staff who presented it to management. The subsequent meeting dragged on for hours but de Valera dismissed it as not being the answer, despite the fact that it had been written by twenty of the most progressive journalists. In July 1987 management went ahead against all advice and decided to make the paper a tabloid and I resigned a month later. The bulk of the best staff left also.[117]

Coogan resigned as editor in August 1987, and although de Valera praised his 'unbroken twenty years as editor' during which 'he put his own personal stamp on the newspaper which came to be identified with him', his resignation did not seem to worry the board.[118] Neither, it seemed, did the fact that Independent Newspapers was negotiating a deal with the British firm Express Newspapers to publish a colour tabloid newspaper (the *Star*) in Ireland. Coogan was replaced as editor by Hugh Lambert who had formerly been a *Sunday Press* production editor. According to Lambert, the decline of the *Irish Press* as a broadsheet was due to the simple lack of resources: 'the competition was continuously upping the ante and giving extra dimensions to their papers. The *Irish Press* was not getting the resources. The rural reading base was shrinking and the morning market was becoming more competitive.'[119] While the *Irish Times* had thirty-two pages and the *Irish Independent* had between twenty-eight to thirty-four pages, the *Irish Press* had to make do with eighteen to twenty pages. The paper was thus 'less value for money' and 'had a poor future as the third national broadsheet'.[120] After 'extensive company-wise discussions' the decision to go tabloid was finally taken: 'the hope was to focus attention on the paper that many felt had so much going for it, to modernise it, to present it anew to the country, to gain new younger readers without alienating older readers'. Fate intervened, however, and 'the decision became known in the industry and as a result, plans for the *Star* were advanced. That paper appeared months before the new *Irish Press* and had more colour, was light and successful'.[121]

It could well be argued that although the *Irish Press* needed to reinvent itself, it should have done so as a quality broadsheet, with investment, better production facilities, more pages and intensive marketing. Although the circulation of the paper was falling and its readership was ageing and rurally based, the paper stood a better chance of upgrading itself as a broadsheet rather than going downmarket as a tabloid, especially given the entry of the British-backed *Star* into the Irish market. In later years the tabloid market would become saturated with Irish editions of British tabloids such as the *Sun* and *Daily Mirror* thus reducing the *Irish Press*' competitiveness even more. It is a fact that while broadsheet newspapers rely more on advertising than circulation revenue for survival, tabloid newspapers rely on mass circulation, since their downmarket status does not appeal to corporate advertisers. In 1983, circulation revenue had accounted for sixty-four per cent of the Press Group's turnover, while advertising revenue had accounted for thirty-six per cent. By 1987, despite the fact that circulation was declining, the respective figures were seventy per cent and thirty per cent.[122] Since advertising revenue was falling, it was thought best for the *Irish Press* to go tabloid, appeal to the masses and seek an increased revenue from circulation. However, with a declining circulation, management should have brought the paper upmarket, aimed it at the urban middle-class market and reaped the rewards of increased advertising revenue. To modernise the paper to target this market, however, necessitated huge long-term financial resources that were beyond the scope of the company. It was easier and cheaper for the *Irish Press* to go tabloid. But there remained the question as to whom the tabloid was to be aimed at. With sixty-four per cent of its readership under thirty-five years of age and sixty-eight per cent of its readership working class, the *Star* had captured both the young and working-class readership markets. Given the *Irish Press*' respective figures – sixty-two per cent and forty-four per cent – it could not hope to compete with the multicoloured and highly marketed *Star*.[123] The *Irish Press* as tabloid was to be Ireland first serious tabloid daily newspaper – a newspaper that the market was to prove fatally hostile towards. In any event, the conversion to tabloid format in April 1988 was hasty in every respect and in the last broadsheet edition of the paper, editor-in-chief Eamon de Valera wrote of his vision of the new tabloid. The new format was to allow for 'easy reading of concise and well written reports and articles' while the smaller page size was to allow for 'a more graphic and brighter presentation'.[124] But the tabloid did not materialise as de Valera prophesied, and it was plagued by technical problems and a lack of resources:

> Our intention was to produce a bright quality tabloid. The aim was to engage and entertain young people without shocking older readers. We thought that a viable tabloid could be produced but it did not

> come out as intended. We could have got it right if we had the resources. The content was fine but the typography was wrong, it was too dull and coarse. We needed to follow the European model – *El Pais* or *Liberation* – rather than the *Mirror* or the *Sun*. Our black typography, necessary because of our printing presses, didn't help. It's fair to say that the paper looked coarser than its content. Although sales continued to drop, the paper was highly rated by other journalists. We had many superb writers and reporters. But we failed to give the tabloid the style it needed.[125]

The tabloid *Irish Press* seemed stuck between markets, prompting the *Phoenix* magazine to comment that the paper was 'neither a real tabloid nor a serious newspaper anymore'.[126] It failed to establish itself in the tabloid market because it concentrated on news rather than fun tabloidism or infotainment. It also lacked colour and was overpriced. While the *Star* cost just fifty-five pence, the *Irish Press* cost seventy pence. Although the journalistic content was of a high quality, it also failed to establish itself in the serious news market because that was the domain of the broadsheets. Without the marketing resources necessary, the paper could not establish a distinctive midway niche in the morning newspaper market. Despite all this, however, the idea of a serious tabloid might have been successful had it not been for the aggressive competition waged against it by Independent Newspapers. The launch of the Fortuna lottery game by that company had a profound effect on sales of the *Irish Press*, causing it to drop by 20,000 copies a day in the game's first week. In response, both the Press Group and the Cork Examiner Group took a High Court action alleging that the game was illegal under the 1956 Gaming and Lotteries Act. While this proved to be correct, the fact that the two newspaper groups were anxious to stop the game only increased public curiosity. When the amended version of the game finally went ahead, the intense publicity generated by the court case translated into thousands of curious new readers for the Independent titles. Although the Press Group fought back with an advertising campaign pointing out the Independent's sneak price increase to cover the cost of Fortuna, it was eventually forced to spend nearly £250,000 on launching its own lottery game to woo back its readership from the Independent titles – money that should have been spent marketing the new tabloid.

> Within weeks of the launch of the tabloid *Irish Press*, Independent Newspapers announced a hugely expensive money give-away game

> across its three titles. Put at its most simple, a substantial war-chest that had been ear-marked for the new tabloid was consumed in weeks in a dismal counter-exercise. The money that would have helped us establish the *Irish Press* in its new guise disappeared in a war of attrition that had nothing to do with journalism. Once Independent Newspapers embarked on its promotion, Burgh Quay had no choice. The *Evening Press* suffered most, so resources intended for the new tabloid were diverted to shore up our three papers instead of marketing the *Irish Press* and getting people used to it.[127]

In a potent sign of the hard times to come, in August 1988 management introduced its five-year corporate plan to revive the company's fortunes. Entitled *Planning for the 1990s*, the survival plan called for voluntary redundancies, the closure of its provincial, Belfast and London offices, the abolition of its transport department and the re-organisation of work practices to allow for direct input.[128] The plan outlined the serious decline in circulation that had afflicted the three Press titles. Between 1983 and 1987, circulation of the *Irish Press* had dropped by 15,000 or sixteen per cent. During the same period, circulation of the *Evening Press* had declined by 14,000 or ten per cent while circulation of the *Sunday Press* had dropped by 55,000 or eighteen per cent. Between 1983 and 1987, the combined circulation of the three titles had declined by fourteen per cent.[129] In addition, the company's dependence on circulation revenue rather then advertising revenue had grown. In 1983, sixty-four per cent of the company's revenue had come from circulation while the remaining thirty-six per cent had come from advertising. By 1987, the respective figures were seventy and thirty per cent.[130]

However, the main stumbling block was the insistence by management that workers accept a five-shift instead of the existing four-shift working week. In response, the NUJ and the Irish Print Union insisted that all elements of the survival plan bar the five-shift week were negotiable. Since the four-shift week had been introduced in 1980 in lieu of a wage increase, to revert to a five-shift week would entail both management and unions going back on their word. Although it accepted the 'inevitability of job losses', the Dublin Printing Trade Group of Unions stated that it had 'lost confidence' in the management.[131] The row over the five-shift week dragged on for almost a year and involved both the Labour Court and an independent arbitrator. In November 1988, the board informed the trustees of the company's pension fund that given the 'failure to secure agreement on the Corporate Plan', the company intended to cease making contributions from mid-1989. At a meeting between NUJ representatives and the trustees, Eamon de Valera 'emphatically denied that a conflict of interest could arise from joint positions as trustees and directors of the company'. In any event, the funding was not cut off. Management finally withdrew the plan altogether – it had made the mistake of insisting on getting 'a full package at once, all or nothing'.[132]

As the Press Group struggled over its future, in 1988 Independent Newspapers began its changeover to modern newspaper production methods when all journalists were required to type their articles on a computer terminal. The articles were then printed, sub-edited and the correct text was then rekeyed by printers. This step-by-step training programme ensured that all journalists became familiar with computer technology before they took the small step to using direct input technology – where the articles would be typed only once by the journalists, transmitted to the sub-editor's terminal, corrected and then positioned on the on-screen newspaper, thus making the function of typesetters obsolete. Later, over one hundred and fifty redundancies were achieved with generous payments and no industrial disruptions.[133] Likewise, at the *Irish Times* the changeover to modern technology was gradual. The company 'engaged in extensive consultation and ensured that there were no compulsory redundancies. Staff were transferred to other areas or given generous severance packages.'[134] Although the Press Group had started off with a two-year lead in the introduction of new technology, by 1988 Independent Newspapers was ahead. The Independent Group had in fact learned from the problems of the Press Group. The latter had taken 'a confrontational approach to technology that Independent Newspapers knew was not a winner'.[135] The Independent Group realised that it 'could not force change through' and as a result the changeover was 'a long and tedious but strife free process'. The company never lost an edition and so it was 'a worthwhile wait that paid dividends in the end'.[136] The following year, 1989, saw the *Sunday Independent* finally outsell the *Sunday Press*, stripping it of the prestige that came with being the premier broadsheet Sunday newspaper. The *Sunday Press* had held that distinction since its foundation in 1949 and being relegated was a severe blow to the paper's morale. That year also saw the reorganisation of the Press Group into three distinct companies. While Irish Press Newspapers would own Burgh Quay and publish the titles, Irish Press Publications would own the titles. A third company, Irish Press Plc, would act as a parent company to the other two. Significantly, ownership of the Press Group's considerable shareholding in the Reuters financial services group remained not with the newspaper company but with the parent company. This decision to fragment the company was to have serious consequences in later years when the company engaged in what it trumpeted as the perfect partnership – a partnership that ultimately killed the Press titles.

In July 1989, Eamon de Valera announced that a partnership agreement had been reached with an American company Ingersoll Publications. How the two companies became involved in discussions in the first place has always been shrouded in mystery. Various intermediaries including a prominent Irish media mogul and an ex-Fianna Fáil leader were rumoured to have played suitor to the two companies. By the deal agreed, a new company, Ingersoll Irish Publications, acquired a fifty per cent equity shareholding in both Irish Press Publications (owner of the three titles) and Irish Press Newspapers (publisher of the three titles) for a price of £5 million and a loan of £1 million. The latter company agreed to pay the Ingersoll company managerial fees of £300,000 per annum for 'a range of management services and resources covering every function of the newspaper business'.[137] Eamon de Valera remained as editor-in-chief of both IPP and IPN while 'ultimate editorial control in respect of political and public policy would rest with the holding company Irish Press Plc'.[138] This deal was the basis for what one editor described as 'the bizarre fifty-fifty division of the company'.[139] In later years, disagreements over who had the right to run the newspapers would cause intense infighting and bitterness. Nonetheless, the *Irish Press* was euphoric as its headline promised a 'New Era for Irish Newspapers'. Described by the paper as the 'perfect partner', Ralph Ingersoll promised investment for extra pages, colour facilities and market research to allow the Press Group 'compete vigorously' and give Independent Newspapers 'a contest they did not expect'. The installation of 'the most advanced newspaper production technology on the planet' was also promised. Dismissing the notion that this would cause industrial unrest, Ingersoll stated there was 'no such thing as a labour problem, only a management problem which can be resolved by better communication'.[140] Reaction to the impending partnership varied. The Dublin Printing Trades Union Group stated that it was regrettable that 'there had to be a foreign involvement' in the Press Group, an investment it believed was 'not in the best interests' of the readers, staff or the newspaper titles themselves.[141] The union also called for the new investment to be tied to new management and expressed its belief that there needed to be 'a drastic improvement in management structure' to improve on 'the dismal performance of the past few years'.[142] In contrast Ralph Ingersoll publicly stated that he 'did not invest to change management' and declared his 'every confidence' in the existing management. While the *Irish Times* welcomed the deal from an ideological viewpoint and hoped that the partnership would lead 'to a new era of security and financial stability for the Press newspapers while preserving their distinct ethos',[143] the *Irish Independent* warned of Ingersoll's harsh business reputation:

> Nothing in Ralph Ingersoll's history suggests he is a man who gives free lunches. Quite the reverse. In the USA, Mr Ingersoll is famous for his business acumen in building up his newspaper empire . . . The *Irish Press* deal appears to fit the pattern so far. The next stage though, is the squeezing for which the group is famed, as costs are pared and extra revenues generated. This has been essential for Ingersoll because the expansion has been paid for with junk bonds – high interest debt which can only be serviced if considerable extra cash is generated from the papers. It is a sensible enough strategy – ensuring that the paper's costs can be brought into line before new money is pumped in – but uncomfortable for those at the receiving end.[144]

Indeed, given his background it was unrealistic to suggest or believe that Ingersoll was going to be a silent partner. Ingersoll's father, also called Ralph, had been one of the most formidable figures of American journalism in the 1940s and 1950s. He had been one of the founders of *Life* and *Fortune* magazines, publisher of *Time* magazine and he later built up an eleven-title regional newspaper chain. It was this that Ralph Ingersoll junior inherited by means of a bitter internal coup.[145] The latter expanded the newspaper empire into a two-hundred title portfolio paid for by the sale of junk bonds sold mostly through Ingersoll's associate, stockbroker Michael Milken, who was later charged with fraud, thus heralding the collapse of the Ingersoll empire.[146] Ingersoll had already ventured into the European newspaper market with the acquisition of the Birmingham Post and Mail Group during the 1980s. While this originally occupied his time, he would eventually turn his attention to his Irish acquisition.

The company's annual general meeting in July 1989 was a stormy affair, when despite all the publicity, the board refused to give shareholders any details about the proposed partnership with Ingersoll. The change of the *Irish Press* to tabloid format and the fact that circulation had dropped from 76,000 in 1988 to 63,287 in 1989 resulted in intense criticism from shareholders. One shareholder claimed that although previously a lifelong *Irish Press* reader, he was now buying the *Guardian* because he wanted a quality newspaper. In response, de Valera replied that the relaunch was 'a success beyond our wildest expectations'.[147] As with almost every other annual general meeting, the issue of the secretive American Corporation was raised. While the 1987 annual report had revealed that the Press Group had acquired 'an interest' in the American Corporation, the board had refused to explain why Irish Press Plc was buying shares in the US-based shareholding trust. This interest was later sold and at the 1989 annual general meeting, one shareholder asked why and to whom. De Valera refused to explain the transaction and claimed that the American Corporation had never had a stake in Irish Press Plc. He did reveal, however, that he intended to 'remain in control' of the company because he was controlling shareholder through shares that he held directly and 'through a trust arrangement . . . as successor to the interests of those' who had gone before him.[148] The share register would, according to de Valera, disclose that Irish Press Plc had members all over the world, but would not include the American Corporation. One may recall how Noel Browne had disclosed to the Dáil in 1959 that Eamon de Valera senior had registered the shares of the American Corporation in his own name, thus giving the appearance that the American shareholders did not exist. The confusion and secrecy generated by the existence of the American Corporation was compounded by the directors of the company who 'exchanged faxes in consultation over means of responding to inquiries about the IPC trust from dissident shareholders'.[149] Who really controlled the company was revealed in November 1989, when de Valera wrote to shareholders informing them that a shareholders' meeting would take place the following month to approve or reject the Ingersoll partnership. The letter also informed shareholders that the directors who controlled fifty-four per cent of the equity (the American Corporation and individual holdings) would vote in favour of the investment.[150] This effectively meant that the decision was already made. At that meeting, the chief executive of Ingersoll Irish Publications, Jim Plugh, stated that the priority of the new investor was to 'break the deadlock which had existed for a number of years between the management and unions'.[151] Asked by one shareholder if he were satisfied with the financial position of Ingersoll, de Valera replied that his inquiries had led him to be 'entirely satisfied'.[152]

Speculation on the possible deal with Ingersoll resulted in increased activity with regard to the American Corporation. In a sworn statement, Elio Malocco claimed that 'he acted as a front-man in assisting Eamon de Valera buy extra "B" shares in the Irish Press Corporation through an Irish registered shelf company, Ataner Ltd'. Jane de Valera (Malocco's wife, Eamon's cousin and daughter of Terry de Valera) was a director of Ataner Ltd. Malocco claimed that 'de Valera transferred $83,000 to Ataner Ltd on June 11 1988 to purchase 100 "B" shares in IPC'.[153] Indeed, in 1989 de Valera formed another American company, USIP, to 'acquire extra Irish Press Corporation shares including those sold by the Carmelite Order in New York'.[154] De Valera subsequently bought 2,500 'A' shares.[155] After the Ingersoll deal was signed, Malocco 'set about buying Irish Press Corporation shares in the US' by placing adverts in the New York papers, the *Irish Voice* and the *Irish Echo*.[156] The mechanisms of the American Corporation itself make for curious reading. Each year, de Valera and Malocco travelled to New York to attend an annual meeting with the Corporation's elderly directors. The board consisted of Jack and Helen Duffy (who were both octogenarians) and Harry Burke (who was in his late seventies). Terry de Valera's nominees to the board consisted of his daughter Jane de Valera and her husband Elio Malocco. The board chairman was Martin Dunne. While these individuals were paid directors' fees of $1,500 each, small shareholders rarely turned up.[157] These directors had been kept in the dark about the negotiations with Ingersoll. In response to queries about the partnership from Irish-American journalists, the Corporation chairman Martin Dunne had replied that there was no truth whatsoever in the rumours. Days later, the deal was announced in Dublin.[158]

Ironically, just as the Press Group had found a perfect partner to save it, so too had Fianna Fáil. The 1989 election produced a hung Dáil and for the first time in its history, Fianna Fáil entered into coalition negotiations with another party. Haughey's decision to negotiate with the Progressive Democrats stunned the Fianna Fáil organisation, but was praised by the *Irish Press* as 'a historic step . . . an acceptance of today's political reality that with the PR system, it is unlikely that any party in the future will command an overall majority'.[159] The thought of entering coalition government saw most rank and file members of the party object to the negotiations. The issue of whether or not the party had a core anti-coalition principle caused a certain amount of confusion. The fact that for decades before the *Irish Press* had consistently demonised the concept of coalition government seemed to suggest that it did. When the coalition agreement was announced, the paper defended Haughey's decision. While conceding that 'opposition to coalition really is a core value' and that resentment within the party was to be expected 'given the suddenness of the u-turn performed on the issue by the leadership and the cabinet', the paper commented that 'the choice Mr Haughey made was probably more painful to him, personally and politically' and that Fianna Fáil 'with the largest number of seats had a duty to provide a government'.[160] Just as in the 1950s, when the party changed policy on free trade and depended on the paper to convince the party faithful to follow suit, in the 1980s it depended on the *Irish Press* to convince the party grassroots to drop the core value of no coalition on the grounds that it was a national necessity.

While in power, Haughey again got involved in a series of controversies involving the *Irish Press*' ex-political correspondent Michael Mills, whom the Fine Gael/Labour coalition had appointed as the country's first ombudsman in 1983. In a 'bitter and embarrassing encounter', cutbacks in government spending eventually ensured that 'the office of Ombudsman was deprived of funds'.[161] As there were cutbacks on all services at the time, 'Haughey's argument was that the office could not be excluded'.[162] However, Mills was obliged to tell the Dáil if he could not carry out his function, a move that Haughey totally disapproved of. According to Mills, 'Haughey's opinion was that public servants should not be allowed into the public arena'. Even though his office acted 'as a voice for those people without a voice' and he 'disliked it being put into the political limelight', Mills persisted in highlighting his case. It was only through the intervention of the Irish Congress of Trade Unions that the funds were eventually restored.[163] Later, when Mills' six-year contract was up, his reappointment became 'a political issue'. According to Mills, Haughey wanted him gone 'and probably would have succeeded except that Fine Gael and Labour asked questions and the Progressive Democrats who were in government with Fianna Fáil told Haughey that they would not support him'. On Mills' last Friday at work, he was driving home not sure whether he would have a job the following Monday when he heard on the radio that he had been reappointed. In Mills' own words, 'Haughey had backed down'.[164] But controversial cutbacks in spending were not confined to the national finances. Over at Burgh Quay, a renewed attempt to implement spending cuts produced unprecedented industrial anarchy during the 1990s.

CHAPTER EIGHT

Endgame – The Collapse of the Irish Press

> The biggest single disaster was Ingersoll. How anybody could decide on such a partnership is beyond me. I was doing a column in the States and I was getting letters from editors and reporters over there asking what the hell was going on? One has to ask what sort of information management were acting on when even the most junior reporter knew what was going on.[1]
>
> *John Kelly on Ingersoll and the* Irish Press

Like the beginning of most other decades, at Burgh Quay the 1990s began with a shock. In June 1990, Ralph Ingersoll's American newspaper empire collapsed and his British holding was subsequently bought out by its management. For the first time since the formation of the 'perfect' partnership, Ingersoll had time on his hands and declared his intention to become more involved in the day-to-day running of the Press Group. This declaration, unlike the initial announcement of the partnership, received a more muted response from Burgh Quay executives who listened helplessly as American accents gradually became more and more common. Shortly afterwards, the partnership attempted to implement an updated version of the failed five-year corporate plan. Entitled the *Supplemental Agreement*, it basically made the same demands as its predecessor – two hundred voluntary redundancies, a move towards new technology and a five-shift instead of a four-shift working week. A pay increase of three per cent for the change in the working week was rejected by unions on the grounds that it represented a weekly productivity increase of twenty-five per cent for less than a quarter of the cost. Again the NUJ and the IPU rejected the plan and in an NUJ vote of no confidence in the management, every staff member and editorial executive at the meeting supported the motion.[2] Talks involving management and the Irish Congress of Trade Unions held under the auspices of Fianna Fáil Minister for Labour, Bertie Ahern, proposed a compromise of a four-and-a-half-shift week. When this was rejected by the workers, the board made it clear that unless an agreement was forthcoming it would cease publishing. Finally, on Friday 20 July 1990, the company's chief executive, Vincent Jennings, wrote to each staff member threatening to take the newspapers off the streets and post the staff's P45s and final pay cheques that he had ready. The following day's edition of the *Irish Press* warned of the looming closure and stated that the fate of the papers 'depended on behind the scene moves'.[3] That day's *Evening Press* also bade goodbye to its readers, noting that the plan 'required considerable understanding and adaptation from staff' that 'in the end they did not at all feel able to accept'.[4] But within three hours of the deadline for agreement, both sides reached a compromise based on the proposals of *Sunday Press* journalist John Kelly. It was Kelly who hit on the idea that the half-shift in the ICTU/management proposal of a four-and-a-half-shift week be used to train staff in the use of new technology. In return for this, greater consultation was to be granted to unions in the key areas of new rosters and newsroom reorganisation.[5] On Sunday 22 July the compromise was accepted by the workers and the following morning the *Irish Press* carried a four-page special on the near death settlement.

That year's presidential election again highlighted the historical if ailing relationship between Fianna Fáil and the *Irish Press*. During the campaign, the party candidate Brian Lenihan (who had written editorials for the *Irish Press* during the 1950s)[6] became embroiled in a controversy. It was alleged that he had telephoned President Patrick Hillery in January 1982, after the collapse of the Fine Gael/Labour coalition, to request that Hillery refuse to grant a dissolution of the Dáil to the Taoiseach Garret FitzGerald and instead invite Charles Haughey to form a government. In a two-page interview with Lenihan, the *Irish Press*' political correspondent, Emily O'Reilly, asked him whether or not he had rung the president. Lenihan replied: 'I wasn't involved. I didn't do it, not personally.' When asked if someone else had rung the president, Lenihan replied 'someone may have done that'.[7] Lenihan was also challenged on the issue by Garret FitzGerald when both men appeared on RTÉ's current affairs programme *Questions and Answers*. On the show, Lenihan again denied that he had rung the president. The following day, the *Irish Press* noted that a 'direct conflict' between Lenihan and FitzGerald had 'arisen over their recollections of events'. The report stated that while Lenihan denied ringing the president, FitzGerald alleged that 'Lenihan and a number of Fianna Fáil TDs made repeated calls to the President'.[8] A few months earlier, Lenihan had conducted a taped interview with a UCD student Jim Duffy for his research thesis on the Irish presidency. On the tape, Lenihan admitted ringing the president. When Lenihan continued to deny that he had rung the president, Duffy took his tape to the *Irish Times* and the paper subsequently released it at a news conference. The fact that Duffy was a former member of Fine Gael was not lost on those looking for irony in the situation.[9] Nonetheless, Fianna Fáil was caught totally off-guard and Lenihan's credibility was badly shaken.

There then emerged a considerable rift among the board of directors, editors and staff at the *Irish Press*: 'in the fortnight leading up to Lenihan's defeat there was considerable recrimination at editorial and boardroom level over a perceived lack of support for him'.[10] Some executives were disappointed at the 'lukewarm approach the papers were taking towards Lenihan'.[11] According to the *Phoenix* magazine, company director Elio Malocco even went so far as to write to Lenihan to assure him that future coverage would improve. The report also stated that political correspondent Emily O'Reilly had had a series of disagreements with senior editorial executives 'who requested that she soft pedal on Lenihan stories such as the tape controversy . . . something O'Reilly refused to do'.[12] However, according to the paper's editor, Hugh Lambert, there was no rift and the Lenihan affair was covered in a 'five-page special that was complimented by management for its balanced approach'.[13] According to Emily O'Reilly, however, the story in the *Phoenix* was correct:

> In the run up to the campaign I did a series of interviews with the candidates, based on a questions and answers format which was to appear in the paper. In the Brian Lenihan interview, I asked him about the Aras phone-calls but some people in the *Irish Press* did not like it. At the time I had little contact with the paper as the political correspondent's office was based in Leinster House where I got a call from the news editor. He said he had a message to be conveyed to me by Malocco to go easy on Lenihan. I was furious. It was the first time there was direct interference with what I was writing. But within a few days the whole thing blew up with the release of the Duffy tapes and Lenihan was fair game after that. After that I had a free reign.[14]

Such sentiments were also expressed by Fianna Fáil deputy leader Mary O'Rourke and former *Irish Press* political correspondent

Michael Mills, who both agreed that by 1990 the 'free reign' given to the paper's political correspondents had grown substantially over the years. While O'Rourke conceded that the paper 'was originally friendly to Fianna Fáil because it was set up for that purpose', in later years 'it was just like any other paper'.[15] According to Mills the paper 'changed greatly in later years' with the political correspondents being 'more critical of things happening in Fianna Fáil which was not possible earlier'.[16] Nonetheless, although the *Irish Press* published the transcript of the tape, the five pages of coverage were mostly uncritical of Lenihan. While the paper stated that 'Mr Lenihan and the Fianna Fáil leadership in general have made some serious errors of judgement in relation to this affair over the past week', it claimed that judging from the reception Lenihan was getting around the country 'the damage may be a lot less than the pundits think'.[17] The paper also called on opposition parties to cool 'the political temperature' and appealed to the party's coalition partners, the Progressive Democrats, to resist the political pressure to punish Lenihan or Haughey. According to the paper, 'whatever reservations the party may have about how the issue was handled by Fianna Fáil, those have to be balanced against the damage that would be done to the economy at this critical time over an incident that happened some eight years ago'.[18] Despite this caution, the Progressive Democrats insisted on Lenihan's resignation as Tanaiste, and when he refused to resign Haughey sacked him. The *Irish Press* carried seven pages on the sacking in which it criticised the venom with which Lenihan had been hounded. Although it acknowledged that 'Mr Lenihan brought much of the disaster down upon his own head', it noted that a 'modicum of iron will have entered the native soul', some of which had 'been engendered as much by the accusers as by the accused'. It criticised the 'zeal with which the attack was pressed home' which it held was both 'merciless and un-edifying'. In an attempt to rally the party faithful, the paper noted that Lenihan remained the Fianna Fáil presidential candidate and that a week was a long time in politics.[19]

Curiously enough, the following day the paper relented and concluded that while the 'anger and resentment' within Fianna Fáil was 'understandable', for the party 'to try to pretend that the trauma' was the fault of the PDs or Fine Gael 'was to miss the painful events of the last week'.[20] It also dismissed the transfer pact between the Labour Party and Fine Gael as 'a strategy simply to stop Fianna Fáil's Brian Lenihan being elected'. The paper accurately pointed out that

Alan Dukes' leadership of Fine Gael depended on the performance of the party's candidate, Austin Currie, and also pointed out that before the Lenihan revelations, Garret FitzGerald had labelled Mary Robinson as being 'unsuitable for the office' because of her opposition to the Anglo-Irish Agreement. Now Fine Gael found it 'politically expedient to change its views and its strategy as the polls changed'. The paper also had harsh words for Robinson herself – it hit out at her for allegedly dumping her left wing beliefs in favour of voter friendly centre politics. This resulted in her 'stumbling on the last lap and losing her ideological balance in her frantic efforts to move out of the left lane'. According to the paper, there was 'nothing wrong with being a left wing candidate or with holding controversial views on social issues'. It was only when such a candidate tried 'to pretend she is someone else that people start to ask questions'.[21] The strategy might have worked had it not been for deputy Padraig Flynn's bizarre radio attack on Robinson's makeover in which he questioned her commitment to her family. The personal attack backfired and in a last ditch effort to get Lenihan elected, the *Irish Press* printed a front page editorial urging its readers to vote for him.[22] According to the editorial, 'by his wide experience and strength of personality' Lenihan was 'uniquely gifted to be our President'.[23] While he had 'shown great courage and resistance in the face of personal and political adversity', the other candidates were 'divided on the Anglo-Irish Agreement'. While 'the election of Mrs Robinson would be seen by some as a form of repudiation of the agreement by the electorate', Austin Currie had 'not been able to establish himself as a candidate with any chance of winning'. Thus Lenihan's 'record of service and loyalty' spoke for itself despite 'the unwarranted vilification' to which he had been subjected. He had 'never betrayed a trust' and he would 'not betray the people of Ireland' who 'should go out and vote for him today'.[24] While the Fianna Fáil vote ensured that Lenihan received the most first preference votes, he was subsequently defeated by the transfer pact between Fine Gael and Labour, leading the *Irish Press* to note that the party could take 'some comfort from the fact that despite everything, its traditional vote held up across the country'.[25]

As Fianna Fáil struggled to keep its coalition with the Progressive Democrats together, over at Burgh Quay the 'perfect' partnership was slowly unwinding as the Ingersoll executives began to make their presence felt more and more. It was this side of the partnership that was mostly responsible for the disastrous relaunch of the *Evening Press* in April 1991. Although sales of the paper had been dropping constantly since 1974, the change shocked many in the newspaper industry. In a 1986 interview, asked if the *Evening Press* would ever undergo a change in format, the group chairman Eamon de Valera had replied, 'basically no. We have a successful formula and we would need to be convinced otherwise. Why change a successful formula? Why launch a new product when the product's current shortcomings you can always improve on?'[26] But change format it did, and the relaunch of the *Evening Press* was headed up by the Ingersoll executives who 'gathered the layout staff and got them to implement the changes they had already decided on'.[27] Relaunched as a twenty-four page, twin-segmented, feature-led newspaper with heavy American input, the first editorial of the new-look *Evening Press* stated that it had been 'redesigned for the nineties' and would be 'more relevant, even better value and easier to read'.[28] The paper was restructured to make its 'different elements . . . more logically segmented and easier to find', while the aim of the two-section format was to 'make the paper more accessible to different members of the family'.[29] Within the paper's new format, the first section contained the news, business and sports pages, while the second section contained the features, classifieds and entertainment pages. The changes implemented saw some regular features moved to new positions while others were moved to different publication days. The change backfired badly, however, as traditional rural readers lost interest in the paper. Changing to a two-section format was 'an act of madness'. Readers preferred 'a solid paper' but the new *Evening Press* was 'shapeless'.[30] It met with less than impressive reviews from the Irish media:

> The relaunch of the paper with two sections and a Coca-Cola editorial flavour has seen sales decline dramatically and the paper has since dropped the two section format. It still, however, retains an emphasis on such as Michael Jackson rather than Big Tom and country readers' loyalty has come under severe pressure without much compensation from the new young readers . . . Things are now so bad at the evening paper that there are reports that it is to lose a substantial chunk of critical advertising revenue due to the fall in sales among the rural population.[31]

The Irish side of the partnership soon realised that changing the format of the *Evening Press* was one of the biggest mistakes ever made: 'the redesign of the *Evening Press* was a complete and utter disaster. The paper lost £1 million in advertising revenue in the first year. For a brief period the circulation graph rose significantly and then plummeted into freefall. The redesign was dreadful. It was more a magazine than an evening paper and the readers hated it. The change was absolute suicide. It was then left to the Irish management to clean up the mess.'[32] In the year following the redesign, circulation of the paper fell from 80,507 in 1991 to 69,567 in 1992. Once regarded in advertising circles as a good professional urban paper able to deliver to a more upmarket readership than the rival *Evening Herald*, the paper began its final decline. Such disastrous results led to mutual recriminations between both partners with each side blaming the other for the redesign debacle. Thus began the longest war in the history of Irish industrial relations. While it had initially brought 'new ideas, good teamwork and a depth of management', the 'perfect' partnership soon 'foundered on the bizarre fifty-fifty division of the company'.[33] This made life almost impossible for those working at Burgh Quay:

> the turmoil at management level meant that it became very difficult for journalists to function. The evenly divided board meant no side prevailed. If Ingersoll wanted to do something they came up against the Irish side and vice-versa. It became impossible for journalists to do anything but work from day to day. As the turmoil worsened, we worked on in hope of some deliverance. Long-term planning became more difficult, as the two sides fought for control.[34]

Shortly after, the transfer of journalists to the newly equipped Parnell House, where over £1 million of new computer technology had been installed, was suspended because of a row over redundancies. Instead, the three newspapers were produced on nineteen ageing computer terminals at Burgh Quay.

The shareholders' meeting of 1991 was a stormy affair. At the meeting it emerged that despite continuing losses and calls for cost cutting, the directors of the company had continually awarded themselves substantial pay rises. For example, although losses for Irish Press Publications reached £2.6 million in 1991, directors' fees rose fifty per cent from £206,000 in 1989 to £308,000 in 1990 – the year that management introduced its cost cutting plan. By 1991, director payments had risen to £327,000. Of this £150,000 came from the parent company Irish Press Plc, while the balance of £177,000 came from the cash-starved Irish Press Newspapers.[35] This company, while calling on journalists to accept a pay freeze, also paid Ingersoll Irish Publications management fees of £378,000 in 1990 and £401,000 in 1991. Alongside these payments, the infighting within the group's various boards severely hampered attempts to turn around the circulation declines of the three Press titles. In February 1992, the chief executive of IPN, Vincent Jennings, was forced to resign by Ralph Ingersoll over editorial and management disagreements. Jennings agreed to go when a golden handshake of £250,000 was agreed upon. His replacement was Pat Montague, whom the Irish side viewed as an Ingersoll advocate. There then began an intense power struggle between the American and Irish partners as a merry-go-round of changes in the boards of the group began. In a move regarded by some directors as 'provocative', de Valera appointed Jennings as chairman of IPP and also reinstated him onto the board of IPN.[36] In a reverse move, Dan McGing resigned as chairman of Irish Press Plc because of 'fundamental differences on policy' with de Valera.[37] De Valera had declared that he had lost confidence in McGing, prompting not only the latter's resignation but also that of fellow Irish Press Plc director Andrew Galligan. In his resignation letter, Galligan declared that McGing 'was not guilty of any negligence or misconduct'.[38] Shortly afterwards, McGing was appointed chairman of Ingersoll Irish Publications and later became chief executive of IPN. By this time, the company had discovered that Elio Malocco had not credited it with payments that it had made to him for libel actions. Such moves and changes of allegiances caused tremendous bitterness: 'when the relationship with Ingersoll turned sour, it became a dreadful situation. While Pat Montague was trying to implement Ingersoll's policy, Eamon de Valera was trying to prevent it and very often the editors were caught in the middle. The subsequent court case was very damaging to the papers'.[39]

As the boardroom tussles continued, the papers continued to lose money, advertising and readers. Management's inability to implement a Labour Court recommendation obliging them to pay a mere three per cent salary increase owed to the staff under the government's Programme for Economic and Social Prosperity led journalists to revert to a four-shift week, instead of the four-and-a-half-shift week they had been working since 1990. In May 1992, there occurred what some regarded as the only success of the partnership – the relaunch of the *Sunday Press*. The paper was increased in size and more colour, new features and an enhanced business section were added. However, the second and third parts of the development were postponed due to disagreements at board level. Such an exercise demonstrated not only that the paper had potential, but that management seemed more interested in gaining control of the boards than enhancing the paper's future. From 1992 onwards, every six months brought more cutback demands: 'although the *Sunday Press* got good resources in comparison to the *Irish Press* and *Evening Press*, we were bedevilled by cutbacks and were forced to cancel the column of former Fine Gael minister John Boland because at £400 a week, it was considered too expensive. The paper lost an experienced voice that was not Fianna Fáil orientated.'[40] The infighting and financial problems at the Press Group presented Independent Newspapers with a golden opportunity to launch an aggressive competitive marketing strategy to overtake the Press titles in circulation and advertising appeal. Rival executives knew exactly what was going on at Burgh Quay and when the right moment came they acted swiftly:

> The main problem at the Press Group was bad management. The *Irish Press* was a massive drain on resources but was kept going because of the Fianna Fáil connection. The *Evening Press* was crucial to the revenue of the Press company but it engaged in an expensive relaunch of the title given the structure of the company. Ingersoll took the *Evening Press* – a splendid paper – and in the best American tradition turned it into a two-section broadsheet. The many problems associated with producing a broadsheet were now doubled. It was the kiss of death within six months. It was marketing director Joe Hayes' decision to attack the Press on three fronts. The Independent Group's response then, was to put a trickle of money into the *Irish Independent* to fight the *Irish Press* which we were ahead of anyway, but we poured money into the *Herald* to attack the *Evening Press* and poured money into the *Sunday Independent* to attack the *Sunday Press*.[41]

Thus at the same time that readers were becoming disillusioned with the new format and tone of the *Evening Press*, Independent Newspapers were investing heavily in improving and marketing the *Evening Herald* as an alternative. While the Press Group's resources were concentrated on trying to market the new style *Evening Press*, the group's other two titles were left with little or no resources to market themselves. This left Independent Newspapers free to capitalise on the vulnerability of the Sunday title in particular by launching a successful marketing campaign to entice readers away from the *Sunday Press* to the more highly visible and highly developed *Sunday Independent*.

During the summer of 1992, Irish Press Plc completely wrote off its investments and loans to Irish Press Newspapers and declared that it was 'no longer committed to financially supporting its related companies'.[42] So although Irish Press Plc still owned fifty per cent of IPN, it was no longer financially responsible for the loss making company. Described as an investment company with assets of £4 million, Irish Press Plc also owned a fifty per cent stake in Irish Press Publications. Although it was doubtful if the newspaper company IPN would ever make a profit again, the Press titles owned by IPP were still extremely valuable. In July 1992, both sides agreed to a dissolution of their partnership and Ingersoll Irish Publications offered to sell its shares in IPN to Irish Press Plc for £8 million. When the offer was rejected, Ingersoll began 'active negotiations with at least five interested Irish parties . . . including a group of business people with Fianna Fáil connections'.[43] By August 1992, relations between the two sides had deteriorated so much that attempts by the consortium of businessmen to buy the newspapers and initiate 'a revamped but back-to-the-roots editorial outlook, a complete refinancing, and a total clean out of existing management' failed when both sides refused to meet together to agree a price for the business.[44] That same month the board of IPN finally approved a joint information pack for potential investors but then split on how or whom it should be distributed to. A six-week delay ensued before the two sides again began to separately seek investors.

At Irish Press Plc's 1992 annual general meeting, shareholders launched a broadside at the directors. What had 'been traditionally a lively meeting turned into a fierce castigation of the Irish Press Plc board with wild accusations of greed and mismanagement coming from the shareholders'.[45] At the meeting, Vincent Jennings astounded shareholders by telling them that Irish Press Plc did not control the newspapers and had no responsibility for their management. This attempt by the board at distancing itself from the disastrous performance of the newspapers provoked laughter from the floor after a shareholder pointed out that four of the five directors of Irish Press Plc also sat on the board of IPN. Until the previous February, Vincent Jennings had been chief executive, Eamon de Valera was still chairman and editor-in-chief, while fellow directors Michael Walsh and Brendan Ryan were operations director and financial controller respectively.[46] When questioned about the £2.7 million loss by IPN in 1991, Jennings revealed that £1 million was spent on the disastrous relaunch of the *Evening Press*, while the same amount had been spent on equipping Parnell House with technology that was never utilised. Again there was widespread criticism of directors' payments, with one shareholder pointing out that while directors' payments had risen sixty-seven per cent over the previous three years, staff had been given a pay increase of only seven per cent. Jennings explained that the enhanced salaries were in response to increased responsibility – a rather curious excuse since the board had denied responsibility for the performance of the newspapers. To sustained applause, the shareholder claimed that the directors' payments were 'scandalous' and that the company's founder, Eamon de Valera, senior, 'must be revolving in his grave'.[47] Another shareholder asked the meeting if it had any confidence in 'those people up there' which drew a unanimous resounding 'no' from the assembled shareholders.[48]

As usual, internal turmoil was not confined to Burgh Quay. Within Fianna Fáil, intrigue had also begun to surface and just as the past had been resurrected to end Brian Lenihan's political career, it also returned to end Charles Haughey's career. In January 1992, his former Minister for Justice Sean Doherty claimed that Haughey had been fully aware in 1982 of the tapping of journalists' telephones to stop leaks from the Fianna Fáil cabinet and that he had handed the transcripts directly to Haughey. The latter again denied any knowledge of the affair and the *Irish Press* initially came down on Haughey's side. According to the paper, the public was confronted with a 'stark choice between the word' of Doherty who had 'contradicted himself on this issue in the past and that of the Taoiseach who had been consistent in his version'.[49] As the pressure mounted, however, the paper became more concerned with the survival of the government than that of Haughey. According to the paper, the question that the Progressive Democrats had to answer was whether or not 'the resurrection of these ten year old allegations by a man who's been untruthful about them in the past merited the downfall of the government'.[50] When the party gave Fianna Fáil the choice of either getting rid of Haughey or disbanding the coalition, the paper came as close as it ever would to urging Haughey to resign by noting that 'during the crisis involving Brian Lenihan last year, the Taoiseach said he was putting the national good first by demanding the then Tanaiste's resignation'. According to the paper, it was 'ironic' that Haughey now found 'himself ransom to that national good'.[51] While it noted that many in Fianna Fáil were angered by the 'PD's threat that either Mr Haughey goes or they pull out of government', it proclaimed that politics was 'a cruel business in which personal survival' came first.[52] As on every such previous occasion, the paper expressed a warm welcome to the new party leader, Albert Reynolds, who took over the party 'with a number of important advantages that his predecessor Mr Haughey never enjoyed'. One such advantage was the 'overall margin of his victory' that left him in 'undisputed control'.[53] With the 'Haughey Factor' at last disposed of, the paper encouraged the party to unify behind the new leader to ensure the survival of the coalition with the party it had once branded as merely an anti-Haughey cabal. According to the paper, Fianna Fáil needed 'a fresh start' to allow it to settle down, rebuild and reorganise after the terrible traumas of recent times'. The 'feuds and the factions of recent years' had produced 'a war weariness in the party'. What the country needed now was 'a period of calm and stability' so that the coalition could 'get back to the real government business'.[54] Despite such sentiments of government stability, the new party leader took an early opportunity to ensure the party faithful that he was committed to single party government. The coalition with the Progressive Democrats, Reynolds declared, was a 'temporary little arrangement'. True to this prediction, the coalition government collapsed within eight months.

The November 1992 election was the last campaign that Fianna Fáil ever contested with the *Irish Press* at its side. Speculation that a coalition of Fine Gael, Labour and the Progressive Democrats would unite to deprive Fianna Fáil of power saw the paper dismiss such a coalition as unworkable. According to the paper, the 'grossest deception being practised on the Irish public' was the attempt by 'opposition parties to portray themselves as part of a potential rainbow coalition'.[55] There was 'no arrangement between any of the opposition parties to present themselves as a combination that would provide an alternative government'. It had become 'increasingly obvious' that not only were 'the policies of some of these parties diametrically opposed to one another' but that there was also 'serious disagreement about who might lead'. It was time to 'stop fantasising' because the opposition were 'being dishonest to portray themselves as anything but individual parties with individual policies'.[56] On polling day, the paper noted that only Fianna Fáil could provide 'a stable and strong government' and that the 'prospect of a rainbow coalition put together after weeks of negotiations' was daunting.[57] According to the paper, 'strong government and confidence were never more needed' because a 'return to the instability of ten years ago would risk a repetition of economic stagnation of the mid 1980s'. That was why 'Fianna Fáil should be returned to government'.[58] The outcome of the election was traumatic for the party. An electoral swing to the left saw Fianna Fáil drop from seventy-seven to sixty-eight seats. In contrast, the Labour Party gained seventeen seats, bringing its strength to an all time high of thirty-three seats. Commenting on the result, the *Irish Press* noted that it was hard to tell whether the dramatic swing 'signalled a real shift in the political landscape' or was 'merely a temporary switch to a party unencumbered by responsibility for our current economic woes'.[59] Nonetheless, it noted that 'given such an overwhelming mandate by the electorate', the Labour Party was 'crucial to the formation of the new government'. Likewise, Fianna Fáil was 'still far and away the largest party in the state with an important contribution to make'. The paper remarked that 'it may yet be that a Labour and Fianna Fáil alliance would prove to be the most compatible partnership on offer'.[60] Despite the hint, the Labour leader Dick Spring spent the next two weeks in negotiations with another left wing party, Democratic Left. Neither Fianna Fáil nor the *Irish Press* was impressed. As the negotiations began, the paper commented that Labour only wanted Democratic Left in coalition to stop it from 'sniping from the sidelines as a left wing opposition' and claimed that the 'uncompromising party's inclusion in any new government would not guarantee stability'.[61] Indeed, 'it would be astonishing if Labour by insisting on the inclusion of a party which had such a minuscule percentage of the vote impeded the formation of a more representative government'.[62] This more representative government was presumably the more compatible Fianna Fáil and Labour alliance already mentioned by the paper. As the negotiations continued into their second week and the seriousness of Spring's intention became clear, the paper totally reversed it position. When Fine Gael and the PDs imprudently ruled out any coalition arrangement involving Democratic Left, the paper accused them of 'showing scant regard for the democratic system or the principle of power sharing with political opposites'.[63] According to the paper, 'the notion that a couple of DL deputies in government . . . would subvert the system and Irish society would not be tenable even if those involved were wide eyed revolutionary threatening communists'. They had been 'democratically elected in precisely the same way as those now bitterly denouncing them in both Fine Gael and the PDs' and had 'the same entitlement to office'.[64] When the inevitable talks between Fianna Fáil and Labour began, the paper commented that the two parties were 'much closer ideologically' than any of the other parties.[65] The Labour Party's main concern had been 'to find a combination in which it could feel comfortable' and the paper held that it 'should find that with Fianna Fáil, the single party which took most votes in the election'.[66] The formation of a coalition and the return to power of Fianna Fáil saw the paper comment that the long wait was over. Commending the 'new maturity' of the Labour Party, the paper praised the 'great responsibility' it took to ensure that the government formed would be a 'lasting one'.[67] Faithful to the last, the paper proclaimed that the most recent poll showed that the new coalition government with Fianna Fáil as the major partner had 'strong support' among the Irish people.[68]

But while the new coalition may have enjoyed strong public support, the same could not be said for the Press Group, where the board infighting had reached fever pitch. In June 1993, Irish Press Plc asked the High Court to terminate its management agreement with Ingersoll Irish Publications claiming that the company was involved in shareholder oppression, that the management of their jointly held concerns was inadequate despite the costly fees and that Ingersoll Irish Publications was not financially sound when it entered into the partnership and thus entered it under false pretences.[69] In its defence, Ingersoll Irish Publications claimed that Irish Press Plc underestimated the capital invested by the company and that the managerial fees charged were well below market prices. In a counter action, the Ingersoll company sought the dismissal of Eamon de Valera as chairman and editor-in-chief, claiming that he continually interfered with and undermined management. It also sought a refund of the payment made to Vincent Jennings when he resigned as chief executive of IPN only to be later reappointed to the board by de Valera. The Ingersoll company also alleged that de Valera had 'failed to act responsibly in the provision of libel protection machinery' by not retaining a reputable law firm that specialised in libel law and further alleged that de Valera acted in his own interests by appointing a relative, Elio Malocco who had subsequently defrauded the company of £64,000.[70] The hearing cost over £2 million and dragged on for thirty-five days, during which it took on 'many of the trappings of a classic divorce case with each side instancing heated examples of what they claim as disruptive, oppressive or underhanded behaviour'.[71] It also revealed 'incredible tales of tension, sackings and secret deals between various directors, executives and some staff'.[72] For those working for the Press titles 'the extended court case was a most debilitating experience':[73]

> Dreadful accusations were made and characters were assassinated. All we could do was carry on while we had ink and newsprint. As long as the papers were coming out, there could be some hope. Looking back, it is clear that we were getting the papers out in the most bizarre and impossible conditions imaginable.[74]

Indeed, the public washing of the Press Group's dirty linen and the details of the constant infighting and bizarre occurrences within the company provided much unfavourable publicity for the Press titles. The details of how IPN chief executive Vincent Jennings had been persuaded by Ingersoll to resign were outlined in evidence. According to Jennings, he was informed that Ingersoll had 'irrevocably decided on a change at the top'. When Jennings recited his contractual rights, Ingersoll replied that he was 'determined to get the change, and if he could not, he would liquidate the company'. Jennings responded by saying that he 'would not consider threats under any circumstances' but left voluntarily when a cash settlement of £250,000 was agreed upon.[75] The court also heard that Jennings' former personal assistant, Joan Hyland, continued on in that post for his replacement Pat Montague. In evidence, she admitted that she had photocopied documents marked 'private and confidential' and passed them on to Eamon de Valera.[76] On another occasion she had photocopied documents and passed them on to Jennings. Hyland agreed that she had 'a duty of confidentiality' to Montague but denied that she had spied on him. According to Hyland, she regarded her actions as 'a duty' to the company and that she had acted 'in the best interest of the company'.[77] When Jennings was recalled to the witness box, he told the court that on one occasion he 'took home a black plastic bag marked "rubbish" that was full of shredded documents from an Ingersoll-appointed executive's office and examined the contents'.[78] An argument then developed within the company as to who owned the shredded documents.[79]

It also emerged that during the 1985 strike, the Press Group had held discussions with the Smurfit Group that were abandoned when it became clear that the latter wished to acquire a majority shareholding in the group. In his evidence, de Valera stated that he had 'friendly and amicable discussions' with Michael Smurfit. When it was put to him that the talks had not proceeded because a 'consequence of continuing the talks would have been that he would have lost control of the newspapers', de Valera replied that he 'always understood that Dr Smurfit's intent would have been for control'.[80] The mysterious American Corporation also raised its head. When counsel for Ingersoll Irish Publications suggested to de Valera 'that he had asked Ingersoll personnel for a £1 million interest-free loan to be placed offshore for "tidying up" purposes in the US, which meant going there to buy Irish Press shares', de Valera replied that 'he had inquired whether finance would be available and that he was interested in clearing up the entire shareholding in the American Corporation but nothing came of it; no such loan was forthcoming'.[81] When asked 'if it would ultimately have been for his personal benefit, de Valera said it would in the very long term'.[82] It was also disclosed that Ralph Ingersoll and IPN chief executive Pat Montague had reached an agreement whereby Montague would receive five per cent of the sale price if he managed to find a buyer for Ingersoll's shareholding.

During the case, it was put to both Jennings and de Valera that the lengthy period of falling circulation of the titles had coincided with their control of the company. Jennings answered the suggestion that the fall in circulation was because 'the papers had become less attractive to readers' by saying that this 'was not necessarily the position'. When it was put to him that 'editorially, it [the *Irish Press*] was not a well produced paper', he replied that this 'was not a simple question'. Pressed to concede that there was 'no hope for the survival of the titles unless editorial direction, policy and control changed', Jennings replied that he 'did not accept this'. When asked if it were 'a coincidence that the decline in circulation started when he became editor-in-chief', Eamon de Valera replied that yes, 'the decline and losses were simply a coincidence with his arrival on the scene'. He 'rejected responsibility totally for the inability' of management 'to implement changes in the newspaper'.[83] Most observers were disappointed, however, when Ralph Ingersoll was not called to give evidence.

In December 1993, having found 'persistent shareholder oppression since late 1991 and an effective repudiation of the management services agreement', Justice Henry Barron ordered Ingersoll Irish Publications to sell its fifty per cent stakes in IPP and IPN to Irish Press Plc for £2.25 million. The latter was also awarded £2.75 million in damages while IPN was awarded compensation of £6 million.[84] While Ingersoll's shareholdings in IPN and IPP reverted to Irish Press Plc, Ingersoll appealed the damages awarded against it. Indeed, in its 1993 annual report, Irish Press Plc conceded that there was little chance of receiving the money awarded to it. According to the report, the company had 'to recognise and be reconciled to the fact' that even if the Supreme Court fully upheld the compensation orders, there was 'little prospect of Ingersoll Irish Publications Ltd being in a position to fully discharge the awards of damages which have been made against it'.[85] As the court case dragged on circulation figures for all three Press titles plummeted. Throughout the last few years of the Press Group's existence, circulation for all three Press titles hit an all-time low. Between 1989 and 1994, circulation of the *Irish Press* fell thirty-nine per cent from 63,345 to 38,848 while circulation of the *Evening Press* dropped forty-seven per cent from 102,000 to 54,000. During the same period, circulation of the *Sunday Press*, the one time money-spinner of the group, fell twenty-eight per cent from 217,000 to 157,000. In the wake of the court revelations, relations between management and workers rapidly deteriorated as the countdown to closure continued.

In April 1994 staff again rejected another cost saving programme that involved further job losses. The following month the company turned down investment from a consortium headed by Independent Newspapers that proposed to buy just under twenty-five per cent of IPN. Separate discussions with a consortium composed of the London-based *Daily Telegraph* and the Irish-based *Sunday Business Post* also collapsed when it sought a majority shareholding. Indeed, consternation within Fianna Fáil caused by the possible investment in the Press Group by a British newspaper prompted Taoiseach Albert Reynolds to state: 'I don't want a British newspaper group to take over the *Irish Press*. I don't even want to contemplate it.'[86] But by the end of August 1994, Irish Press Newspapers had literally run out of money. Faced with an impending financial crisis, the company made a direct approach to Independent Newspapers and negotiated a possible £2 million loan and a £15 million investment package from the company.[87] In mid-October, however, it disengaged from the negotiations after Independent Newspapers sought two directorships in return for the investment. Less than three weeks later, financial reality forced the Press Group to engage AIB Corporate Finance to help it secure investment. On 9 November 1994, AIB wrote to both Independent Newspapers and the *Sunday Business Post* consortium and stated that Irish Press Plc was willing to sell its entire holding in IPN, but that a £2 million investment was needed immediately. On 23 November, the *Sunday Business Post* consortium offered an interest free loan of £2 million for one hundred days to secure the exclusive option to purchase the company after examining its account books. The maximum the consortium was prepared to pay for the company was £4.5 million with a total financial commitment of £20 million. In a follow-up letter, the consortium also asked that the loans to IPN from Irish Press Plc and Ingersoll Irish Publications be written off.[88] Although Fianna Fáil Minister for Finance Bertie Ahern acted as a facilitator for the bid, it was subsequently turned down on 22 December.[89] According to one editor, the consortium 'wanted the papers for nothing. The deal did not stand up businesswise, although from a public relations approach, it looked like intransigence on the management's part'.[90] Instead, the Press Group opted for a deal with Independent Newspapers. On 22 December 1994, Irish Press Plc announced that it had sold just under twenty-five per cent of IPN and IPP to Independent Newspapers. Most of the workforce at Burgh Quay was shocked at the decision: 'we were puzzled and could not make sense of it. They were our lifelong competitors. Was our future to be a lap-dog to Tony O'Reilly? But the investment was welcome because it kept us going for six months. The decision was brought about by a touch of desperation – there was no other course.'[91]

The Press Group's historical ally against Independent Newspapers, the *Irish Times*, was virtually excluded from the negotiations on the future of the Press titles. This despite the fact that on 2 December 1994, the company had written to the Irish Press Plc expressing an interest in purchasing a shareholding in IPN. Even after Independent Newspapers had invested in IPN and IPP, the *Irish Times* still offered investment, but only if it could examine the future development plans for the Press titles. At a meeting on 5 January 1995, Vincent Jennings informed the *Irish Times* that unlike Independent Newspapers, it could not help draw up a business plan for the future of IPN because it was not a shareholder. The *Irish Times* replied that it could only invest when given information that would normally be in any company prospectus seeking investment, but the information was still refused. Thus Independent Newspapers invested on its own in the Press companies and as such held the purse strings from which the life of the titles hung. The decision to allow only Independent Newspapers to invest in the Press Group was certainly an act of desperation and was slightly disingenuous given the company's submission to the Competition Authority on the Independent Group's purchase of just under thirty per cent of the *Sunday Tribune* two years earlier. That submission claimed that the purchase would have detrimental ideological and competitive consequences for the *Sunday Tribune*. According to its submission, the Press Group was:

> extremely concerned at the commercial implications of the proposal, which would further enhance the dominant position of Independent Newspapers in the Irish newspaper market . . . editorial policy could not in practice be separated from the controls of a paper and from commercial considerations . . . both the political and commercial aspects of a paper were influenced by the paymasters . . . The publishers appointed the editors and gave them policy directions, even if there was no day-to-day interference. Competition could be distorted in a contrived manner, with one paper in a group giving a particular policy point of view and another giving a different slant, but in a measured way. It [the *Sunday Tribune*] needed financial independence, otherwise it would get watered down or practical or economic problems would intervene.[92]

Now the Press Group had reversed its position and allowed the very company it had accused of being capable of editorial and financial manipulation to buy shares in its own companies. Although no shareholder meeting was convened to discuss the prospective deal, in December 1994 Independent Newspapers Plc acquired an interest in both IPN and IPP for just over £1 million and a loan of £2 million. Significantly though, the money for the share of Irish Press Newspapers was paid over to Irish Press Plc thus leaving the cash-starved newspaper company no better of as a result of the investment. Rather than getting an injection of new capital to relieve its financial pressures, all the newspaper company got was the £2 million loan that it could not afford. Independent Newspapers also secured the three Press titles as security for the loan.[93] The investment was condemned by the NUJ as 'designed to drip feed the only real source of competition to the Independent Newspaper Group'.[94] Likewise, after having been asked to investigate the deal, the Competition Authority found that 'the acquisition by Independent Newspapers of a shareholding in the *Irish Press* and the provision to it of loans by the Independent, represented both an abuse of a dominant position contrary to Section 5 of the Competition Act and an anti-competitive agreement, contrary to Section 4 of the Act'.[95] According to the authority, the purchase would 'further strengthen Independent's dominance in the various relevant markets for newspapers and advertising'. The authority found that 'the share purchase was designed to prevent a rival of Independent Newspapers acquiring control of the *Irish Press*' and noted that 'at the very least Independent Newspapers will exercise some influence, direct or indirect, over the commercial conduct of the *Irish Press*'.[96] In the circumstances, the authority 'recommended that the Minister take action under Section 6 of the

Competition Act against these arrangements'.[97] Section 6 of the Act allowed for the enforcement of the regulations of the Competition Act by way of High Court action on behalf of the Minister for Enterprise and Employment, if the case were believed to be of 'especial public importance'.[98] One member of the authority went so far as to present a minority report that stated that 'failure to take action in a case such as this would seriously undermine the credibility and effectiveness of the Competition Act'.[99] Despite this, the Competition Act was never used to challenge the deal. The previous November, the Fianna Fáil/Labour coalition had collapsed amid acrimonious circumstances and had been replaced without an election by the rainbow coalition of Fine Gael, Labour and Democratic Left. Many within Fianna Fáil believed that things would have worked out differently under a Fianna Fáil government. According to one deputy, the pressure from the parliamentary party would have been far too strong not to have done something.'[100]

On 15 May 1995, a belated extraordinary general meeting of Irish Press Plc shareholders was convened to give the directors 'permission to sell all or part of Irish Press Plc's shareholding in IPN and IPP on such terms and at such times as the directors of the company in their discretion decide'.[101] According to chief executive Vincent Jennings, the move 'was necessary if the directors were to have the flexibility necessary to act in the best interests of the newspapers and the employees'.[102] The motion was proposed by Jennings and seconded by de Valera and was passed by 537,506 votes to 2,443. Several shareholders were vocal in their criticisms of management, with one shareholder asking whether the Press titles were to suffer 'the same fate as the *Freeman's Journal* in 1924'. Another shareholder claimed that 'the rot set in when the *Irish Press* put the liberal agenda before republicanism'. In a potent protest at the end of the meeting, a female shareholder, Loretta Clarke, 'walked up to the top table, accused Jennings of being "a Judas" and dropped thirty pieces of silver on the table. The silver turned out to be old English one shilling pieces, with the head of King George V, the king on the British throne when the *Irish Press* was founded.'[103]

Publication of the Press titles finally ceased on 25 May 1995, after the dismissal of business editor and shareholder Colm Rapple for 'disloyalty to the company' after the publication by the *Irish Times* the previous day of an article he had written. Although the alleged disloyalty centred on Rapple's suggestion of a 'reconstructed *Irish Press* under new management',[104] the business plan of the company drawn up by its board the previous April clearly indicated that it was 'the view of the present board of IPN that new appointments to top management should be made at an appropriate early date. This would include the appointment of a new chief executive or managing director to oversee the major changes that will be necessary.'[105] Indeed, two weeks previous to the publication of Rapple's article, he had voiced similar opinions at the Forum on the Future of the Newspaper Industry organised by the Minister for Enterprise and Employment, Richard Bruton – a forum that Press Group management had refused to participate in. Indeed, management had failed to follow the agreed procedures between itself and the NUJ for the handling of disciplinary cases. No notice of disciplinary action was given and Rapple was not afforded the opportunity of representation by a union officer as laid down by the agreement. He was simply summoned to Vincent Jennings' office and handed a letter that stated that his position as a senior executive was untenable, that he had shown extreme disloyalty and that the views expressed in the article were in total conflict with the interests of the management of the company. It also stated that if he did not resign by noon he would be automatically sacked. Jennings then went to the Supreme Court to hear its verdict on Ingersoll's appeal on the compensation orders made against it by the High Court the previous year. The verdict quashed the compensation orders and instead of being owed money by Ingersoll, the Press Group now owed Ingersoll £4 million in unpaid loans – £1 million of which was secured on the Burgh Quay newspaper building.[106] Jennings then returned to his office and formally dismissed Colm Rapple. In response, the company's NUJ chapel held a mandatory meeting that subsequently called for the dismissal to be lifted so that talks could begin. When management rejected this option stating that it knew of 'no grounds' for lifting the dismissal, the chapel remained in mandatory session to organise a ballot of strike action.[107]

The non-appearance of the Press titles the following day resulted in four hundred and fifty non-journalistic staff being laid off. A board meeting was held on 27 May and when management ordered the securing of the building – in effect beginning a lock-out – thirty journalists vowed to remain inside until Rapple was reinstated. The board rejected Fianna Fáil leader Bertie Ahern's offer to act as a mediator and also turned down a shareholder's request for an extraordinary shareholders' meeting. Determined not to be silenced, the journalists began to publish their own newspapers to tell their side of the story. The *Irish XPress*, the *Evening XPress* and the *Sunday XPress* were sold by the journalists on the streets of Dublin and had an average circulation of 25,000. The first edition of the *Irish XPress* carried messages of support for the workers from several Fianna Fáil politicians. Deputy Hugh Byrne accused the board of 'using a sledge-hammer to crack a nut' while MEP Jim Fitzsimons said that as a lifelong reader of the *Irish Press* he was appalled at the board's action and accused it of using Rapple's action as 'an excuse to close the *Irish Press* down'.[108] Northern Ireland politicians, both nationalist and unionist, also expressed their support. The Sinn Féin leader Gerry Adams expressed concern that journalists were 'locked out of the *Irish Press*' and stated that the Press titles had played an 'important role in reporting on the conflict in the six counties and in recent times on the development of the peace process'. Likewise, unionist politician Chris McGimpsey stated that the behaviour of management was 'contrary to the cause of free speech which all newspapers are supposed to support'. He also said that management's treatment of Colm Rapple was 'a deliberate attempt to provoke a confrontation with the NUJ at the *Irish Press*.'[109] The occupation of Burgh Quay by journalists received phenomenal public support after high profile visits by public figures such as Jack Charlton and the Irish soccer team, world boxing champion Steve Collins, comedian Brendan O'Carroll, Oscar-winning film-maker Jim Sheridan and film director Neil Jordan. As legendary journalist Con Houlihan recalled: 'the workers' determination and the public support made it feel like being on the barricades in Paris during the revolution. People of all classes and creeds came to help us . . . If the people in Burgh Quay had had the same initiative, the same imagination and drive as my comrades had, we'd still have three great papers.'[110] Instead, water, heating and electricity supplies to the building were cut off, access points to the roof of the building were sealed off and the fire alarm was tested in the early hours of the morning.

On 29 May, management issued a statement warning that should the *Sunday Press* miss another publication, the Group's position would become 'irretrievable'. The statement also dismissed the interim report of the Competition Authority as a 'flawed' document and ironically asserted that it was 'not the business of the Minister to broker deals over the heads of shareholders'.[111] The following day, the Press workers organised a march to Leinster House attended by over one thousand people. Representatives from all political parties addressed the rally and pledged support for the workers. Despite this, the workers were denied social welfare assistance on the grounds that they were involved in an industrial dispute. The march then proceeded to Burgh Quay where the last of the remaining journalists within the building ended their occupation with an emotional reunion with their family and colleagues. In a Dáil debate on the plight of the Press Group, the deputy leader of Fianna Fáil Mary O'Rourke called on the board 'to suspend the correspondence which led to this impasse' and stated that it was 'ironic that the *Irish Press* which was set up in 1931 to give the voiceless a voice now finds itself threatened by the same forces which led to the need for its establishment'.[112] O'Rourke took up the workers' cause because she 'had a deep-set interest in trying to save the jobs and in ideas on how they might be saved'.[113] These survival plans 'were very far advanced but then dropped through the floor. It was extremely sad and tragic for the workers. The cause of the collapse was bad management – the decision to go tabloid was very wrong and ill-judged. Management showed a lack of grasping the nettle and making the hard decisions. They had little regard for what they inherited.'[114] In response to O'Rourke's efforts, de Valera wrote to her claiming that he was 'astonished' at the comments and accused her of listening 'too closely to those with no responsibility for IPN' who proposed 'facile solutions'.[115] He added that he and the board were 'appalled by the behaviour of Fianna Fáil in this matter', which he described as 'irresponsible'.[116] O'Rourke was also threatened with legal action over comments made by her regarding the dispute. Such exchanges show only how far apart Fianna Fáil and the Press Group had drifted.

Labour Court talks between the NUJ and management began on 31 May but lasted only a few hours. According to the union, 'no attempt was made solve the problem. Management refused to discuss it at a meeting in the Labour Court and exacerbated the difficulties by saying that all that could be discussed was a phased return to work with the company selecting the staff to return.'[117] The following day at a board meeting of IPN, it was decided to liquidate the company and managing editor Niall Connolly and personnel director Catherine Griffin were dispatched to the Labour Court to inform it of the board's decision. It was, recalled a Labour Court spokesperson, 'one of the most discourteous encounters ever'.[118] Fianna Fáil leader Bertie Ahern described the announcement as 'a tragedy for the workforce, the investors and the loyal readership' and committed the party to helping 'facilitate the re-emergence of the uniquely individual voice of the Press Group in public and political comment'.[119] When Independent Newspapers stated that it 'would view with concern the possible demise of a great Irish publishing institution',[120] the NUJ retorted that the company's 'only possible interest in taking a stake in the *Irish Press* was to prevent it being taken over by a new investor with the cash and expertise to provide effective competition for the Middle Abbey Street Empire'.[121]

News of the proposed liquidation of Irish Press Newspapers led to a Dáil debate that saw Fianna Fáil politicians criticise Fine Gael's Minister for Enterprise and Employment Richard Bruton for not implementing the Competition Authority report. In a lengthy reply, Bruton declared that he was 'deeply concerned' at the overall situation facing the Press titles but stated that there was no role for him to play in the process on which the company had embarked upon. Nonetheless, he castigated the board's actions and stated that 'it would have been more honest if the board, instead of seeking to blame others, had publicly recognised their failure to produce a commercial operation'.[122] According to Bruton, he had reached a decision on the Competition Authority's report just before the board's decision to liquidate IPN, an action that now required 'further assessment'. He stated that 'the question of taking court action to seek to have Independent Newspapers divest itself of its existing hold over IPN' remained to be decided and that the issue was 'dramatically changed by the decision of IPN to put the paper [*sic*] into liquidation'.[123] Although Bruton feared that Independent Newspapers would fight the High Court action thereby locking up the titles for several months or even years, a ministerial decision on deinvestment was crucial to the survival of the newspapers, simply because the Press titles were secured by Independent Newspapers against the loan that it had given to IPN. If the company were forced to deinvest, then the titles would be free of the charge it held over them. It was unrealistic to expect other investors to invest if Independent Newspapers still held a charge over the titles. In any event, Bruton's refusal to make an immediate decision angered Fianna Fáil. Deputy leader Mary O'Rourke accused him of 'pussyfooting around' and 'deliberately' helping the downfall of the Press newspapers, while deputy Seamus Brennan pointed out that there would 'be no Irish Press Newspapers by the time the Minister decides'.[124] Overall, the government apathy to both the plight of the workers and the loss of the titles shook the Fianna Fáil party:

> It was a horrific thing to happen. Over six hundred people were thrown on the scrapheap. Management showed incompetence and a lack of sensitivity. It was ruthless. The *Irish Press* should have been owned by the shareholders and not by one person or one family as happened. The party as a whole was upset, not about the titles, but about the workforce and the manner in which they were treated. The episode has left a scar on the psyche of a lot of us. The Government could have done more. It had no feeling or sympathy for the *Irish Press*. Then again there was the market forces element – the strong operations survive while the weak go to the wall. But I thought Democratic Left would have done more for the workers. I would like to think things would have been different under a Fianna Fáil government. Brian Lenihan's efforts in America would have been helped, and at least the manner of its demise would have been different.[125]

On 10 June, arrangements were made for the staff to collect their personal belongings from Burgh Quay. When the board insisted that an editor be present to supervise, *Sunday Press* editor Michael Keane volunteered. However, when Keane and the workers arrived at the building, they were refused entry by the security guards on duty who said that the only instruction they had received was to keep everyone out of the building. No one from the board had contacted them to say that six hundred people would descend on the building to collect their belongings. The situation turned into a farce as Keane used his mobile phone to ring the board members, none of whom were available to take his call on a Saturday afternoon. The board later blamed the farce on 'a breakdown in communication and misunderstood instructions from management'.[126] The board also threatened legal action against the NUJ, claiming that the Press chapel had breached copyright by its publication of the Irish, Evening and Sunday *XPress* titles. The board demanded that the chapel discontinue the use of the Press trade marks or else be liable for the 'damage' caused to the company. In response, journalists changed the name of the daily title to the 'XPress'. The new publication was launched outside the Dáil with the help of a de Valera lookalike who walked around the streets of Dublin advertising his new enterprise. The first edition carried the first interview with Irish band U2 for over two years, giving the paper its first and last scoop.

The decision by management to liquidate IPN was, however, challenged by its staff. A High Court petition on behalf of the workers to seek the appointment of an examiner outlined their views on where the origins of the situation lay. The petition blamed the situation on 'a lack of financial and management input over recent years and the impact of a number of unfortunate management decisions and derelictions dating back over a decade'.[127] These included the purchase of Southside Publishing in 1985, changing the *Irish Press* to a tabloid, the *Evening Press* transformation debacle, the failure to maintain adequate editorial budgets and the failure to capitalise on the new technology productivity agreements. According to the affidavit, during a meeting with union representatives on 16 June 1995, 'the chief executive of IPN said that the closure associated with this dispute had simply advanced the decision to go into liquidation by a couple of days'.[128] The workers' action was challenged by IPN, IPP, Irish Press Plc and Ingersoll Irish Publishing but was not challenged by Independent Newspapers. Hugh Cooney was appointed as examiner to both IPN and IPP and found that there were several consortiums interested in buying the titles. The most serious of these were an Irish consortium and an Irish-American consortium whose motivation had more to do with politics than with business opportunity:

> The Yanks' motivation has as much to do with politics as money. They were outraged at the . . . *Sunday Independent* and its line on the North – especially in the lead up the IRA ceasefire when John Hume, the SDLP, US Ambassador Jean Kennedy-Smith, et al were savaged by the Sindo's rottweilers . . . As one of them put it recently, 'it is sickening to have to choose between Fleet Street and Abbey Street when it comes to the Irish media and the North'.[129]

Indeed, there was a deep sense of loss regarding the silencing of the distinctive nationalist voice of the Press titles – they were the only Dublin titles that initially supported the peace process:

> When the Humes-Adams talks became public, some doomladen commentators predicted outright civil war within months. We, on the other hand, criticised other papers for using the term pan-nationalist front . . . We stood alone in supporting Mr Hume in those lonely months of 1993 and 1994, while others treated him with derision for deciding to speak to Mr Adams. When they accused Cardinal Cathal Daly of being naive and foolish in encouraging these talks, we reported on his genuine belief in the integrity of the main players in their endeavours. We also encouraged the Sinn Féin leader to take the risk for peace, with all its dangers for him. While Section 31 was still in force, time after time we carried lengthy, probing interviews with Mr Adams on the emerging Peace Process . . . The *Sunday Press* was the first newspaper to confidently predict an IRA ceasefire in August 1995.[130]

With the death of the three Press titles came the prospect of both Fianna Fáil and nationalism again being left voiceless. As the peace process gained momentum and as pressure mounted to 'accept a settlement at any price', nationalism would 'require powerful advocates to articulate its fears and defend its rights'. While Fianna Fáil could 'be depended upon to champion the cause', the death of the Press titles could result in a return to the media situation of the 1930s when the Fianna Fáil message would 'be ignored by those busily peddling sex and gossip in Middle Abbey Street or suffocated by the "on-the-one-hand" brand of D'Olier Street liberalism'.[131]

But despite the strongly expressed interest from investors, IPN did not own the titles – it merely published them. Ownership of the three titles still rested with IPP, now owned by Irish Press Plc (75.1%) and Independent Newspapers (24.9%). To expect investors to pump money into a company that didn't even own the titles was unrealistic. Thus, the examiner, Hugh Cooney, had to convince the owners to sell or at least lease them to new investors. In his interim report, Cooney called on the owners of the titles to 'adopt a realistic approach to the future ownership and management of the company'. If required, they should 'be prepared to transfer their shares to a new investor for a nominal sum'.[132] This call fell on deaf ears as it entailed Independent Newspapers selling its shares in IPP and IPN to enable a competitor to revive the titles with fresh capital. Shortly afterwards, the Irish consortium pulled out because it wanted to buy the titles outright – a proposal rejected by both Irish Press Plc and Independent Newspapers. Cooney then requested a fourteen-day extension to negotiate with the Irish-American consortium that had been brokered by Brian Lenihan. Both Irish Press Plc and Independent Newspapers opposed Cooney's proposal. Although the extension was granted by the High Court, the scheme devised by Cooney whereby the purchasers of IPN would be allowed to lease and print the titles while paying IPP a royalty, with an option to buy the titles after five years, was also turned down. Even before negotiations could begin, senior counsel for Irish Press Plc, Colm Allen, informed the court that the proposal would not be agreed to by IPP shareholders.[133] Such sentiments differed greatly from those expressed in September 1994, when Vincent Jennings told *Business and Finance* magazine that the board of Irish Press Plc was 'prepared to retain an interest as a minority partner with a fresh investor or sell out completely'.[134] The Irish-American consortium was forced to pull out and the plan that would have saved up to two hundred jobs and netted an estimated £2 million a year for the shareholders fell through. In response, NUJ members vowed never to work for any newspaper managed by de Valera or Jennings who publicly stated their ambitions to relaunch the titles. Fianna Fáil also expressed its anger, with the party's deputy leader Mary O'Rourke stating that although she wished that 'an appeal from the leadership to the shareholders would lead to a change of heart', she knew 'full well that it would be the reverse'.[135]

In what was described as 'the final indignity for the *Irish Press*', IPN's wind-up meeting was held in September 1995 in the main hall of the Royal Dublin Society, 'once a bastion of the British Establishment and the antithesis of all things Republican'.[136] At the six-hour meeting, 'there was a strange mixture of emotions . . . The predominant one was anger, seething anger emanating from the workers . . . And there was sadness, although some people seemed just too tired and fed up with the situation to grieve. Bewilderment too, as to how on God's earth things had come to this.'[137] While Tom Grace was appointed as liquidator to IPN, which by then had debts of £19 million, several creditors, mostly staff, availed of the opportunity to vent their anger at chairman Eamon de Valera and chief executive Vincent Jennings. One journalist told de Valera that he had betrayed his grandfather and all the people who had gone to America to raise the funds to set up the *Irish Press*.[138] Another stated that the board had been 'biggest impediment to getting investment in the *Irish Press*.'[139] Indeed, the meeting heard many recriminatory remarks to the effect that both de Valera and Jennings had not wanted the High Court examiner to succeed in his task of finding new investors because they wanted the newspaper titles for themselves.[140] But perhaps the final say should go to an elderly employee who succinctly summed up how unpredictable life at the Press Group always was: 'On my first day in the Press, I was employed, sacked and re-employed all in the one day. It hasn't changed at all in thirty years, all because of management ineptitude.'[141] Thus the much loved newspaper titles that had brought so many political and journalistic luminaries into public prominence for over six decades bowed out of existence with as much acrimony as that which had marked their very foundation.

Epilogue

> I urge all the members of Fianna Fáil to support the efforts of the *Irish Press* workers in whatever way they can. Not just for old times sake, but for the sake of the future. Fianna Fáil has had a special relationship with the *Irish Press* in the past and it retained the loyalty of many Fianna Fáil minded people for its differing public and political viewpoint. At times, it was perhaps the least inimical of newspapers to Fianna Fáil, but at its best for many years and on many occasions, it expressed the alternative Fianna Fáil point of view and understood what Fianna Fáil was trying to achieve.[1]
>
> *Bertie Ahern on the impending demise of the Irish Press*

With the demise of the three Press titles, Fianna Fáil is again left without a supportive media voice. According to David Andrews, 'Fianna Fáil miss the Irish Press'.[2] It seems that the old anti-Fianna Fáil bias that existed in the 1920s and 1930s is still present today and according to Andrews, 'there is a lack of balance – particularly in RTÉ and on the radio'.[3] Indeed, in a 1997 survey of political affiliations among Irish journalists, the Labour Party emerged strongest with twenty-nine per cent support. While Fine Gael secured just over ten per cent, Fianna Fáil trailed at five and a half per cent – reinforcing Andrews' assertion that the party is at a media disadvantage since the demise of the *Irish Press*.[4]

That same year, the party contested its first general election since 1932 without the support of the *Irish Press*. Ironically, the party found a new and most unlikely ally in the *Irish Independent*. The electorate had the choice of returning the outgoing Fine Gael, Labour and Democratic Left rainbow coalition or electing a Fianna Fáil and Progressive Democrat alternative. In the year previous to the election, a subsidiary company of Independent Newspapers, Princes Holdings had conflicted sharply with the rainbow coalition. The company held an MMDS licence that allowed it to distribute British television channels to subscribers. However, several communities in counties Mayo and Donegal had their own systems for the distribution of the same channels. When these systems were outlawed, Princes Holdings demanded that the coalition enforce the law and shut down these systems. But fearful of a backlash in the forthcoming election, the coalition took no action. Although several meetings between representatives of both Independent Newspapers and the coalition took place, no compromise was forthcoming.

At the final such meeting, the government representatives were informed that unless action was taken, the coalition would 'lose Independent Newspapers Plc as friends'.[5] On the day before polling, the *Irish Independent* took the unusual step of publishing its editorial on its front page. Under the headline 'Payback Time', the editorial criticised the economic and taxation policies of the rainbow coalition and urged its readers to vote for the Fianna Fáil/Progressive Democrats alternative.[6] When details of what had transpired at the last meeting became public knowledge courtesy of the *Irish Times*, Independent Newspapers denied that there was any connection whatsoever between the meeting and the editorial. Instead, the statement simply meant that Independent Newspapers could no longer continue its friendly intermediate role between its subsidiary company and the outgoing government. Editorial policy was, the company declared, 'a matter for editors, not senior executives'.[7]

The controversy over whether or not the editorial helped bring Fianna Fáil back to power obscured the fact that the party vote was the second lowest in its history. So low was the party support, that it reneged on a central pre-election promise to hold a referendum on Ireland joining the NATO led Partnership for Peace military alliance. Since the demise of the *Irish Press*, the lack of a supportive media voice has occupied the minds of the upper echelons of the party. This explains perhaps, attempts by leading party figures to stimulate the recreation of the titles. In 1997, Fianna Fáil Senator Donnie Cassidy registered a company called 'The Press on Sunday Ltd', but it has remained inactive. Since retaking office, the party has been continually embarrassed by a multitude of financial scandals, centred primarily around payments to politicians and non-resident off-shore bank accounts. The various revelations, that involved party figures such as former Taoiseach Charles Haughey, former minister Ray Burke, former EC Commissioner Padraig Flynn, and backbenchers Liam Lawlor, Beverly Cooper-Flynn and Denis Foley have damaged the integrity of the party in the public eye and exposed it to increased media scrutiny. Devoid of the *Irish Press*, the party is effectively voiceless.

The party's fáilure to convince the electorate to ratify the Nice Treaty in June 2001 also raised questions about its effectiveness in getting its message across. The question remains as to whether or not the presence and support of the three Press titles would have made any difference. In an Ireland that has changed so much in so little time, the question may be purely academic. Celtic Tiger Ireland is a world away from the Gaelic Ireland envisioned by de Valera and espoused in the editorials of the *Irish Press*. Although mostly ruled by Fianna Fáil since independence, modern Ireland is an increasingly secular, urbanised consumer society, dominated by the presence of foreign multi-national firms – the very opposite of what de Valera and the *Irish Press* had advocated. In an Ireland obsessed with image rather than substance, the old certainties of Catholicism, nationalism and republicanism have been gradually replaced by the vulgarities of consumerism, pragmatism and a brand of consensual politics that is more akin to voter management than voter representation. A new generation of voters who never read the *Irish Press* has taken the place of the de Valera faithful and as Ireland moves towards closer European integration, the future of Fianna Fáil looks increasingly fragmented.

So what ultimately caused the demise of the three Press titles? In the case of the *Irish Press*, the paper fáiled to sufficiently re-orientate itself from its political leanings and repackage its core ideology for a changing Ireland. Until the day it died, it retained the reputation of being the 'kept paper' of the Fianna Fáil party. In stark contrast to the reinventions of the *Irish Times* and the Independent titles, the paper's fáilure to reinvent itself gave it a jaded look. In the succinct words of John Waters, the decline within the Press Group was the 'result of a fáilure to understand how Irish society was changing and to refine the Irish Press products in an appropriate manner'.[8] According to Waters, 'the people who used to read the Irish Press newspapers have not ceased to exist. What happened was that the newspapers they read ceased to keep abreast of the complex reality of their changing lives'.[9] Constant renewal through keeping abreast of and reflecting social and political change is essential to the survival any newspaper. According to Waters:

> not only did this not happen at the Press Group but, such was the complacency at managerial and editorial levels that, when the crisis loomed, there no longer existed anything but the remotest connection with what was going on in society. The only options available were blind pursuit of off-the-peg marketing strategies and imitation of the methods employed by the Press' competitors. As a consequence of the blind pursuit of the phantom ABC1, who would not be seen dead with a Press newspaper anyway, there developed within the Press Group a deep hatred of the readers who were its very bread and butter.[10]

Much has been made of the de Valera family's role in the creation, control and demise of the Press titles. Whatever terminology one employs to describe the American Corporation, the basic fact remains that trusteeship or guardianship of it brought with it control of the whole company. Control of the American Corporation passed down through three generations of the de Valera family. According to Cahill, companies owned or highly influenced by family concerns are generally slower to adopt new strategies and structures. Very often such companies become dynastic systems, with policy being directed mainly to maintain family control rather than change the status quo and modernise.[11] One possible result of this is product stagnation, loss of market orientation and ultimate collapse.

Perhaps the titles' only redeeming factor was their solid support for the Hume–Adams talks that otherwise occurred amid media wariness and hostility. In contrast, the Press titles refrained from consigning republican ideologies and politicians to pariah status at a time when it was both popular and profitable to do so. Unlike most other southern media, the titles were prescient in seeing that no solution was possible without bringing republicans in from the cold. The resultant peace process as championed by the titles is the greatest example that it wasn't the nationalist ideology propagated by the titles that became outdated, but rather the overall presentation of the products themselves. The proof of this scenario lies in the change that other national titles have undergone in latter years. Having spent decades demonising republicanism, in the wake of the peace process, southern media have come to recognise republicanism as a view as valid as any other – a cornerstone philosophy of the *Irish Press*.

Given its unshakable association with Fianna Fáil, its declining readership, and its unattractiveness to advertisers, the question arises as to whether the Press Group should have ceased publishing (even temporarily) the *Irish Press* and instead concentrated its energies and resources on its evening and Sunday titles? These two titles were always less associated with the party in the public mind and were also always more commercially successful. Whatever the historical implications of dropping the title, commercially the paper was being pushed out of the market anyway. Besides the growing volume of British tabloids saturating the Irish morning market, both the *Irish Independent* and the *Irish Times* offered more than the *Irish Press* could ever hope to. In contrast, there was only one national evening newspaper for the *Evening Press* to compete with and although the circulation of the *Sunday Press* had declined, it was still competitive and had a respectable readership that could have been built on. At the time of its demise, the paper was selling more than the *Sunday Business Post* and the *Sunday Tribune* combined.[12] In the six months following the collapse of the Press titles, sales of both the *Evening Herald* and the *Sunday Independent* jumped by over thirty per cent each.[13] Indeed, by November 1995, a number of former editorial staff were working on a relaunch of the *Sunday Press*. The plan was aborted the following January after Independent Newspapers withdrew its support on the grounds of costs and the fear of a protracted legal battle with a government that had ruled against any further investment by Independent Newspapers.

By 1997, the once proud but always cash-starved Irish Press Plc had been reduced to a company whose main assets were the 75.1% share of the defunct newspaper titles and investments worth approximately £2 million.[14] The board eventually became reconciled to the fact that the company would never relaunch the titles on its own. According to company chairman Vincent Jennings, the relaunch of one or more of the newspapers required 'the commitment of very substantial sums far in excess of the resources' available to the company.[15] Arguably, this was also the case in 1995. If the board had agreed to the sale or leasing of the titles in 1995, the company may have preserved the value of the titles, saved jobs and perhaps even rewarded shareholders. By 1997, the titles were virtually worthless. That year, consultants Deloitte and Touche were appointed to advertise the three titles for sale nationally and internationally. Despite enquiries, no concrete proposal for the purchase of the titles was received.[16]

At the company's 1997 annual general meeting, the board ruled that a shareholders' resolution to wind up the company because it no longer fulfilled the function for which it was formed, could not be accepted as it had not been given the required twenty-one days' notice. During that meeting, both Eamon de Valera and Vincent Jennings 'endured two-and-a-half hours of trenchant criticism'.[17] Many shareholders 'expressed puzzlement' about managing director Eamon de Valera's role and the salary that he earned in a company that did not appear to trade. They were duly informed that the company retained an office in Merrion Square at an annual cost of £20,000 and employed two secretarial staff. They were also informed that de Valera earned £75,000 per year with 'minimal expenses' and a company car. His main task was to manage the company's investments.[18] Vincent Jennings stated that he was paid £5,000 a year as a director and confirmed that the company had a pension fund for de Valera. However, he emphatically stated that there was 'no question of giving lifelong salaries' and noted that the company was 'not a pension fund'.[19] Many shareholders opposed Jennings' re-election as company chairman. De Valera stated that Jennings was the most successful editor of the *Sunday Press* – an assertion hotly disputed by shareholders. Nonetheless, he was re-elected by the proxy votes held by the board.[20]

In November 1998, the company offered to buy back 100,000 shares from shareholders at the price of £2.50 per share. The company was, according to its chairman, 'anxious to return value to shareholders'.[21] At the meeting to pass the special resolutions to allow the company to engage in the buy-back scheme, the board again met with protracted opposition and criticism. As on previous occasions, the motions were carried by the voting strength of the board. When asked why there had been no independent or professional share price evaluation, Jennings referred the questioner to the company documentation that indicated how the board had reached the price of £2.50 per share. He also denied that there was 'a nefarious plan to privatise the company'. The board had not opted for a dividend 'because a large amount would have got to Dr de Valera's interests and not so much would have flowed to what may be described as the small shareholder'.[22] Shareholders representing 53,699 shares later availed themselves of the offer.[23] No member of the board took advantage of the buy-back scheme. In 1999, the company purchased just under thirty per cent of County Tipperary Radio Ltd and later purchased Thom's Dublin Street Directory. Whatever the future of the company, it is extremely unlikely that the three Press titles will ever again see the light of day.

Notes

CHAPTER ONE

1 Connolly, J. (1996) p. 283.
2 Dáil Éireann Report, Vol. 22, col. 1615.
3 De Valera Papers, UCDA, File 1410/2.
4 *Irish Press*, 5 September 1931.
5 FF/26, UCDA, Letter from de Valera to John Hearn, Treasurer of AARIR (1922).
6 MacManus, M. J. (1944) p. 279.
7 *Irish Times*, 19 May 1976.
8 Connolly, J. (1996) p. 282.
9 *idem.*
10 *The Bell*, February 1945, p. 386.
11 Oram, H. (1983) p. 321.
12 *ibid.*, p. 76.
13 *The Bell*, January 1945, p. 290.
14 Interview with Conor Brady.
15 Oram, H. (1983) p. 187.
16 *The Bell,* January 1945, p. 290.
17 Joseph McGarrity Papers, NLI, MS 17441.
18 Coogan, T. P. (1993) p. 157.
19 FF/27, UCDA, Newspaper Cuttings.
20 Joseph McGarrity Papers, NLI, MS 17441.
21 *Wall Street Journal*, 4 Feb. 1919; Cited in Coogan (1993) p. 159.
22 Lavelle, P. (1961) p. 148.
23 Coogan, T. P. (1993) p. 210.
24 Rumpf, E. and Hepburn, A. (1977) p. 69.
25 O'Mahoney, P. and Delanty, G. (1998) p. 136.
26 Rumpf, E. and Hepburn, A. (1977) p. 73.
27 *idem.*
28 Prager, J. (1986) p. 205.
29 Tierney, M. (1988) p. 108.
30 *ibid.*, p. 112.
31 Dunphy, R. (1995) p. 83.
32 O'Mahony P. and Delanty, G. (1998) p. 157.
33 Prager, J. (1986) p. 205.
34 *ibid.*
35 Garvin, T. (1981) p. 3.
36 Devane, R. (1927) p. 545.
37 *idem.*
38 *idem.*
39 *ibid.*
40 *ibid.*
41 *ibid.*
42 FF/29, UCDA, Proceedings of Second Ard Fheis 1927.
43 Dáil Éireann Report, Vol. 48, col. 1321.
44 Interview with Tim Pat Coogan.
45 *The Nation*, 26 March 1927.
46 FF/26, UCDA, Letter from Frank Walsh to bondholders, 1927.
47 *ibid.*
48 National Archives, File S, 9972.
49 Dáil Éireann Report, Vol. 48, col. 1322.
50 National Archives, File S, 9596.
51 FF/26, UCDA, Letter from M. Conbey to F. Walsh, 1928.

52 *ibid.*, letter from F. Walsh to M. Conbey, 1928.
53 *ibid.*, letter from de Valera to M. Conbey, 1928.
54 *ibid.*, letter from M. Conbey to de Valera, 1928.
55 William Martin Murphy Papers, National Archives Business Records Survey (Meath 11).
56 *The Nation*, 26 March 1927.
57 Dáil Éireann Report, Vol. 48, col. 1751.
58 Joseph McGarrity Papers, NLI, MS 17441.
59 Frank Gallagher Papers, NLI, MS 18361.
60 Sarbaugh, T. (1985) p. 16.
61 FF/26, UCDA, The Need for a National Daily Newspaper in Ireland.
62 *idem.*
63 Frank Aiken Papers, UCDA, P104/2636.
64 *idem.*
65 *ibid.* (de Valera's emphasis).
66 English, R. (1998) p. 32.
67 Sarbaugh, T. (1985) p. 18.
68 Frank Aiken Papers, UCDA, P104/2640.
69 *ibid.*, P104/2639.
70 FF/26, UCDA, Letter from de Valera to W. Lyndon, Secretary of AARIR, 1929.
71 *ibid.*, letter from P. Carolan to de Valera, 1928.
72 Joseph McGarrity Papers, NLI, MS 17441.
73 *ibid.*
74 Sarbaugh, T. (1985) p. 19.
75 FF/27, UCDA, San Francisco Leader; 19 April 1930.
76 *Magill,* August 1978.
77 Joseph Smartt Papers, NLI, MS 33738.
78 Coogan, T. P. (1993) p. 419.
79 FF/26, UCDA, Letter from J. Carroll to de Valera, 1931.
80 *Hibernia*, 13 June 1975.
81 *Irish Times*, 2 July 1993.
82 *Magill*, August 1978.
83 Dáil Éireann Report, Vol. 48, col. 1862.
84 *ibid.*
85 Interview with Michael O'Toole.
86 Frank Gallagher Papers, NLI, MS 18361.
87 Frank Aiken Papers, UCDA, P104/2636.
88 Company Registration Office, Irish Press Ltd. File No.1. Shares Prospectus, p. 2.
89 FF/26, UCDA, Letter from P. Carolan to de Valera, 1928.
90 Browne, N. (1986) p. 202.
91 *The Irish Press* (Philadelphia), 23 March 1918.
92 Frank Gallagher Papers, NLI, MS 18361.
93 *ibid.*, Irish Press Articles of Association; Article 77.
94 O'Toole Papers.
95 *ibid.*
96 Company Registration Office, Irish Press Ltd Shares Register.
97 FF/26, UCDA, Letter from de Valera to W. Lyndon, Secretary AARIR, 1929.

CHAPTER TWO

1 Companies Registration Office, *Irish Press* File, 1931.
2 FF/26, UCDA, Letter from Sean MacEntee to de Valera, 1931.
3 *ibid.*, Letter from Sean Dunne to de Valera, 1931.
4 *ibid.*, Letter from Maire Devane to de Valera, 1931.
5 *ibid.*, letter from de Valera to Maire Devane, 1931.
6 *ibid.*, Letter from de Valera to several applicants, 1931.
7 *ibid.*, Letter from J. Considine to de Valera, 1931.

8 *ibid.*, Letter from de Valera to J. Nix, 1931.
9 Browne, N. (1986) p. 202.
10 Frank Gallagher Papers, NLI, MS 18361.
11 *idem.*
12 Connolly, J. (1996) p. 283.
13 Frank Gallagher Papers, NLI, MS 18361.
14 *idem.*
15 *The Nation*, 12 September 1931.
16 Interview with Jim Walsh.
17 Kelly, J. (1995) p. 58.
18 Interview with Michael O'Toole.
19 Frank Gallagher Papers, NLI, MS 18361.
20 *Irish Times*, 1 September 1931.
21 *ibid.*, 3 September 1931.
22 Frank Gallagher Papers, NLI, MS 18361.
23 *idem.*
24 *The Nation*, 22 August 1931.
25 Company Registration Office, Irish Press Ltd Shares Register.
26 O'Toole Papers.
27 O'Toole, M. (1992) p. 62.
28 The first edition of the *Irish Press* appeared on 5 September 1931.
29 Sarbaugh, T. (1985) p. 21.
30 *Irish Press*, 5 September 1931.
31 *idem.*
32 *idem.*
33 Interview with Vincent Doyle.
34 Interview with Hugh Lambert.
35 *Irish Press*, 5 September 1931.
36 Interview with Douglas Gageby.
37 Interview with Douglas Gageby.
38 *Irish Times*, 5 September 1931.
39 *ibid.*, 7 September 1931.
40 Frank Gallagher Papers, NLI, MS 18361.
41 *Irish Press*, 28 October 1931.
42 Interview with Michael O'Toole.
43 Browne, N. (1986) p. 232.
44 Dáil Éireann Report, Vol. 40, col. 364.
45 *ibid.*
46 Cumann na nGaedheal and Fine Gael Archives, UCDA; P/39/MIN/2.
47 *idem.*
48 National Archives, File S, 2858.
49 *Irish Press*, 5 September 1932 – Anniversary Supplement.
50 National Archives, File S, 2858.
51 *idem.*
52 O'Toole, M. (1992) p. 70.
53 Interview with Douglas Gageby.
54 Oram, H. (1983) p. 176.
55 *Irish Times*, 22 March 1932.
56 National Archives, File S. 4915.
57 *idem.*
58 *idem.*
59 *idem.*
60 *idem.*
61 *Irish Times*, 22 March 1932.
62 *ibid.*, 6 April 1932.
63 *ibid.*, 22 April 1932.
64 *idem.*
65 *ibid.*, 10 May 1932.
66 Interview with Michael O'Toole.

67 Oram, H. (1983) p. 176.
68 De Valera Papers, UCDA, File 1453/1.
69 *Irish Press*, 5 September 1981 – 50th Anniversary Supplement.
70 *ibid.*, 5 September 1932.
71 Andrews, C. (1982) p. 91.
72 Connolly, J. (1996) p. 284.
73 *Irish Press*, 9 September 1931.
74 *ibid.*, 10 December 1931.
75 *idem.*
76 *ibid.*, 1 December 1931.
77 Andrews, C. (1982) p. 91.
78 *Irish Press*, 5 September 1932.
79 *Irish Independent*, 7 February 1932.
80 *ibid.*, 1 January 1932.
81 *ibid.*, 30 January 1932.
82 *Irish Press*, 9 February 1932.
83 *idem.*
84 *ibid.*, 29 January 1932.
85 *ibid.*, 15 February 1932.
86 *ibid.*, 16 February 1932.
87 *Irish Times*, 16 February 1932.
88 De Valera Papers, UCDA, File 1453/1.
89 *idem.*
90 *Irish Press*, 21 April 1932.
91 *ibid.*, 20 May 1932.
92 *The Irish Digest* 1929–1938; col. 266.
93 *Evening Press*, 6 July 1932.
94 *ibid.*, 7 July 1932.
95 *idem.*
96 *idem.*
97 NUJ Files, Irish Press Chapel Minute Book, 1932.
98 *Irish Press*, 5 July 1932.
99 *ibid.*, 14 July 1932.
100 Fanning, R. (1983) p. 114.
101 *Irish Press*, 5 January 1933.
102 *idem.*
103 *idem.*
104 *idem.*
105 *ibid.*, 6 January 1933.
106 *idem.*
107 Frank Gallagher Papers, NLI, MS 18361.
108 *Irish Press*, 26 January 1933.
109 *idem.*
110 *ibid.*, 27 January 1933.
111 *idem.*
112 *ibid.*, 28 January 1933.
113 *The Bell*, February 1945, p. 392.
114 *idem.*

CHAPTER THREE

1 Dáil Éireann Report, Vol. 172, col. 582.
2 Frank Gallagher Papers, NLI, MS 18361.
3 Interview with Michael Mills.
4 NUJ Files, Irish Press Chapel Minute Book, 1933.
5 Interview with Michael O'Toole.
6 Interview with Tim Pat Coogan.

7 Frank Gallagher Papers, NLI, MS 18361.
8 *idem.*
9 *idem.*
10 *idem.*
11 *idem.*
12 *idem.*
13 *idem.*
14 *idem.*
15 *idem.*
16 *idem.*
17 Dáil Éireann Report, Vol. 48, col. 1735.
18 *ibid.*, col. 1751.
19 *Irish Press*, 3 July 1933.
20 *idem.*
21 *idem.*
22 Dáil Éireann Report, Vol. 48, col. 1325.
23 *ibid.*, col. 1324.
24 *ibid.*, col. 1328.
25 *ibid.*, col. 1830.
26 *ibid.*, col. 1880.
27 *ibid.*, col. 1328.
28 *ibid.*, col. 1884.
29 *ibid.*, col. 1758.
30 *ibid.*, col. 1762–1782.
31 *idem.*
32 *idem.*
33 Coogan, T. P. (1993) p. 442.
34 *Irish Press*, 6 July 1933.
35 Dáil Éireann Report, Vol. 48, col. 1755–1760.
36 Frank Gallagher Papers, NLI, MS 18361.
37 *Irish Press*, 13 September 1933.
38 *Irish Times*, 30 December 1933.
39 *idem.*
40 Frank Gallagher Papers, NLI, MS 18361.
41 *idem.*
42 *idem.*
43 *idem.*
44 *idem.*
45 *idem.*
46 *idem.*
47 O'Toole, M. (1992) p. 138.
48 Frank Gallagher Papers, NLI, MS 18361.
49 Connolly, J. (1996) p. 283.
50 Frank Gallagher Papers, NLI, MS 18361.
51 *idem.*
52 *idem.*
53 *idem.*
54 Brown, S. (1971) p. 49.
55 *The Bell*, February 1945, p. 394.
56 Foley, J. and Lalor, S. (eds). (1995) p. 123.
57 NUJ Files, Irish Press Chapel Minute Book, 1937.
58 *Irish Press*, 8 July 1937.
59 *ibid.*, 13 October 1937.
60 *idem.*
61 Litton, H. (1991) p. 214.
62 *Irish Press*, 13 October 1937.
63 *idem.*
64 Mansergh, M. *The History of Fianna Fáil*, 1996.
65 NUJ Files; Irish Press Chapel Minute Book, 1937.

66 *Irish Times*, 12 November 1937.
67 *ibid.*, 16 November 1937.
68 *idem.*
69 *idem.*
70 *idem.*
71 O'Toole Papers.
72 *Irish Press*, 26 April 1938.
73 *idem.*
74 *idem.*
75 *Irish Press*, 4 May 1938.
76 *ibid.*, 8 June 1938.
77 *ibid.*, 9 June 1938.
78 *ibid.*, 17 June 1938.
79 *ibid.*, 20 June 1938.
80 *ibid.*, 4 September 1939.
81 O'Grada, C. (1997) p. 8.
82 *ibid.*, p. 18.
83 *Irish Press*, 1 June 1943.
84 *ibid.*, 2 June 1943.
85 *ibid.*, 4 June 1943.
86 *ibid.*, 3 June 1943.
87 *ibid.*, 21 June 1943.
88 *idem.*
89 *ibid.*, 22 June 1943.
90 *ibid.*, 26 June 1943.
91 *ibid.*, 26 May 1944.
92 Mansergh, M. *The History of Fianna Fáil*, 1996.
93 National Archives, File D/FA, (Sec). p. 51.
94 *ibid.*, File D/J, Press Censorship Reviews.
95 *idem.*
96 *ibid.*, File D/J, no. 1.
97 *ibid.*, File D/FA, (Sec). p. 51.
98 Duggan, J. (1989) p. 87.
99 National Archives, File D/J, Press Censorship Reviews.
100 *idem.*
101 *Irish Press*, 5 September 1981 – 50th Anniversary Supplement.
102 *Irish Independent*, 12 May 1945.
103 *Irish Times*, 12 May 1945.
104 *Irish Press*, 12 May 1945.
105 *idem.*
106 Interview with Douglas Gageby.
107 *idem.*
108 NUJ Files, Irish Press Chapel Minute Book, 1943 and 1944.
109 *ibid.*, 1947.
110 Interview with Jim Walsh.
111 Cousins, M. (1999) p. 35.
112 *Irish Times*, 9 May 1976 – Fianna Fáil 50th anniversary supplement.
113 *Irish Press*, 2 January 1948.
114 *ibid.*, 22 January 1948.
115 *ibid.*, 7 January 1948.
116 *ibid.*, 16 January 1948.
117 *ibid.*, 14 January 1948.
118 *ibid.*, 4 February 1948.
119 *Irish Independent*, 5 February 1948.
120 Browne, N. (1986) p. 110.
121 *idem.*
122 Interview with Douglas Gageby.
123 Browne, N. (1986) p. 192.
124 Dáil Éireann Report, Vol. 113, col. 732.

125 National Archives, File S/14518 / Dáil Éireann Report, Vol. 155, col. 923.
126 *Irish Press*, 1 July 1949.
127 *idem.*
128 Interview with Douglas Gageby.
129 Interview with Jim Walsh.

CHAPTER FOUR

1 *Magill*, August 1985.
2 *Irish Press*, 17 March 1949.
3 Interview with Douglas Gageby.
4 *idem.*
5 *idem.*
6 Interview with Conor Brady.
7 *Sunday Press*, 4 September 1949.
8 *idem.*
9 *Irish Press*, 5 September 1949.
10 Interview with Michael O'Toole.
11 *idem.*
12 Coogan, T. P. (1993) p. 675.
13 Tierney, M. (1988) p. 347.
14 *Irish Press*, 5 May 1951.
15 *ibid.*, 26 May 1951.
16 *ibid.*, 19 May 1951.
17 Interview with Michael O'Toole.
18 O'Mahony, P. and Delanty, G. (1998) p. 161.
19 *Irish Press*, 25 November 1952.
20 Garvin, T. (1978) p. 346.
21 Rumpf, E. and Hepburn, A. (1977) p. 189.
22 *Irish Press*, 15 January 1954.
23 Garvin, T. (1978) p. 346.
24 *Irish Press*, 7 May 1954.
25 *ibid.*, 5 May 1954.
26 *ibid.*, 13 May 1954.
27 *ibid.*, 17 May 1954.
28 *ibid.*, 21 May 1954.
29 Interview with Michael Mills.
30 *idem.*
31 Interview with John Kelly.
32 Acts of the Oireachtas, 1954.
33 National Archives, 2000/10/3377.
34 *idem.*
35 *idem.*
36 *idem.*
37 *idem.*
38 *idem.*
39 Interview with John Kelly.
40 Interview with Douglas Gageby.
41 *idem.*
42 *idem.*
43 Interview with Tim Pat Coogan.
44 Interview with Douglas Gageby.
45 *idem.*
46 Interview with John Kelly.
47 Interview with Michael O'Toole.
48 *Evening Press*, 2 September 1954.
49 *ibid.*, 1 September 1954.

50 Interview with John Kelly.
51 *Evening Press*, 2 September 1954.
52 *Evening Mail*, 1 September 1954.
53 *Evening Herald*, 31 August 1954.
54 Interview with Douglas Gageby.
55 *Irish Times*, 20 December 1954.
56 *Evening Press*, 20 December 1954.
57 *ibid.*, 21 December 1954.
58 *ibid.*, 22 December 1954.
59 *ibid.*, 23 December 1954.
60 *ibid.*, 24 December 1954.
61 *ibid.*, 26 January 1955.
62 Interview with Jim Walsh.
63 Coogan, T. P. (1993) p. 681.
64 NUJ Files, Irish Press Chapel Minute Book, 1954 and 1958.
65 *Irish Press*, 18 January 1955.
66 *idem.*
67 *idem.*
68 *ibid.*, 12 October 1955.
69 *idem.*
70 *idem.*
71 *idem.*
72 *ibid.*, 13 October 1955.
73 *Sunday Press*, 19 February 1956.
74 *idem.*
75 *ibid.*, 1 July 1956.
76 *ibid.*, 19 February 1956.
77 *Irish Press*, 18 January 1957.
78 *Sunday Press*, 20 January 1957.
79 Farrell, B. (1983) p. 96.
80 *Irish Press*, 5 February 1957.
81 *ibid.*, 11 February 1957.
82 *ibid.*, 2 March 1957.
83 *ibid.*, 1 March 1957.
84 *ibid.*, 5 March 1957.
85 Interview with Tim Pat Coogan.
86 Interview with Michael Mills.
87 NUJ Files, Irish Press Chapel Minute Book, 1958.
88 Interview with John Kelly. The 'Sean South saga' refers to an IRA ambush in the 1950s, during which an IRA member (Sean South) was killed. He was later immortalised in song.
89 *idem.*
90 Interview with Douglas Gageby.
91 *idem.*
92 Interview with John Kelly.
93 *idem.*
94 *idem.*
95 Dáil Éireann Report, Vol. 183 col. 1–2.
96 National Archives, File S, 1957/63.
97 *idem.*
98 Coogan, T. P. (1993) p. 671.
99 Browne, N. (1986) p. 231.
100 Interview with Michael O'Toole.
101 Browne, N. (1986) p. 234.
102 *idem.*
103 Dáil Éireann Report, Vol. 171, col. 2169.
104 *ibid.*, col. 2169–2196.
105 *idem.*
106 *idem.*
107 *idem.*

108 *idem.*
109 *idem.*
110 *idem.*
111 Browne, N. (1986) p. 235.
112 Dáil Éireann Report, Vol. 171, col. 2169–2196.
113 *idem.*
114 *idem.*
115 *idem.*
116 *ibid.*, and Vol. 172, col. 127–132.
117 Dáil Éireann Report, Vol. 172, col. 139–141.
118 *ibid.*, col. 582.
119 *ibid.*, col. 586–594.
120 *ibid.*
121 *ibid.*
122 *Irish Times*, 15 January 1959.
123 Dáil Éireann Record, Vol. 172 col. 586–594.
124 *idem.*
125 *idem.*
126 *idem.*
127 Coogan, T. P. (1993) p. 675.
128 *Irish Press*, 15 January 1959.
129 *Irish Independent*, 20 May 1985.
130 Interview with Jim Walsh.
131 Andrews, C. (1982) p. 236.
132 *Irish Press*, 16 June 1959.
133 *ibid.*, 19 June 1959.

CHAPTER FIVE

1 O'Toole, M. (1992) p. 94.
2 *Irish Press*, 23 June 1959.
3 Baker, S. (1986) p. 57.
4 *Irish Press*, 24 June 1959.
5 *idem.*
6 *ibid.*, 14 August 1959.
7 *ibid.*, 21 April 1961.
8 *ibid.*, 24 June 1959.
9 *ibid.*, 20 June 1960.
10 *idem.*
11 *idem.*
12 *idem.*
13 *idem.*
14 *idem.*
15 *ibid.*, 9 November 1960.
16 *ibid.*, 11 November 1959.
17 *ibid.*, 15 January 1960.
18 *ibid.*, 30 September 1961.
19 *ibid.*, 3 October 1961.
20 *ibid.*, 7 October 1961.
21 *ibid.*, 12 October 1961.
22 *idem.*
23 Horgan, J. (1997) p. 226.
24 *Irish Press*, 18 July 1963.
25 Dillon, M. (1989) p. 22.
26 *idem.*
27 O'Toole, M. (1992) p. 94.
28 Dáil Éireann Report; Vol. 224, col. 1046.
29 Interview with Michael O'Toole.

30 Kimberly, J. and Miles, R. (1980) pp. 2–4.
31 O'Toole Papers; 'Some Points for Use in the Preparations of Copy etc. for the Irish Press' 1961.
32 Interview with Douglas Gageby.
33 Interview with Michael O'Toole.
34 Interview with Douglas Gageby.
35 Interview with John Kelly.
36 *idem.*
37 Interview with Michael Keane.
38 Interview with John Kelly.
39 *idem.*
40 *idem.*
41 NUJ Files, Irish Press Chapel Minute Book, 1960s.
42 *idem.*
43 *idem.*
44 Interview with Michael O'Toole.
45 Interview with Tim Pat Coogan.
46 Interview with John Kelly.
47 Interview with Michael O'Toole.
48 *Hibernia*, 13 June 1975.
49 Interview with Michael O'Toole.
50 Interview with Michael Mills.
51 Interview with Tim Pat Coogan.
52 Interview with Hugh Lambert.
53 *idem.*
54 *idem.*
55 *Irish Press*, 8 October 1964.
56 *idem.*
57 *ibid.*, 9 October 1964.
58 *ibid.*, 9 March 1965.
59 *ibid.*, 12 March 1965.
60 *ibid.*, 29 March 1965.
61 *ibid.*, 17 March 1965.
62 *ibid.*, 27 March 1965.
63 *ibid.*, 7 April 1965.
64 Oram, H. (1983) p. 275.
65 Interview with Douglas Gageby.
66 *idem.*
67 *Irish Times*, 8 July 1981.
68 Interview with Conor Brady.
69 Interview with Michael Mills.
70 *Irish Press*, 31 October 1966.
71 Interview with Michael Mills.
72 Walsh, D. (1986) p. 91.
73 Collins, S. (1992) p. 20.
74 *Irish Press*, 5 November 1966.
75 Sean MacEntee Papers, UCDA, P67/734.
76 Horgan, J. (1997) p. 338.
77 *Irish Press*, 10 November 1966.
78 Interview with Hugh Lambert.
79 O'Toole Papers.
80 Interview with Tim Pat Coogan.
81 O'Toole Papers.
82 *Irish Times*, 20 July 1973.
83 Interview with Tim Pat Coogan.
84 *Hibernia*, 13 June 1975.
85 Interview with John Kelly.
86 Interview with Michael Mills.
87 Interview with Michael O'Toole.
88 *idem.*

89 Interview with John Kelly.
90 Interview with Michael O'Toole.
91 Interview with John Kelly.
92 *idem.*
93 Oram, H. (1983) p. 302.
94 Interview with John Kelly.
95 *idem.*
96 Interview with Michael Keane.
97 Interview with Michael Mills.
98 Interview with Tim Pat Coogan.
99 *idem.*
100 Interview with Hugh Lambert.
101 Interview with John Kelly.
102 Interview with Michael Mills.
103 Interview with David Andrews.
104 Interview with John Kelly.
105 *Irish Press*, 15 October 1968.
106 *Irish Times*, 18 October 1968.
107 *Irish Press*, 17 June 1969.
108 *ibid.*, 5 June 1969.
109 *ibid.*, 6 June 1969.
110 Mansergh, M. *History of Fianna Fáil*, 1996.
111 See *Magill*, May, June and July 1980 for a comprehensive analysis of the arms crisis.
112 *idem.*
113 *Irish Press*, 5 May 1970.
114 See footnote 105.
115 *Irish Press*, 7 May 1970.
116 *idem.*
117 Interview with Tim Pat Coogan.
118 Interview with Michael Mills.
119 *Irish Press*, 7 May 1970.
120 *idem.*
121 *ibid.*, 8 May 1970.
122 *ibid.*, 9 May 1970.
123 *idem.*
124 Three others, Irish intelligence officer Captain James Kelly, northern nationalist John Kelly and Belgian businessman Albert Luykx were similarly charged. While the case against Blaney was dropped for lack of evidence, all the others were subsequently found not guilty of the charge.
125 *Irish Press*, 29 May 1970.
126 *idem.*
127 *Irish Times*, 13 April 2001.
128 *Irish Press*, 5 June 1970.
129 Coogan, T. P. (1987) p. 22.
130 *idem.*
131 *Irish Press*, 23 June 1970.
132 *ibid.*, 20 September 1971.
133 Interview with John Kelly.
134 *Irish Press*, 24 October 1970.
135 *ibid.*, 26 October 1970.
136 *ibid.*, 5 November 1970.

CHAPTER SIX

1 Interview with Michael O'Toole.
2 Mansergh, M. *History of Fianna Fáil*, 1996.
3 *Irish Press*, 2 October 1971.

4 *idem.*
5 *ibid.*, 24 November 1972.
6 *ibid.*, 26 November 1972.
7 *ibid.*, 28 November 1972.
8 *ibid.*, 29 November 1972.
9 *ibid.*, 30 November 1972.
10 *ibid.*, 6 February 1973.
11 *ibid.*, 24 February 1973.
12 *ibid.*, 12 February 1973.
13 *ibid.*, 24 February 1973.
14 *ibid.*, 27 February 1973.
15 *ibid.*, 3 March 1973.
16 *ibid.*, 2 March 1973.
17 *idem.*
18 *In Dublin*, 20 August 1987.
19 *Magill*, June 1983.
20 Kenny, I. (1994) p. 116.
21 Interview with Michael O'Toole.
22 Interview with Hugh Lambert.
23 *idem.*
24 Interview with Michael Keane.
25 *Irish Press*, 7 June 1973.
26 *Irish Times*, 14 July 1973.
27 Collins, S. (1992) p. 27.
28 Waters, J. (1991) p. 150.
29 Interview with David Andrews.
30 *Irish Times*, 16 March 1974.
31 Dáil Éireann Report; Vol. 273, col. 1613.
32 *Irish Press*, 30 August 1975.
33 Interview with Michael Mills.
34 *Irish Press*, 16 February 1976.
35 Collins, S. (1992) p. 31.
36 Dáil Éireann Report, Vol. 292, col. 482.
37 Interview with Tim Pat Coogan.
38 *Irish Times*, 6 September 1976.
39 *idem.*
40 *Irish Press*, 4 September 1976.
41 *idem.*
42 *idem.*
43 Interview with Michael Mills.
44 *idem.*
45 Interview with Tim Pat Coogan.
46 *Irish Press*, 4 September 1976.
47 *idem.*
48 Dáil Éireann Report, Vol. 292, col. 474–479.
49 *ibid.*, col. 615.
50 *ibid.*, col. 474–479.
51 *ibid.*, col. 542.
52 *Irish Press*, 8 September 1976.
53 *idem.*
54 Dáil Éireann Report, Vol. 292, col. 576–1079.
55 *idem.*
56 *ibid.*, col. 578.
57 *Irish Press*, 15 September 1976.
58 *idem.*
59 *idem.*
60 Interview with Tim Pat Coogan.
61 *idem.*
62 Lenihan, B. (1991) p. 126.

63 Kerrigan, G. and Brennan, P. (1999) p. 287.
64 *Irish Press*, 20 October 1976.
65 *ibid.*, 23 October 1976.
66 *idem.*
67 *Irish Times*, 25 October 1976.
68 *idem.*
69 O'Toole Papers.
70 *idem.*
71 Interview with John Kelly.
72 O'Toole Papers.
73 *Hibernia*, 13 June 1975.
74 Interview with Tim Pat Coogan.
75 *Hibernia*, 13 June 1975.
76 Interview with Michael Keane.
77 Interview with John Kelly.
78 *idem.*
79 Irish Times Trust Memorandum of Association, D II A / C 1 and 2.
80 Interview with Conor Brady.
81 Interview with Vincent Doyle.
82 *idem.*
83 *idem.*
84 *Business and Finance*, 1 September 1983.
85 Interview with Vincent Doyle.
86 *idem.*
87 *idem.*
88 Kenny, I. (1994) p. 207–224.
89 *The Phoenix*, 16 December 1994.
90 *idem.*
91 *idem.*
92 The paper later acknowledged that Casey was not interviewed 'in any normal sense of the word'.
93 *Sunday Independent*, 22 October 2000.
94 Interview with John Kelly.
95 NUJ Files, Irish Press Chapel, 1970s.
96 *idem.*
97 O'Toole, M. (1992) p. 136.
98 Healy, J. (1978) p. 65.
99 *Irish Press*, 4 June 1977.
100 *ibid.*, 2 June 1977.
101 *ibid.*, 15 June 1977.
102 *idem.*
103 *idem.*
104 *ibid.*, 16 June 1977.
106 *ibid.*, 18 June 1977.
107 *ibid.*, 20 June 1977.
108 *Irish Press*, 5 October 1979.
109 Interview with Michael Mills.
110 *The Kerryman*, 3 March 2000.
111 *idem.*
112 *idem.*
113 *Irish Press*, 25 October 1979.
114 *ibid.*, 7 Nov. 1979.
115 *ibid.*, 9 Nov. 1979.
116 Interview with Michael Mills.
117 *Irish Press*, 10 November 1979.
118 *idem.*
119 *idem.*
120 *ibid.*, 15 November 1979.
121 *ibid.*, 21 November 1979.

122 *idem.*
123 *ibid.*, 6 December 1979.
124 *ibid.*, 8 December 1979.
125 Dáil Éireann Report, Vol. 317 col. 1326–1327.
126 *idem.*
127 *Irish Press*, 12 December 1979.
128 Interview with Michael O'Toole.
129 *Irish Press*, 12 November 1980.
130 *idem.*
131 Interview with Michael O'Toole.
132 *Sunday Business Post*, 14 November 1999.

CHAPTER SEVEN

1 Interview with Tim Pat Coogan.
2 *Business and Finance,* 13 September 1984.
3 Irish Press Plc. 1982 Annual Report.
4 *Business and Finance*, 13 September 1984.
5 *Irish Press*, 10 June 1981.
6 *ibid.*, 22 May 1981.
7 *ibid.*, 23 May 1981.
8 *ibid.*, 26 May 1981.
9 *idem.*
10 *ibid.*, 8 June 1981.
11 *idem.*
12 *ibid.*, 18 June 1981.
13 Keogh, D. (1994) p. 356.
14 *idem.*
15 *Irish Press*, 1 October 1981.
16 *idem.*
17 *ibid.*, 28 January 1982.
18 *ibid.*, 29 January 1982.
19 *ibid.*, 10 February 1982.
20 *idem.*
21 *idem.*
22 *ibid.*, 18 February 1982.
23 *ibid.*, 22 February 1982.
24 *idem.*
25 Keogh, D. (1994) p. 359.
26 *Irish Press*, 25 February 1982.
27 *idem.*
28 *idem.*
29 *ibid.*, 11 March 1982.
30 Joyce, J. and Murtagh, P. (1997) p. 255.
31 *Irish Press*, 5 October 1982.
32 *ibid.*, 7 October 1982.
33 *ibid.*, 8 October 1982.
34 *ibid.*, 6 November 1982.
35 *ibid.*, 18 November 1982.
36 *ibid.*, 17 November 1982.
37 *ibid.*, 20 November 1982.
38 *ibid.*, 24 November 1982.
39 *ibid.*, 25 November 1982.
40 *ibid.*, 21 January 1983.
41 *ibid.*, 22 January 1983.
42 *ibid.*, 21 January 1983.

43 *Sunday Press*, 23 January 1983.
44 *Irish Press*, 27 January 1983.
45 Interview with John Kelly.
46 Interview with Tim Pat Coogan.
47 Interview with Michael Mills.
48 Interview with Michael Keane.
49 Interview with David Andrews.
50 *Irish Press*, 28 January 1983.
51 *idem.*
52 *Evening Press*, 28 January 1983.
53 Kerrigan, G. and Brennan, P. (1999) p. 8.
54 *Irish Press*, 3 February 1983.
55 *ibid.*, 4 February 1983.
56 *Sunday Press*, 6 February 1983.
57 Interview with Michael Keane.
58 *idem.*
59 *Irish Press*, 7 February 1983.
60 *idem.*
61 *ibid.*, 8 February 1983.
62 Cahill, E. (1997) p. 297.
63 Interview with Tim Pat Coogan.
64 *idem.*
65 Interview with John Kelly.
66 O'Toole Papers.
67 Irish Press Plc, 1983 Annual Report.
68 *Irish Independent*, 20 May 1985.
69 *Business and Finance*, 9 May 1985.
70 *Irish Independent*, 20 May 1985.
71 NUJ Files, Irish Press Chapel, 1980s.
72 *idem.*
73 Interview with Tim Pat Coogan.
74 *Business and Finance*, 22 July 1993.
75 *Irish Independent*, 20 May 1985.
76 Irish Press Plc, 1985 Annual Report.
77 *Irish Times*, 26 July 1986.
78 *idem.*
79 *idem.*
80 Irish Press Plc, 1985 Annual Report.
81 Interview with John Kelly.
82 *Irish Independent*, 20 May 1985.
83 *Sunday Press*, 19 May 1985.
84 *Business and Finance*, 23 May 1985.
85 O'Toole Papers, Letter from management to staff, 24 June 1985.
86 Interview with Tim Pat Coogan.
87 *Business and Finance*, 7 August 1986.
88 *Evening Press*, 2 July 1985.
89 Interview with Hugh Lambert.
90 Interview with Tim Pat Coogan.
91 Interview with Michael Keane.
92 Irish Press Newspapers Ltd Employee's High Court Petition.
93 *Irish Press*, 20 November 1984.
94 *Sunday Press*, 6 May 1984.
95 *ibid.*, 20 May 1984.
96 Interview with Michael Keane.
97 Interview with Michael O'Toole.
98 *Irish Press*, 23 December 1985.
99 *idem.*
100 Mansergh, M. *History of Fianna Fail*, 1996.
101 Interview with Tim Pat Coogan.

102 *Irish Press*, 25 June 1986.
103 *Irish Times*, 26 July 1986.
104 *Irish Press*, 28 June 1986.
105 *ibid.*, 24 January 1987.
106 *idem.*
107 *ibid.*, 17 February 1987.
108 *ibid.*, 10 February 1987.
109 Keogh, D. (1994) p. 375.
110 NUJ Files, Irish Press Chapel Files, 1980s.
111 *idem.*
112 Interview with Michael Keane.
113 *idem.*
114 *idem.*
115 Interview with Tim Pat Coogan.
116 *The Phoenix*, 26 August 1988.
117 Interview with Tim Pat Coogan.
118 *Irish Press*, 7 August 1987.
119 Interview with Hugh Lambert.
120 *idem.*
121 *idem.*
122 *Business and Finance*, 11 May 1989.
123 *The Phoenix*, 6 October 1989.
124 *Irish Press*, 9 April 1988.
125 Interview with Hugh Lambert.
126 *The Phoenix*, 1988 Annual.
127 Interview with Hugh Lambert.
128 *Planning for the 1990s*, Irish Press Plc Corporate Plan 1989–1993.
129 *idem.*
130 *idem.*
131 *Business and Finance*, 11 May 1989.
132 NUJ Files, Irish Press Chapel Files, 1980s.
133 Interview with Vincent Doyle.
134 Interview with Conor Brady.
135 Interview with Vincent Doyle.
136 *idem.*
137 *Irish Times*, 11 December 1989.
138 *ibid.*, 16 November 1989.
139 Interview with Hugh Lambert.
140 *Irish Press*, 8 July 1989.
141 *Irish Independent*, 8 July 1989.
142 *ibid.*
143 *Irish Times*, 8 July 1989.
144 *Irish Independent*, 15 July 1989.
145 *Magill*, October 1989.
146 *Irish Times*, 16 June 1993.
147 *ibid.*, 15 July 1989.
148 *idem.*
149 *Business and Finance*, 11 June 1992.
150 *Irish Times*, 16 November 1989.
151 *ibid.*, 11 December 1989.
152 *ibid.*, 12 December 1989.
153 *Business and Finance*, 11 June 1992.
154 *idem.*
155 *Irish Times*, 2 July 1993.
156 *Business and Finance*, 11 June 1992.
157 *idem.*
158 *The Phoenix*, 14 July 1989.
159 *Irish Press*, 7 July 1989.
160 *ibid.*, 9 July 1989.
161 Interview with Michael Mills.

162 *idem.*
163 *idem.*
164 *idem.*

CHAPTER EIGHT

1 Interview with John Kelly.
2 O'Toole, M. (1994) p. 135.
3 *Irish Press*, 21 July 1990.
4 *Evening Press*, 21 July 1990.
5 *Irish Independent*, 23 July 1990.
6 Downey, J. (1998) p. 19.
7 *Irish Press*, 22 October 1990.
8 *ibid.*, 23 October 1990.
9 O'Reilly, E. (1991) p. 101.
10 *The Phoenix*, 16 November 1990.
11 *idem.*
12 *idem.*
13 Interview with Hugh Lambert.
14 Interview with Emily O'Reilly.
15 Interview with Mary O'Rourke.
16 Interview with Michael Mills.
17 *Irish Press*, 27 October 1990.
18 *idem.*
19 *ibid.*, 1 November 1990.
20 *ibid.*, 2 November 1990.
21 *ibid.*, 5 November 1990.
22 *ibid.*
23 *ibid*, 7 November 1990.
24 *idem.*
25 *ibid.*, 9 November 1990.
26 *Business and Finance*, 7 August 1986.
27 Interview with John Kelly.
28 *Evening Press*, 22 April 1991.
29 *idem.*
30 *In Dublin*, 16 January 1997.
31 *The Phoenix*, 7 August 1992.
32 Interview with Michael Keane.
33 Interview with Hugh Lambert.
34 *idem.*
35 *The Phoenix*, 18 September 1992.
36 *Business and Finance*, 11 June 1992.
37 *idem.*
38 *Irish Times*, 25 June 1993.
39 Interview with Michael Keane.
40 *idem.*
41 Interview with Vincent Doyle.
42 *Business and Finance*, 2 December 1993.
43 *ibid.*, 2 July 1992.
44 *The Phoenix*, 21 August 1992.
45 *Business and Finance*, 1 October 1992.
46 *idem.*
47 *idem.*
48 *idem.*
49 *Irish Press*, 23 January 1992.
50 *idem.*

51 *ibid.*, 24 January 1992.
52 *ibid.*, 25 January 1992.
53 *ibid.*, 7 February 1992.
54 *idem.*
55 *ibid.*, 19 November 1992.
56 *idem.*
57 *ibid.*, 25 November 1992.
58 *idem.*
59 *ibid.*, 27 November 1992.
60 *ibid.*, 30 November 1992.
61 *ibid.*, 2 December 1992.
62 *idem.*
63 *ibid.*, 5 December 1992.
64 *idem.*
65 *ibid.*, 12 December 1992.
66 *ibid.*, 25–28 December 1992.
67 *ibid.*, 11 January 1993.
68 *idem.*
69 *Irish Independent*, 16 June 1993.
70 *idem.*
71 *Business and Finance*, 22 July 1993.
72 *ibid.*, 18 November 1993.
73 Interview with Hugh Lambert.
74 *idem.*
75 *Evening Xpress*, 9 June 1995.
76 *Irish Times*, 16 July 1993.
77 *idem.*
78 *ibid.*, 22 July 1993.
79 *idem.*
80 *Evening XPress*, 9 June 1995.
81 *Irish Times*, 2 July 1993.
82 *idem.*
83 *Evening XPress*, 9 June 1995.
84 *Business and Finance*, 19 May 1993.
85 Irish Press Plc, 1993 Annual Report.
86 *Sunday Press*, 17 April 1994.
87 *ibid.*, 16 April 1995.
88 *idem.*
89 *Irish Times*, 16 May 1995.
90 Interview with Michael Keane.
91 Interview with Hugh Lambert.
92 Competition Authority Report 1992.
93 *The Phoenix*, 20 January 1995.
94 *Irish Times*, 23 December 1994.
95 Competition Authority Annual Report 1995.
96 Competition Authority Interim Report of Study on the Newspaper Industry.
97 *idem.*
98 Competition Authority, *A Guide to Irish Legislation on Competition.*
99 Competition Authority Interim Report of Study on the Newspaper Industry.
100 Interview with David Andrews.
101 *Irish Times*, 16 May 1995.
102 *idem.*
103 *idem.*
104 *ibid.*, 24 May 1995.
105 *The Phoenix*, 13 October 1995.
106 *Irish Times*, 26 May 1995.
107 *Irish Independent*, 27 May 1995.
108 *Irish XPress*, 27 May 1995.
109 *Evening XPress*, 29 May 1995.
110 *In Dublin*, 16 January 1997.

111 *Irish Times*, 30 May 1995.
112 Dáil Éireann Record, Vol. 453, col. 1404.
113 Interview with Mary O'Rourke.
114 *idem.*
115 *Irish Times*, 19 August 1995.
116 *idem.*
117 Irish Press Newspapers Ltd Employee's High Court Petition.
118 *Evening XPress*, 1 June 1995.
119 *ibid.*, 2 June 1995.
120 *idem.*
121 *ibid.*, 5 June 1995.
122 Dáil Éireann Report, Vol. 454, col. 97–109.
123 *idem.*
124 *idem.*
125 Interview with David Andrews.
126 Interview with Michael Keane.
127 Irish Press Newspapers Ltd Employee's High Court Petition.
128 *idem.*
129 *The Phoenix*, 4 August 1995.
130 *XPress*, 15 June 1995.
131 *idem.*
132 *Business and Finance*, 27 July 1995.
133 *Irish Times*, 10 August 1995.
134 *Business and Finance*, 1 September 1994.
135 *Irish Times*, 19 August 1995.
136 *Irish Independent*, 9 September 1995.
137 *idem.*
138 *idem.*
139 *idem.*
140 *idem.*
141 *Irish Times*, 2 June 1995.

EPILOGUE

1 *XPress*, 15 June 1995.
2 Interview with David Andrews.
3 *ibid.*
4 Corcoran, M. and Kelly-Browne, H. *Political Partisanship Among Irish Journalists* (1998).
5 *Irish Times*, 14 June 1997.
6 *Irish Independent*, 5 June 1997.
7 *Sunday Independent*, 15 June 1997.
8 *Irish Times*, 30 April 1996.
9 *ibid.*
10 *ibid.*
11 Cahill, E. (1997) p. 14.
12 *Irish Times*, 27 January 1996.
13 *ibid.*
14 *ibid.*, 17 November 1998.
15 *ibid.*, 14 October 1997.
16 *ibid.*
17 *Irish Times*, 6 November 1997.
18 *ibid.*
19 *ibid.*
20 *ibid.*
21 *ibid.*, 17 November 1998.
22 *ibid.*, 10 December 1998.
23 *ibid.*, 8 September 1999.

Bibliography

Interviews

David Andrews, Conor Brady, John Brophy, Tim Pat Coogan, Vincent Doyle, Douglas Gageby, Michael Keane, John Kelly, Hugh Lambert, Michael Mills, Emily O'Reilly, Mary O'Rourke, Michael O'Toole, Jim Walsh.

Private Papers

Frank Aiken Papers, University College Dublin Archives
Eamon de Valera Papers, University College Dublin Archives
Frank Gallagher Papers, National Library of Ireland
Sean MacEntee Papers, University College Dublin Archives
M. J. MacManus Papers, National Library of Ireland
Joseph McGarrity Papers, National Library of Ireland
William Murphy Papers, National Archives, Business Records Survey
Sean T. O'Kelly Papers, National Library of Ireland
Michael O'Toole Papers, Private Collection
Hanna Sheehy Skeffington Papers, National Library of Ireland
Joseph Smart Papers, National Library of Ireland

National Archives

Department of the Taoiseach; S–1957/63, S–2858, S–4915, S–5749, S–9596, S–9972, S–14518
Department of Foreign Affairs; D/FA; (Secretary's Files)
Department of Justice; D/J; Press Censorship Reviews, D/J; No. 1
File 2000/10/3377; Attorney General's Office

University College Dublin Archives

Cumann na nGaedheal and Fine Gael Files; P39/2
Fianna Fáil Files; FF/26, FF/27 and FF/29

Companies Registration Office

Articles of Association and various annual reports for Irish Press Plc, Independent Newspapers Plc and The Irish Times Trust Ltd

National Union of Journalists

Irish Press Group Chapel Files, 1932–1995

Government Publications

Dail Éireann Reports
Acts of the Oireachtas 1954, Stationery Office, Dublin, 1955
Competition Authority Report of Investigation of the Proposal whereby Independent Newspapers Plc would increase its Shareholding in the Tribune Group from 29.9% to 53.9%, 1992
Competition Authority; A Guide to Irish Legislation on Competition, 1992
Competition Authority Interim Report of Study on the Newspaper Industry, 1995
Competition Authority Annual Report 1995
Report of the Commission of Inquiry into the Newspaper Industry, 1996

Newspapers and Periodicals

Business and Finance, Dublin Opinion, Evening Herald, Evening Mail, Evening Press, Evening XPress, In Dublin, Irish Business, Hibernia, Hot Press, Irish Independent, Irish Press, Irish Times, Irish XPress, Magill, Sunday Business Post, Sunday Independent, Sunday Review, Sunday Press, Sunday XPress, The Examiner, The Irish Digest, The Kerryman, The Nation, The Phoenix, The Word.

Unpublished Documents

Corcoran, M. and Kelly-Browne, H. *Political Partisanship Among Irish Journalists*. Paper presented to the 25th annual conference of the SAI, 1998
Irish Press Newspapers Ltd Employees' High Court Petition
Mansergh, M. *The History of Fianna Fáil*. Speech given to UCD History Society, 1996
Planning for the Future: Statement by Irish Press Limited to its Employees, 1983
Planning for the 1990s: Irish Press Plc Corporate Plan 1989–1993
Torde, B. *Discursive Dependency or is the Irish Press Independent?* Paper presented to the 5th annual conference of the SAI, 1978

Published Works

Allen, K. *Fianna Fáil and Irish Labour; 1926 to the Present*. Pluto Press, 1997, London.
Andrews, C. *A Man of No Property*. Mercier Press, 1982, Dublin.
Arnold, B. *What Kind of Country? Modern Irish Politics 1968–1983*. Jonathan Cape, 1984, London.
Baker, S. *Nationalist Ideology and the Industrial Policy of Fianna Fáil; The Evidence of the Irish Press*. Irish Political Studies; Vol. 1 (1986) p. 57.
Bew, P. and Patterson, H. *Sean Lemass and the Making of Modern Ireland 1944–1966*. Gill & Macmillan, 1982, Dublin.

Boland, K. *The Rise and Decline of Fianna Fáil*. Mercier Press, 1982, Dublin.

Bowman, J. *De Valera and the Ulster Question*. Clarendon Press, 1982, Oxford.

Brasier, A. and Kelly, J. *Harry Boland; A Man Divided*. New Century Publishing, 2000, Dublin.

Breen, R. *et al. Understanding Contemporary Ireland*. Gill & Macmillan, 1990, London.

Browne, N. *Against the Tide*. Gill & Macmillan, 1986, Dublin.

Browne, S. *The Press in Ireland; A Survey and a Guide*. Lemma Publishing Corp, 1971, New York.

Browne, T. *Ireland; A Social and Cultural History 1922–85*. Fontana, 1985, London.

Cahill, E. *Corporate Financial Crisis In Ireland*. Gill & Macmillan, 1997, Dublin.

Clancy, P. *et al. Ireland; A Sociological Profile*. IPA/SAI, 1986, Dublin.

Coakley, J. and Gallagher, M. (eds) *Politics in the Republic of Ireland*. PSAI Press, 1993, Limerick.

Collins, S. *The Haughey File; The Unprecedented Career and Last Years of the Boss*. O'Brien Press, 1992, Dublin.

— *The Power Game; Fianna Fáil since Lemass*. O'Brien Press, 2000, Dublin.

Connolly, J. *The Connolly Memoirs*. Irish Academic Press, 1996, Dublin.

Coogan, T. P. *De Valera; Long Fellow Long Shadow*. Hutchinson, 1993, London.

— *Disillusioned Decades; Ireland 1966–87*. Gill & Macmillan, 1987, Dublin.

Cousins, M. *The Introduction of Childrens Allowances in Ireland 1939–44*. Irish Economic & Social History; Vol. 26 (1999) p. 35.

Curran, C. *Fianna Fáil and the Origins of the Irish Press*. Irish Communications Review; Vol. 6 (1996) p. 7.

Daly, M. *Industrial Development and Irish National Identity, 1922–1939*. Syracuse University, 1992, Syracuse.

Devane, R. *Suggested Tariff on Imported Newspapers and Magazines*. Studies; Vol. 16 (1927) p. 545.

Dhonnchadha, M. and Dorgan, T. *Revising the Rising*. Field Day, 1991, Derry.

Dillon, M. *Culture, Rationality and Modernity*. UMI, 1989, Michigan, USA.

Downey, J. *Lenihan, His Life and Loyalties*. New Island Books, 1998, Dublin.

Duggan, J. *Neutral Ireland and the Third Reich*. Lilliput Press, 1989, Dublin.

Dunphy, R. *The Making of Fianna Fáil Power in Ireland 1923–48*. Clarendon Press, 1995, Oxford.

Dwyer, T. R. *De Valera's Finest Hour; In Search of National Independence, 1932–1959*. Mercier Press, 1982, Dublin.

— De Valera; *The Man and the Myths*. Poolbeg, 1981, Dublin.

English, R. *Ernie O'Malley, IRA Intellectual.* Clarendon Press, 1998, Oxford.

Fanning, R. *Independent Ireland.* Helicon, 1983, Dublin.

Farrell, B. *Sean Lemass.* Gill & Macmillan, 1983, Dublin.

— *The Founding of Dail Eireann; Parliament and Nation Building.* Gill & Macmillan, 1971, Dublin.

— *Communications and Community in Ireland.* Mercier Press, 1984, Dublin.

FitzGerald, G. *All in a Life; An Autobiography.* Gill & Macmillan, 1992, Dublin.

Foley, J. and Lalor, S. (eds). *Annotated Constitution of Ireland.* Gill & Macmillan, 1995, Dublin.

Garvin, T. *1922; The Birth of Irish Democracy.* Gill & Macmillan, 1996, Dublin.

— *The Evolution of Irish Nationalist Politics.* Gill & Macmillan, 1981, Dublin.

— *The Destiny of the Soldiers; Tradition and Modernity in the Politics of de Valera's Ireland.* Political Studies; Vol. 26 (1978) p. 328.

Girvin, B. *Between Two Worlds; Politics and Economy in Independent Ireland.* Gill & Macmillan, 1989, Dublin.

— *Political Culture, Political Independence and Economic Success in Ireland.* Irish Political Studies; Vol. 12 (1997) p. 48.

Girvin, B. and Sturm, R. *Power and Society in Contemporary Ireland.* Gower, 1986, Hampshire.

Gray, T. *Mr. Smyllie, Sir.* Gill & Macmillan, 1991, Dublin.

Hannon, P. and Gallagher, J. *Taking the Long View; Seventy Years of Fianna Fáil.* Blackwater Press, 1996, Dublin.

Healy, J. *Nineteen Acres.* Kenny's Bookshop, 1978, Galway.

Horgan, J. *Sean Lemass; The Enigmatic Patriot.* Gill & Macmillan, 1997, Dublin.

— *Irish Media; A Critical History Since 1922.* Routledge, 2001, London.

Hutchinson, J. *The Dynamics of Cultural Nationalism; The Gaelic Revival and the Creation of the Modern Irish State.* Allen & Unwin, 1987, London.

Jacobsen, J. *Chasing Progress in the Irish Republic; Ideology, Democracy and Dependent Development.* Cambridge University Press, 1994, New York.

Joyce, J. and Murtagh, P. *The Boss.* Poolbeg, 1997, Dublin.

Kearney, R. *Post-Nationalist Ireland; Politics, Culture and Philosophy.* Routledge, 1997, London.

Kelly, J. *Bonfires on the Hillside.* Fountain Publishing, 1995, Belfast.

Kennedy, K (ed). *Ireland in Transition.* Mercier Press, 1986, Dublin.

Kenny, I. *Talking to Ourselves.* Kenny's Publishing, 1994, Galway.

Keogh, D. *Twentieth Century Ireland; Nation and State.* Gill & Macmillan, 1994, Dublin.

Kerrigan, G. and Brennan, P. *This Great Little Nation; The A–Z of Irish Scandals and Controversies.* Gill & Macmillan, 1999, Dublin.

Kiberd, D. (ed) *Media in Ireland; The Search for Diversity.* Open Air, 1997, Dublin.

Kilfeather, F. *Changing Times; A Life in Journalism.* Blackwater Press, 1997, Dublin.

Kimberly, J. and Miles, R. *The Organizational Life Cycle.* Jossey-Bass Publishers, 1980, San Francisco.

Lavelle, P. *James O'Mara; A Staunch Sinn Feiner.* Clonmore & Reynolds, 1961, Dublin.

Lee, G. and Bird, C. *Breaking the Bank; How the NIB Scandal was Exposed.* 1998 Blackwater Press. Dublin.

Lee, J. *Ireland 1912–1985; Politics and Society.* Cambridge University Press, 1989, New York.

Lenihan, B. *For the Record.* Blackwater Press, 1991, Dublin.

Litton, H. (ed) *Revolutionary Woman; Kathleen Clarke.* O'Brien Press, 1991, Dublin.

Longford, Lord and O'Neill, T. *Eamon de Valera.* Arrow Books, 1970, London.

MacManus, M. J. *Eamon de Valera; A Biography.* Talbot Press, 1944, Dublin.

Mair, P. *The Autonomy of the Political; The Development of the Irish Party System.* Comparative Politics; Vol. 11 (1979) p. 445.

McDermott, E. *Clann na Poblachta.* Cork University Press, 1998, Cork.

Mercier, V. *The Irish Times;* The Bell; Vol. 9, Issue 4 (January 1945) p. 290.

— *The Irish Press*; The Bell; Vol. 9, Issue 6 (March 1945) p. 475.

Murphy, B. *Patrick Pearse and the Lost Republican Ideal.* James Duffy, 1991, Dublin.

Murphy, J. and O'Carroll (eds). *De Valera and His Times.* Cork University Press, 1983, Cork.

Oram, H. *The Newspaper Book; A History of Newspapers in Ireland, 1649–1983.* M.O. Books 1983, Dublin.

— *Paper Tigers.* Appletree Press, 1993, Belfast.

Orridge, A. *The Blueshirts and the Economic War; A Study of Ireland in the Context of Dependency Theory.* Political Studies; Vol. 31 (1983), p. 351.

O'Donnell, D. *The Irish Independent*; The Bell; Vol. 9, Issue 5 (February 1945) p. 386.

O'Donnell, J, (ed). *Ireland; The Past Twenty Years; An Illustrated Chronology.* Institute of Public Administration, 1986, Dublin.

O'Drisceoil, D. *Censorship in Ireland 1939–45; Neutrality, Politics and Society.* Cork University Press, 1996, Cork.

O'Grada, C. *A Rocky Road; The Irish Economy Since the 1920s.* Manchester University Press, 1997, Manchester.

O'Mahony, P. and Delanty, G; *Rethinking Irish History.* Macmillan Press, 1998, London.

O'Mahony, T. *Jack Lynch; A Biography.* Blackwater Press, 1991, Dublin.

O'Reilly, E. *Candidate; The Truth Behind the Presidential Campaign.* Attic Press, 1991, Dublin.

— *Veronica Guerin; The Life and Death of a Crime Reporter.* Vintage. 1998, London.

O'Toole, M. *More Kicks than Pence; A Life in Irish Journalism.* Poolbeg, 1992, Dublin.

Prager, J. *Building Democracy in Ireland; Political Order and Cultural Integration in a Newly Independent Nation.* Cambridge University Press, 1986, New York.

Rumpf, E. and Hepburn, A. *Nationalism and Socialism in Twentieth Century Ireland.* Liverpool University Press, 1977, Liverpool.

Sarbaugh, T. *Eamon de Valera and the Irish Press in California 1928–1931.* Eire Ireland; Vol. 20 (1985) p. 15.

Schlesinger, P. *Media, State and Nation.* Sage, 1991, London.

Schudson, M. *Discovering the News; A Social History of American Newspapers.* Basic Books, 1978, United States of America.

Tierney, M. *Ireland Since 1870.* Fallon, 1988, Dublin.

Tobin, F. *The Best of Decades; Ireland in the 1960s.* Gill & Macmillan, 1984, Dublin.

Walsh, D. *The Party; Inside Fianna Fáil.* Gill & Macmillan, 1986, Dublin.

Waters, J. *Jiving at the Crossroads.* Blackstaff Press, 1991, Belfast.

Young, J. *Erskine H. Childers; President of Ireland.* Colin Smythe, 1985, Buckinghamshire.

Index

I. INDIVIDUALS

II. SUBJECTS